PREGNANT WITH THE STARS

Watching and Wanting

the Celebrity Baby Bump

RENÉE ANN CRAMER

STANFORD LAW BOOKS
An Imprint of Stanford University Press
Stanford, California

Stanford University Press
Stanford, California

Printed on acid-free, archival-quality paper

Printed and bound in Great Britain by
Marston Book Services Ltd, Oxfordshire

Library of Congress Cataloging-in-Publication Data

Cramer, Renée Ann, author.
Pregnant with the stars: watching and wanting the celebrity baby bump / Renee Ann Cramer.
  pages cm—(The cultural lives of law)
Includes bibliographical references and index.
ISBN 978-0-8047-9255-4 (cloth: alk. paper)—ISBN 978-0-8047-9674-3 (pbk.: alk. paper)
1. Pregnant women—Legal status, laws, etc.—United States. 2. Fetus—Legal status, laws, etc.—United States. 3. Pregnancy in popular culture—United States. 4. Celebrities in popular culture—United States. 5. Pregnancy—Social aspects—United States. I. Title. II. Series: Cultural lives of law.
KF478.C73 2015
342.7308'78—dc23

                                        2015007276

ISBN 978-0-8047-9679-8 (electronic)

Typeset by Bruce Lundquist in 10.25/15 Minion

I dedicate this to Wyatt,

who was the bump,

who became the boy.

And who, in both regards,

instigated the book.

CONTENTS

ACKNOWLEDGMENTS

This has been a terrifically fun book to write—and writing acknowledgments has been a joyful process of remembrance. Thank you to all listed here for your assistance and encouragement.

For being the best colleague and friend a scholar could want, many thanks to Jeff Dudas. He read the entire manuscript more than once, commented critically and kindly on each draft, and saw, early on, the importance of Mila Kunis. Similar thanks to Claire Rasmussen for her helpful engagement with the entire text and for sharing her work in progress where it dovetailed with some of the arguments I am making. Thanks, too, to generous and thoughtful anonymous reviewers at Stanford University Press and to Michelle Lipinski— she's a terrific reader and a great editor. Thank you, Austin Sarat, for passing my manuscript proposal along to her capable hands—and for your support of cultural analysis within legal studies.

Thanks go to Julia Jordan-Zachery for three reasons: her engagement with the introduction and chapter two, her role in keeping me accountable for celebrating and working, and her friendship. Thanks, too, to Janine Holc for accountability help and to the Scrappy Scribblers! for support, celebration— and yes, accountability—especially scribblers Nikol Alexander-Floyd (inter-sectionality scholar extraordinaire) and Beth Posner Ginsburg (who I have known since grad school and whose dad performed the ceremony marrying Aaron and me).

I appreciate all of these friendships daily.

I am similarly grateful to the following people for their engagement with several of the chapters: Megan Brown, Sandi Patton-Imani, Amy O'Shaughnessy, and Nancy Berns. For early critique and commentary, thanks to Judith Grant, Marjorie Jolles, Susan Burgess, and participants at the Drake Women's and Gender Studies colloquium, Law and Society Association meetings, and the Western Political Science Association meetings. For early and enthusiastic encouragement, as well as helping earlier versions of the text to "pop," thanks to Shira Tarrant. Mary Dudas presented a paper on "the consumptive passions," at Law and Society—that paper helped to shape my thinking in chapter five.

For telling me that he thought the book was a bad idea—and challenging me to convince him otherwise—thanks to Sasha Gorman!

Thank you to the folks at TedXWomen Des Moines for the opportunity to turn the entire book into a seventeen-minute notes-free speech.

While working on this book, two other professional endeavors pulled my attention. First, I was chairing my department and must offer my thanks to Will Garriott in particular for being such a wonderful departmental colleague—explaining gently to students why I wasn't around (even when I was), teaching brilliantly, and engaging parts of this text with intelligence and care. I was also working to lead a team assessing our campus climate and culture for faculty, staff, and students of color—and using that assessment to create a strategic plan for diversity and inclusive excellence. My colleagues on that leadership team, Melissa Sturm-Smith and Mike Couvillon, deserve special thanks and high praise for understanding the juggling act I was undertaking, for supporting my time away, at times, to write and think—and for seeing the connections between this project and ours. Special thanks, too, to Melissa for her reading of several chapters and her willingness to talk about critical race and feminist theory. And thanks to the entire Strategic Diversity Action Team for your commitment to the We Make Drake! project. All the scholarly analysis in the world is for naught if we don't try to make our corner of the world better.

For collegiality, friendship, and a willingness to chat about these—and other—scholarly things, a hearty thank-you to Melissa Michelson, Anna Maria Marshall, Laura Beth Nielsen, Erika Iverson, Heather Pool, Nina Flores, Olivia Garcia, Petra Lange, Laura Hatcher, Christine Harrington, Jean Carmalt

(I miss you!), Jon Gould, Aaron Lorenz, Shelby Bell, Paul Passavant, Paula Mohan, Tony Tyler, Sarah Cote Hampson, Jennifer Harvey, Jose Marichal, Joanna Mosser, Hadar Aviram, Shannon Portillo, Nancy Mullane, Benjamin Fleury-Steiner, Jennifer Perrine, Darcie Vandegrift, Jinee Lokaneeta, Julie Novkov, Amanda Hollis Brusky, Jennifer Perrine, Josh Wilson, Peter Hovde, Scott Lemieux, Sandi Patton-Imani, Danelle Stamps, Michael Renner, Roger Hartley, Art Sanders, and Rebecca Spence.

For the examples they set of joyful productivity and a commitment to justice, thanks to Kerry Ann Rockemore, Brene Brown, and Jennifer Louden— I only know you via social media, but I love you!

A hearty thank-you to everyone who brought me pictures of pregnant celebrities—whether you tore them from magazines, emailed links, or posted pics on my Facebook wall. I won't remember all of you—but I know that I owe special gratitude to Tami Drew (my sister!), Amanda Krafft, Kristi Martel, Nicole Fenton, Charlynn Rick (we miss you!), Andrew Fowler, Tracey Sommerville, Megan Day Suhr, Frederique Courard-Hauri, Samantha Wagner, Kayla Craig, Jamie Brightman, Katie Kruger, Molly Bassford, Lena Fox, and Adrienne Erazo.

Thanks to the three iterations of my undergraduate class Reproductive Law and Politics for helping me think through these things—especially chapter one. Thanks as well to students in my Law, Politics, and Society senior seminar (fall 2014) for their critical engagement with the introduction. And thank you to Mikhala Stutzman (I call her "the comma killer") for being a terrific undergraduate research assistant. It's a delight to have a student who you can trust with both substantive and stylistic edits, while also enjoying long conversations about feminist theory, cultural politics, and legal studies.

The majority of this book was written while on a semester-long sabbatical from teaching, as well as over the course of a wonderful summer. I am grateful to Drake University for the sabbatical time, to the College of Arts and Sciences for funding related to that time off, to the provost's office for research support, and to the Drake Center for the Humanities for essential financial support at the end of the project. Thank you to Carla Herling for fabulous administrative support.

Because it was where I formed my understanding of scholarship and teaching, I always must acknowledge the profound impact that my undergraduate years at Bard College have on the person I am and the scholar I am becoming.

The book was written while listening to the following essential music: M.I.A., Lorde, Macklemore, Eminem, Matisyahu, Trevor Hall, Michael Franti and Spearhead, the Decemberists, Iron and Wine, Dawes (always Dawes—live, on CD, via Spotify, in the car . . .), U2, Iris Dement, The Head and the Heart (including live shows at critical moments), Taylor Swift (yes, Taylor Swift), Katy Perry, the Avett Brothers, Lupe Fiasco, Beyoncé, Pink, Ani DiFranco, the Mountain Goats, the Decemberists, Trampled by Turtles, and D'Angelo. I recommend them all for writing and running. Thank you to Gayle, Lena, Mary Kate, and Ben—the yoga classes you taught were just as necessary as the music and the running.

This book was also written over the course of multiple cups of coffee and tea and amazing veggie food at the best coffee shop in Des Moines, Iowa: Ritual Café. Thanks, ladies, for your hospitality. And thanks, Lars, for the Thursday morning conversations while we both took breaks from our writing and editing.

I am grateful to media watchers and media makers whose obsession with the celebrity baby bump made this book possible and to the celebrities willing to make private portions of their lives public.

There would be no book, no reason to write, and no fun after the work without my family: my husband, Aaron, and our son, Wyatt. There aren't words to tell you of my gratitude and my joy at sharing life with you.

PREGNANT WITH THE STARS

OBSESSION WITH THE CELEBRITY BABY BUMP

IN OCTOBER 2011, when Beyoncé Knowles announced her due date, and Jennifer Garner began the second trimester of her second pregnancy, the website BumpShack.com received more than 345,000 visitors from the United States. With worldwide traffic, the site—devoted solely to coverage of celebrity pregnancies—saw more than 500,000 hits that month. Celebitchy.com, a celebrity-watching website that often features pregnant stars, had more than 200,000 U.S. visitors.[1]

Cultural obsession with celebrity pregnancy is evident in print journalism, too. *People* magazine offers readers multiple pages of glossy photos of pregnant and mothering celebrities, week after week. *In Style* magazine has articles about famous women's "Pregnancy Style." The industry standard *Entertainment Weekly* often prints stories about celebrity pregnancy, and the impact that pregnancy has on story line, plot development, and stars' marketability.[2] And, of course, supermarket tabloids and magazine headlines are full of speculation:

Is Katie pregnant?
Is Jennifer expecting?
Will Kim have a baby girl?
Will the Royal Baby be a boy?
How long will it take Jessica to lose her baby weight?

Yet popular culture obsession with pregnant celebrities and their "baby bumps" is not only a guilty pleasure. The baby bump itself is more than just a trending topic on a Twitter feed or a headline grabber for infotainment venues. Rather, the visibly pregnant celebrity body, on display in hundreds of popular culture sources, is both an indicator of rapidly changing contemporary understandings of pregnancy in the United States and a lens through which we can interpret a complex set of social and legal regulations of pregnant women and their bodies. Images of pregnant celebrities—focusing on their baby bumps—and press coverage of these women's postbaby bodies saturate our contemporary media; we watch these popular culture representations and are told to want them, as well. These activities, watching and wanting, embroil us in a relationship to celebrity pregnancy that has ramifications for our behavior as consumers and citizens.

When we *watch* the pregnant celebrity, we can see how our culture judges which bodies are acceptable and desirable—which performances of femininity and pregnancy are considered ideal. In the coverage of these pregnancies, we see the exoticization of women of color, the valorization of the super-wealthy, and the imperative to extreme slimness. We are also encouraged, in the invitation to watch the celebrity bump, to surveil, to gossip, and to judge. Ultimately, we are enlisted in the regulation of the bodies of pregnant women, even as we are called on to accept and internalize our own regulation. As we judge and regulate the bodies of pregnant celebrities, we are simultaneously accepting and internalizing the very same regulations of ourselves.

When we *want* the pregnant celebrity body, we are confronted by the objectification of that body and multiple modes of commodification: of pregnancy, of the child itself—or at least its image, and of the "rockin' beach-worthy post-baby body." We are confronted with normative ideals of femininity and family that depend upon race, ethnicity, and citizenship, as well as socioeconomic class status and access to high fashion, good nutrition, and round-the-clock help. And, even as we are confounded by our inability to attain what we are told is perfection, women are provided strategies and products that promise rescue, for a cost.

A Neoliberal Biopolitics of Consumption, Surveillance, and Regulation

In these two ways—by compelling us to watch and to want—media coverage of the pregnant celebrity body becomes an interpretive lens through which to view the twin pillars of the state in late neoliberalism: an expansion of technologies of governance through proxies that enable state- and self-regulation and totalizing commodification via global capitalism. Neoliberalism, as a historical moment in the United States, commenced with the Reagan presidency with massive industry deregulation and continued during the Obama administration apace with global capital expansion. It is an economic ideology based on unrestricted trade and unfettered competition, and a political ideology that seeks to limit the seeming size of government in favor of privatization of most goods and services traditionally provided by the state.[3] Neoliberalism's deregulation and privatization are accompanied by a hyperfocus on individuals as consumers, rather than citizens or political actors.

For all of the deregulation undertaken in the economic sector, however, citizen-consumers find themselves, and their individual choices, increasingly monitored, surveilled, and regulated. This regulation often takes the form of "biopolitics"—theorized by Foucault as power exercised over living beings, *as* living beings, at the level of both the aggregate and the individual.[4] As we have less and less control over the forces shaping our daily lives, we have also become more and more responsible for how we live them.

In popular culture representations of celebrity pregnancies, biopolitical governance and commodity fetishism work in tandem to reassert formal and informal control over women's bodies, especially through a charged political discourse advocating a proliferation of fetal protection measures. Paradoxically, this occurs even as press coverage trumpets tales of women's liberation and our increasing cultural openness to pregnancy. Pregnant women are governed by a complex web of regulatory policy and informal social control, meant to structure their patterns of consumption and delimit access to autonomy and meaningful choice, in the name of contemporary "motherhood."

In the past decade, as press coverage of pregnant celebrities has proliferated, invasive and radical fetal protection and anti-abortion measures regulating and criminalizing the average woman and her pregnancy have emerged as public policy. At the same time, the general public's willingness to interfere in women's pregnancies also seems to have markedly increased.

Sarah Buttenwieser's witty and biting contribution to the feminist publication *Bitch!* noted the "rabid gestation speculation" of the popular press as it stalked and publicized celebrity pregnancies. Buttenwieser presciently noted that media coverage of celebrity pregnancy focuses on joy and glamour, on the "odd, unreal, and idealized version of celeb pregnancy—part dewy-eyed, part hot-pants"[5]—while the same publications' coverage of the average, everyday, normal pregnancy focuses on risk and danger and discomfort. The message is clear: celebrity pregnancies can be watched in order to be wanted; but regular pregnancies must be watched in order to be regulated and controlled.[6]

Fetal protection laws proposed in the 2010s stalk and discipline women in ways similar to approaches taken by the star-crazed media; ideas of "good motherhood" in the media portrayals of some celebrity's bumps are reinforced by and replicated in law. The National Abortion Rights Action League (NARAL) reports a steady increase in anti-choice measures enacted nationally since 1995, when 18 such measures were in place, to 2012, when that tally reached 755. These laws are not simply controls on access to termination of pregnancy (such as South Dakota's nearly universal ban on abortion); they are extensions of surveillance and criminal control over women's bodies in the specious name of fetal protection. These laws are not only proliferating, they are increasingly punitive. And the Supreme Court is increasingly willing to uphold these laws: restricting buffer zones for protest around clinics that provide reproductive health services and allowing employers to deny their workers access to birth control via company health plans.

I am not making a causal claim here. Viewing images of pregnant celebrities does not cause legislators to write bills mandating transvaginal ultrasounds, nor does it lead regulatory actors to advise against too many servings of fish or lunch meat. Rather, my claim is interpretive: we are in a unique moment of cultural, political, and legal convergence in which strangers feel entitled to warn women off sushi and mandated transvaginal ultrasounds seem to make as much sense (even if they do not sell as many magazines) as does surveilling Kate Middleton for the first glimpse of her "royal bump."

An Interpretive, Feminist Approach

The methodology I use in this book is interpretive. Interpretive methods allow scholars to read closely, to attend to complexity, and to situate particular phenomena within a cultural context that helps them be more legible.[7] These methods also give the scholar a wide choice of frames or lenses through which to view the issues at stake. Rooted in traditions of immanent critique through dialectical and hermeneutic methods, interpretivist scholars do not use their work in order to make causal claims, but rather to see connections.[8]

I am therefore interested in situating images of pregnant and mothering celebrities more deeply within the context in which they appear and with which they form a constitutive relationship. Pregnant women in America don't only see images of Angelina Jolie; they also see Jennifer Garner, MIA, Britney Spears, Gwen Stefani, their best friend Tina, their coworker Nancy, and their partner Amelia. Contemporary American women live in a society that devalues their work (figuratively and financially) and treats them in discriminatory ways based on their racial or ethnic identity, sexual orientation, and feminine/masculine presentation. They live in a culture of continuous battles within a constructed "culture war" that seems to make meaningless or impossible any deep conversation about reproductive freedom. And they live in a culture that is structured by the impulse to consumption and purchase that typify late neoliberal global capital.

My questions became what the proliferation of images of pregnant celebrities says about contemporary American law and culture, how we can read shifts in legality and governance through them, and how they grow from a particular history of pregnancy. Grounded in an analysis of changing popular and legal understandings of pregnancy in the United States since the 1970s, and focusing on the normative idealizations of certain pregnancies and pregnant bodies through popular culture representations of the pregnant celebrity body, this book examines our increasing comfort with governing pregnant bodies through the neoliberal processes of regulation, surveillance, and commodification. By taking an interpretive approach to social science research, the book argues that our obsessive attention to celebrity pregnancies is a reflection of, and reflected in, legal and political discourses of pregnancy. Tracing regulation of motherhood over time, I investigate popular culture representations of pregnancy to understand contemporary legislation and political discourse. In other words, *I am less interested in what these images do to us and much more interested in what they tell us about ourselves.*

I first came to this research wondering what the obsession with "the bump" said, in fact, about me. I first became aware of the celebrity baby bump as a popular culture phenomenon in 2004, when I was expecting our son and living in southern Los Angeles County. I was pregnant at the same time that Julia Roberts was, and many of the women I knew through pregnancy—from yoga, from birth classes, from La Leche League meetings—and from my scholarly research on midwifery and homebirth[9] were also interested in Roberts's pregnancy. We had conversations about what she wore and ate and how she planned to give birth (reportedly, she planned a water birth at Cedars Sinai). The idea for this book was planted there, as I watched myself watching Roberts and her pregnancy and wondering what it meant about how I was living mine.

In 2008, I began to write a chapter to contribute to a book on fashion and feminism; the chapter discusses mainstream portrayals of celebrity pregnancy fashion as the expression of particular tropes of femininity and womanhood. While researching the topic, I collected and analyzed print and web images of pregnant celebrities.

I tore photos out of magazines—at the gym, at my mom's house, at hair salons, at the dentist, and in our family's doctors' offices—and I taped them to my office wall. Nearly everyone who walked into my office asked about the photos and often would return with stacks of torn-out photos of their own to add to my collection. Soon my office was papered in hundreds of these images. I eventually took down the pictures of those women who were merely sensational and not celebrity; I removed pictures of those who were daughters of famous people, or married to famous men, or those whose fame I expected to be fleeting or was somehow more niche-like than broadly based. And although cultural obsession with her pregnancy is exceedingly interesting, this book does not engage the significant subject of Kate Middleton's pregnancy. A royal baby is somehow different from a celebrity baby, though the lines are not hard and fast. Though I make passing reference to media obsession with Kate's bump, I do not analyze treatment of her pregnancy in this text, nor do I discuss Chelsea Clinton's recent pregnancy, for similar reasons.

The photos that remained on my wall, and that are represented in this book, are those of iconic women. Ultimately, the celebrity pregnancies that I chose to focus on were embodied by women like Katie Holmes, Nicole Kidman, Angelina Jolie, Jennifer Garner, Julia Roberts, Britney Spears, Salma Hayek, Halle Berry, Jennifer Lopez, Beyoncé Knowles, and others—women famous for their own work, if also for their partners.

Having narrowed the field of potential pregnancies to analyze, I used *People* magazine's archives to search for all articles and photos in that publication related to these particular women. This search turned up thousands of pieces of data to interpret. I also performed web searches in Google, using key terms composed of each star's name, plus "pregnancy," "pregnant," "bump," and "baby"—as well as searches that specified certain publications and televised "infotainment" programs *(Us! Weekly, Entertainment Tonight,* and *TMZ).* Soon, hundreds more photos inhabited my hard drive. Finally, I lurked on highly trafficked celebrity websites such as *Just Jared, Celebitchy,* and *BumpShack.* Quite quickly, I began to see themes in the coverage of the pregnancies and births: easily recognizable tropes of femininity, which form the basis of the first article I wrote, as well as much of the third chapter of this book.

That first analytical pass generated an intersectional, feminist analysis. Approaching my work with a feminist analysis means first and foremost that I am attentive to gendered experiences, with an eye to social justice. Central to my analysis are standpoint epistemology[10] and intersectionality.[11] Standpoint epistemology is the claim that we know, and experience what we know and experience, because of where we are located within political, economic, and social structures, as well as how we are situated culturally, in our families, and in our own psyches. Standpoint epistemology exposes the "taken-for-granted" aspects of daily life and situates that life institutionally, contextually, and temporally.

Standpoint epistemology acknowledges that some ways of being and knowing and acting are foreclosed to some individuals because of their gender identity, location in geography and history, racial identity, and class positionality. Conversely, other novel and important ways of being and knowing are opened by those same aspects of positionality, though those perspectives have often been marginalized by dominant masculine and heterosexist discourses and powers.

Intersectionality is the anti-essentialist position that members of groups, while able to participate in identity politics based on their held identities, are also discrete and unique individuals with multiply held identities related to their social, temporal, and cultural contexts.[12] An intersectional analysis understands that some identities gain primacy, or are deployed, based upon the context an individual is acting within. For example, I am a wife in a heterosexual marriage, a biological mother and active parent to a son, a white (non-Hispanic), a progressive, a professor, and a cis female. My professional identity is not as salient at my son's school as is my identity as one of his parents; my whiteness affords me unearned privilege in front of a classroom, even as my female identity offers challenges in the same context.

Embodiment is a third important aspect of my feminist analysis and an area to which this book holds debts. Robin West early articulated a theory of hedonic feminism that recognized the embodied aspects of women's existence;[13] Sara Ruddick's work on mothering also understands the embodied aspects of women's lived experiences[14] and the way those experiences contribute to political beliefs and actions. Latina writers Gloria Anzaldua and Cherrie Moraga, as well as African American womanist writers Alice Walker and Audre Lorde placed significant focus on what it means to live in the body of a woman of color.[15] How, they asked, does it feel threatening, or powerful, or unsafe? How are some female bodies read as overly voluptuous and fertile or, alternatively, as cold and sterile? Feminists and women of color writers make it clear that the body is both a cultural battleground and a site of pleasure. Additionally, stylized figures and narratives of these bodies—scripts of "the black butt," for example—impact popular understandings of women and their lives.[16]

The import for my work of these understandings has been as strong for me as the insight from feminists in an earlier generation, that "the personal is political."[17] Grounding experiences of feminism deeply in the body enables us to understand feminist politics and theory as rooted in everyday, lived, embodied experience. It also enables feminists to understand bodies as locations upon which politics and law are worked out and contested, to read particular bodies as cultural texts, and to understand the legal regulations and pressures upon them. And doing so allows for an exploration of the implications for regulatory policy and legality of particular bodies as they are understood in particular ways.[18] Thus, pregnancy—an embodied, extraordinary, and unique (while simultaneously mundane and everyday) series of moments experienced only by women—offers a particularly rich site for intersectional feminist analysis.[19]

Looking at images of pregnant celebrities, I asked, "What norms of gender, racial, and class identity are visible via the bump? What messages do women receive when they look at thousands of images of pregnant celebrity icons?" What resulted from that analysis was first published in the book *Feminism, Fashion, and Flair* as a chapter titled "The Baby Bump Is the New Birkin," which I have expanded upon and offer as chapter three of this text. The title of that original chapter hints at a second level of analysis, which is only marginally developed in that piece, but which serves as the basis of chapters four and five here. This analysis investigates the baby bump—and the pregnant body in total—as a site of consumption, as a product to possess. As a site of both consumption and production, the pregnant female body emerges as a worthy and necessary object of state and social control.

As I began analyzing the images of pregnant celebrities, it became clear that those wearing and buying and eating the "right" things are portrayed not just as ideal mothers, but also as ideal consumers and ideal citizens. One paparazzi photo shows a glowingly fresh-faced and pregnant Jennifer Garner shopping for groceries; the camera zoom enables us to see that her handwritten list includes "hot dogs" and "macaroni and cheese." How quintessentially American! And, paired with a basket already full of produce, how healthy! A photo of Britney Spears, on the other hand, features the star in dingy sweat pants and a shaved head carrying a venti-sized coffee. The picture is accompanied by caption text suggesting that she buys more potent—and illegal— uppers at other times of the day. One woman is clearly a good consumer, a good American, and, thus, a good mother; the other is drawn toward the criminal, the subversive, and the unacceptable and is clearly portrayed as a bad mom.

Examination of images like these makes it evident that the obsession around celebrity pregnancy does not merely reaffirm normative idealizations of femininity that are racialized and eroticized. It also enables women to feel comfortable with, accept, and even welcome the dual powers of neoliberal governance: social control through commodification on the one hand, and regulatory surveillance on the other. This control is achieved through the internalization of norms and the deployment of a disciplinary social gaze, to be sure. But it is also achieved politically, through legislation and political rhetoric, as well as juridically, through court decisions. And it is achieved through the use of proxies—nonstate actors like medical professionals, restaurant wait staff, friends and neighbors, and the media. Women's bodies are sites of contestation in the contemporary American culture wars being fought socially, politically, and juridically. This book is animated by an interest in law and governance—their relationship to culture and as cultural powers in themselves—as we see them in contemporary obsession with pregnant celebrities.

A Law and Society Take on Law and Popular Culture

Is there any place a law and society scholar will not go to understand law in its magnificent variety, complexity, and possibility?

—Austin Sarat, "Imagining the Law of the Father"[20]

As a sociolegal scholar, I explore changes in law and state regulatory power, as well as political discourses around them, from the point of view that law, culture, and society are mutually constitutive.[21] Both pregnancy and popular culture are wonderful places from which to do this. Understanding that realities of social and cultural life are reflected in law at the same time that law creates many of the conditions within which social and cultural life is organized, law and society scholars are aware of the presence of law and legality in the areas of social and cultural life that are conventionally understood as "informal" or "not legal."[22] They are attentive to both that legality and the potential for reification of the dichotomy crafted by just such a discourse of formality and informality, legal and extralegal.[23] As such, work on law and society/law and culture understands that legal, social, and cultural aspects of lived experience have similar import; this work attends to the uniquely legal (that is, state-sanctioned) use of power as it impacts people, and to the quotidian, the seemingly nonlegal, extralegal or informal, as it impacts laws and legality.[24]

One of the places sociolegal scholars have looked, of late, to examine law where it might not "at first glance" appear to be[25] are popular culture representations of legality in film and television. Scholars interested in popular culture often examine films and television shows for what they say and demonstrate about law in the culture that produced them.[26] They show how these forms of cultural production can be interpreted in a way similar to the interpretation of legal texts and propose to use analysis of them "to get a better purchase on [the] study of how law operates in the larger culture."[27] This work often examines televised and filmic representations of formal legal moments in order to show the importance of legal conventions, such as the trial, to contemporary drama and the prevalence of legality as a dramatic trope in popular culture.[28] They see, in popular culture, representations and reflections of the legal. They argue that film can help us understand legal power and that an examination of film can shed light on the contingencies and possibilities inherent in a legalized social order. They also make the constitutive point that law is crafted through discursive and representational practices.[29]

These analyses of law and popular culture almost always return to a focus on formal moments of and in law—usually via popular culture representations of the trial. The majority of the work focuses on representations of law in films, via characters, plot lines, and metaphor—they focus, that is, on examples of popular culture production that are *meant to* represent and discuss something "legal."[30]

However, pregnant celebrity bodies, and our obsessive cataloguing of them, are not intended as legal texts, nor as representations of law. They are not overtly legal; they do not ask viewers to think of, invoke, or reflect upon law as such. And yet, they construct legal meaning and reflect contemporary legal ideologies.

Law and culture scholars understand that just as often as they refer to overtly legal images, popular culture sources can also be read to understand and construct particular ideologies. Elayne Rapping, for example, has shown that conservative partisan ideologies are expressed in popular culture televised crime dramas like the *CSI* and *Law and Order* franchises.[31] Sarat and Kearns have noted that popular culture has been tied, via political discourse, to identity politics, in ways that serve to advance the "culture wars" that are, at core, about defining "American identity" through both popular culture and law.[32] Rosemary J. Coombe draws on Althusser's theory of interpellation to argue, "Law must be understood not simply as an institutional forum or legitimating discourse to which social groups turn to have pre-existing differences recognized, but, more crucially, as a central focus for the control and dissemination of those signifying forms with which difference is made and remade."[33] In Coombe's view, "cultural flows are legally regulated, imagined, managed, and contested"[34] via regulatory policy, in terms of broadcast, customs, and the like. Drawing on Angela McRobbie's work, Coombe writes, "Regimes of law are constitutive of the cultural conditions of production and reproduction of representations."[35] Sarat and Kearns' introduction to Coombe's contribution to their volume stresses that cultural studies "connects [cultural] texts with larger cultural contexts."[36]

I do not disagree; yet I find that the relationship between law and cultural production is more complex, and more mutual, than this. I argue the constitutive other side of Coombe's statement: cultural forms also inform—help us imagine, accept, tolerate, welcome, manage, and contest—the legal controls of the regulatory state, beyond the realm of cultural production itself. These "signifying forms," to adopt Coombe's usage of Althusserian language—the texts and images of cultural production—are interpellated, to constitute legality via governance and regulation.[37]

Haltom and McCann make a similar argument, referring to popular culture treatment and media coverage of contemporary tort litigation and the political arguments for tort reform. They argue that mass media is central in the production of cultural narratives that subsequently impact policy. Haltom and McCann are interested in the way that these popular culture narratives help to constitute and inform a set of institutions, individual actors, and ideologies that constrain and open particular interpretations of and possibilities within law. They argue that these narratives, scripts, and logics are objects of public interest that can help us crystallize conversations about important legal and political issues, abstract legal concepts, and the way that we construct identities like race, class, and gender.[38]

The analysis here relies on a framework of law "in" and "on" sites of popular culture, and the constitutive interaction of popular culture as seen in representations of the celebrity baby bump with political life and legality. Such a constitutive circle is made possible, in large part, by the paradoxical proliferation of regulatory governance typified by late modern capital in neoliberalism, a point to which we turn at the end of this introduction. Pregnant and mothering celebrity bodies—and cultural obsession with them—are sites of legal and political contestation and learning. These bodies have nothing overt to do with law and politics, but they are deeply embedded in contemporary practices of law and governance and reflected in them. Ideologies of mothering and pregnancy, neoliberal capitalism and control, regulation and risk, become manifest and visible in our popular culture obsession with pregnant celebrities and in a simultaneous proliferation of laws meant to control pregnant women.

Regarding Celebrities as Cultural Texts with Legal-Political Implications

Celebrity as a general category has a long history of inclusion in analysis of Western popular culture and politics. Celebrity provides a powerful means by which to understand emerging cultural trends and through which to read contemporary politics.[39] David Marshall's early definition of celebrity has become standard. He writes:

> In the public sphere, a cluster of individuals are given greater presence and a wider scope of activity and agency than are those who make up the rest of the population. They are allowed to move on the public stage while the rest of us watch. They are allowed to express themselves quite individually and idiosyncratically while the rest of the members of the population are constructed as demographic aggregates. We tend to call these overtly public individuals *celebrities*.[40]

Marshall's definition understands that athletes and politicians can achieve celebrity status just as readily as the "stars" focused on in this book: film actresses and musical performers. His focus is on the power accorded celebrity status and the way that status functions in popular culture imaginings.[41]

Whether understood as the physical embodiment of a particular set of "signs," as a "system," or as a set of "symbols," celebrity functions to valorize particular cultural messages. As Marshall explains: "The power of celebrity status appears in business, politics, and artistic communities and operates as *a way of providing distinctions and definitions of success* within those domains. Celebrity status also confers on the person a certain discursive power: within society, the celebrity is a voice above others, a voice that is channeled into the media systems as being legitimately significant."[42] With this discursive power, "the celebrity . . . allows for the configuration, positioning, and proliferation of certain discourses about the individual and individuality in contemporary culture."[43]

Many of those who focus on celebrity in a scholarly way share general agreement on four propositions that are important to this book:

1. Celebrities express ideologies of the wider culture.

2. Celebrities channel cultural anxieties, often through representations of particular identities.

3. Celebrities stand at the junction of "ordinary life" and the "extraordinary."

4. Celebrities cultivate a wide range of desires.

Most important for most scholars of celebrity, that designation helps express a culture's founding ideologies and contemporary priorities. Dyer argues that stars have particular ideological meanings and functions and that particular stars become important at particular cultural moments in order to crystallize and assert particular ideologies.[44] In the context of the United States, celebrity is widely acknowledged to express (and justify) a focus on "conceptions of individuality that are the ideological ground of Western culture."[45] For instance, it is well documented that Ronald Reagan, the president, was able to channel the persona of Ronald Reagan, the film star—traditionalist, rugged individualist, masculine—in order to attain political success by merging conservative American ideals with his celebrity status.[46]

Even as celebrity popularizes particular ideologies, it also channels cultural anxiety. Dyer sees these as related; he argues that stars serve to reinforce the status quo, and in particular to reinforce particular values that are considered "under threat."[47] The star might do that by embodying those values for the popular culture to emulate. Or a star's transgressive acts might serve to reinforce traditional values by embodying the "threat" of, for instance, the female sexuality of Madonna in the 1980s, or the gender-queering performances of David Bowie in the 1970s; Lady Gaga in 2010; and Miley Cyrus in 2013.

Given the focus on hyperindividuality underlying Western cultural ideologies, it is unsurprising that some of the cultural anxieties being transmitted and mediated through celebrity regard issues of identity and boundary crossing or transgressing. Celebrity confronts questions of identity on the national stage. Sometimes, celebrity offers reassurance about stereotyped identities. As Pamela Robertson Wojcik puts it: "The star system . . . relies on recognizability, marketability, and the necessity for known commodities. . . . [I]nsofar as the actor represents human characters, film acting relates to changing conceptions of identity and identity politics, and thus the actor will inevitably negotiate stereotypes and represent identities inflected by race, gender, and ethnicity."[48]

But stars often embody contradictions within, and contestations over, identity. Marshall argues, "The celebrity offers a discursive focus for the discussion of realms that are considered outside the bound of public debate in the most public fashion."[49] We can see this in obsession over which stars are gay or not—in the obsessive coverage, in the popular press and tabloids, of John Travolta's sexuality, and Hugh Jackman's, and Jodie Foster's. As we obsess on the private sexual lives of real (famous) people, we work out, culturally, the proper role of sex—and what kind of sex is proper—in public debate.

The same is true of pregnancy. In the early 1980s, when talk of pregnancy was still largely taboo, celebrity was one of the vehicles through which it became public. There remains a tension among notions of motherhood, womanhood, feminism, power, and identity. Accordingly, we continue to use the pregnant celebrity body as a location from which we can have conversations about pregnancy, motherhood, and gender roles for contemporary American women.

Pregnancy is arguably a mundane and ordinary event—millions of women are pregnant every day of every year—but pregnancy is experienced, and culturally celebrated, as a unique and extraordinary moment in an individual's life. This strange and incompletely realized dichotomy—the blurred line between the exceptional and the ordinary—is also at the heart of celebrity and is the third hallmark of its power. Celebrity is always both about "a capacity to attract attention," and about "some degree of 'ordinariness.'"[50] Here, for example, we find stories of the average, rural, teenager (Ashton Kutcher, for instance) brought to fame by a television show (*That 70s Show*) nominally about daily life in average, small-town America—made extraordinary by his wealth, marriage to, and divorce from Demi Moore—later becoming a parent with bump-watched Mila Kunis.

Celebrities are exceptional; yet in order to maintain a connection to their fan base, they must also be somewhat accessible, their personas at least marginally attainable. The insistence on the partial ordinariness of celebrities enables the rest of us to use stars as embodiments of, or imaginary templates for, the ways that we will live our lives.[51] This is part of the reason we see "make-over" features in women's magazines that purport to make average women look like Beyoncé or Gwyneth Paltrow. It is why popular culture is fascinated by average or not famous people who happen to look like celebrities, without makeover manipulation. This need for ordinariness contributes to the contemporary interest in "un-Photoshopping" glamorous magazine advertisements and photojournalistic editorial spreads, and to paparazzi photos of celebrities out "without makeup" or "looking horrible" or "average."

The audience, Marshall argues, yearns to know the star "authentically."[52] They seek to be able to say, with certainty, "this is what celebrity *is*, and is not." Increasingly, such authentic knowledge is achieved through photojournalism that endeavors to show celebrities doing everyday activities: grocery shopping, taking children to school, getting their hair done. In *US!* magazine, there are pages devoted to coverage of celebrities that trumpet the headline "They're just like us!" Stars like Katy Perry and James Franco promote themselves and their work through "selfies" and Instagram; the internet is full of memes of Ryan Gosling and Hugh Jackman (as feminists, no less), engaging in ordinary life.

Celebrity would not be nearly as pleasurable or enjoyable if it were off limits to those of us consuming it; rather, celebrity status becomes the embodiment of our aspirations.[53] Simon Dixon's analysis of photojournalistic coverage of celebrity homes makes the same point. He writes, "For all the decadence of stardom, a key ingredient is . . . an 'ordinariness' of background, something that makes the star typical."[54]

Marshall argues that our obsession with the "real" lives of celebrities is incredibly important in the construction of the celebrity sign itself. He writes, "the disjuncture and intertextuality of the working life and the real life of the celebrity configures celebrity itself."[55] Celebrity, then, creates its own desire to know the (often ordinary) "truth" or "reality" of those celebrated as extraordinary. Even if we cannot attain celebrity status, or successfully look or shop like a celebrity, a particularly (bitter)sweet tension within celebrity is our deep desire to uncover the "real person" under the persona.[56]

Celebrity's final function—this creation of desire—plays a significant role here as well. We learn to crave the movie star's aesthetic: "With its close connection to the construction of consumer lifestyles, the film celebrity's forays into recreational pursuits helped define the parameters of pleasure through consumption for all segments of society."[57] Dixon argues that "the star's residence has in general been less a home than a temporary theater for the display of living."[58] And we go further, Marshall argues: we match our morality and personality with the star's morality, lifestyle, and psychological personality.[59] He concludes, "Perhaps the best example of this expansive and proliferating power to influence the entire society has been the growing centrality of the Hollywood image of the healthy body."[60]

The celebrity body, then, is a text, a sign, something to be read and understood.[61] It tells us what is construed as healthy, what is construed as decadent, what is construed as desirable. Dyer stresses the need to understand the context from which particular stars emerge and in which they operate;[62] Marshall asks us to attend to the ideologies behind the construction of particular celebrity personalities. We can learn much about the star by attending to the context and ideology surrounding her. As with popular legal culture analyses, the constitutive relationship holds true: we can learn much about the context, and the cultural ideologies at play, by attending to the embodied star.

Governance through Celebrity: A Sociolegal View

The sociolegal literature has not yet theorized celebrity as a legal text nor attended to celebrity in the same way that it has attended to film or literature. But the pregnant celebrity body is a particularly important sign to be read and contextualized at this particular time because it serves as a uniquely powerful proxy of governance in neoliberalism. Pregnancy, as it is represented in these celebrity bodies, reflects the changing role of the state vis-à-vis the pregnant body. We can learn much by observing our popular culture's mediated relationship with pregnant female celebrities.

French social theorist Michel Foucault was one of the first to define and describe the processes of state and social control related to neoliberalism in late capital, though he did not term them such. Writing just prior to the initiation of neoliberal consolidation under the Reagan (in the United States) and Thatcher (in Britain) regimes, Foucault delivered thirteen lectures between 1970 and 1984 that outlined his theory of governmentality. Key to Foucault's theory is that in late modernity, developed societies shifted from a "disciplinary society"—one where institutions were emphatic and obvious in the ways that their rules and physical organization shape behavior, to a "society of control" via, in large part, the individual internalization of the rules we have been disciplined to accept. Drawing on the plans for a prison made by Jeremy Bentham, Foucault shows us that the "panopticon"—a physical structure for incarceration with a centralized guard tower and open-to-view cells—makes surveillance unnecessary, as eventually the prisoners internalize the presence of the guards and discipline themselves. Under panoptical power, the state no longer relies solely on governmental institutions with overt rules to gain compliance with norms.

Foucault further theorized "biopower"—power exercised over humans *as* living beings, both as individuals and as members of collectivities. Biopower exerts control over individual bodies by "prohibiting conduct such as masturbation, defining some activities as perverted, or celebrating other activities, such as heterosexual sex, as natural."[63] Biopolitical power works on larger populations by, for example, "measuring and calculating the demographics associated with how and when a child is fed, adjusting the social environment to promote the desired outcome."[64] Once individuals have internalized the panoptical gaze and the biopolitical imperative, Foucault theorized that they would act appropriately most of the time, even absent overt rules and laws.

What, then, becomes of the state? Theorists of neoliberalism widely accept that we have made the shift posited by Foucault from discipline to control, but differ in their views on the role and size of the state in such a society. To the extent that there remain deviant and undisciplined subjects whose presence justifies a need for state discipline and intervention, state surveillance and discipline remains necessary.

Counter to those who have argued that neoliberalism's move toward privatization of social control has diminished the role of the state, a wide range of scholars have argued that the state remains an important site of contestation and control in neoliberalism.[65] Indeed, these scholars argue that institutions of neoliberal capital expansion are *dependent* upon the neoliberal state, which focuses its biopower on the personal lives of discrete individuals.[66] In addition to increased surveillance and regulation tied to criminal law and anti-terror campaigns, commodification and consumption become increasingly important sites for the locus of social control. Dean writes: "the individualization of politics into commodifiable 'lifestyles' and opinions subsumes politics into consumption. That consumer choices may have a politics— fair trade, green, vegan, woman-owned—morphs into the sense that politics is nothing but consumer choices, that is, individuated responses to individuated needs."[67]

Rather than having fixed identities that they mobilize through protest or voting, contemporary citizens are offered, through neoliberalism, "multiple, imaginary identities" and are "encouraged to remake themselves, to see themselves as mutable projects ever available to improvement and refashioning."[68] In the service of this project, we are offered easy ways to engage politically (join a virtual petition, click a "like" button, shop at Whole Foods or The Body Shop), as well as a plethora of goods and services to purchase.

This focus on consumers as individuals dovetails with an upswing in popular culture obsessions with discrete, singular, individual stars—celebrities.[69] And because one aspect of the political agenda of neoliberalism is the tendency to "politicize all aspects of family life and lived experience, [and] seek the intervention of law on their behalf,"[70] it makes sense that pregnant women and their bodies are increasingly the subjects of discipline via surveillance and social control.[71] Popular culture obsession with the celebrity baby bump enables biopolitical governance of women's bodies for conservative ends, consonant with neoliberalism.

We can see biopower at work in the way that women are governed and disciplined through the images of celebrity pregnancies they receive in the popular press. Much of this biopolitical governance and discipline reinscribes norms of femininity, yet this is not the extent of the governance and disciplining of women through these images; such governance is also present in the commodification of products and bodies associated with pregnancy and in the rendering of criminal those women who perform their pregnancies in deviant ways through a desire for an abortion, through prenatal neglect, or by miscarriage. The state in neoliberalism is *not* absent nor declining in its power or presence in women's lives or on their bodies; rather, it appears in different forms, with different intent and function. State power in neoliberalism may be more diffuse and dispersed; it is not, however, any less powerful.

Very few theorists of law and culture have attended to neoliberalism as part of the context within which representations of law in the popular culture are made and consumed. Ouellette, though, posits that the proliferation of reality television shows dealing with justice (judge shows and "cop" shows) seem to "be situated within [a] broader political reimagining of responsibility for civic life and public services."[72] She does not term this "broader political reimagining" as neoliberalism, but it seems appropriate to do so. She writes that within this broader context, "the point to be made is not that control is totalizing or seamless, but that 'real justice' entertainment stitches commercial television into a range of intersecting strategies for managing populations conceived as risky or at risk."[73] Coverage of the celebrity baby bump serves a similar purpose; it enables the general public to work out and develop strategies for managing pregnant bodies—those that deviate from idealized and normalized performances as well as those disciplined enough to maintain them.

Law, Again

Informed by feminist theory and an understanding of the unique context provided by global neoliberalism and neoliberal governance, a view of law through the baby bump is attentive to cultural production and allows us to see law and culture as mutually constitutive, as mutually self-reinforcing, and as mutually regulatory. Representations of pregnancy within popular culture coverage of celebrities are figures upon which our cultural tolerance for and expectations of regulation are constituted. Press coverage of celebrity pregnancy is a manifestation of seemingly paradoxical American cultural shifts begun in earnest in the 1970s—shifts that seemed to result in increased freedoms, rights, and equality for pregnant women, but which actually brought about a responsibilization of women and a set of doctrines, policies, and discourses that constrain women's freedom in the name of fetal protection.

We live in a society where significant numbers of politicians seem increasingly desperate to control women's reproducing bodies, where a significant minority of the population does not trust that the panopticon is working—does not trust that women are adequately disciplined and docile. The extension of surveillance and the expectation of self-governance have not reduced the requirement for state intervention into women's reproductive lives. Laws are not suspended as we reach postmodernity; rather, as Jodi Dean argues, they are operating in different ways, favoring some actors and interests, rather than others,[74] with increasing focus on discrete individual acts of citizen-consumers.

By paying attention to popular obsession with the celebrity baby bump—the pregnant celebrity body—we also attend to law, patriarchy, late capitalism, and neoliberalism, as they work on the reproductive bodies of women living within them. What we view when we attend to these obsessions are not only the pregnancies of Beyoncé, Britney, and Julia; rather, through them, the celebrity baby bump becomes a window through which we gaze back in at law in late modern capitalism.

This is a book about celebrity and popular culture, about normative idealizations of women's bodies, and about consumerism and neoliberal governance through surveillance and biopower. This is also a book about law and politics and pregnancy and mothering in late neoliberalism. And it is a book about the way institutions and policymakers have struggled to adapt to cultural change regarding pregnancy in the 1970s and 80s. It is about law and its politicization in the early part of the twenty-first century as a technique for controlling unruly women's bodies; and, ultimately, about how law and politics have adapted to the necessities of surveillance in late capitalism—where we have become exceedingly comfortable with, and implicated in, watching ourselves and each other.

CHAPTER 1

LAW, POPULAR CULTURE, AND PREGNANCY IN AMERICA

IN 1991, *Vanity Fair* magazine broke ground by placing an image of a nude and pregnant Demi Moore on its cover. The resulting media firestorm was intense, and the controversy helped the cover become iconic. The magazine broke records, selling more than one million copies (in contrast to a regular distribution at the time of around 800,000) and receiving voluminous correspondence, both in support of and angry about the cover.[1]

The *Vanity Fair* cover and the attention given it helped to change how pregnancy was seen and represented in the contemporary press. In the last twenty-five years, in large part because of celebrity openness about their pregnant physiques in the wake of the Demi Moore cover, the pregnant body has mostly lost its reputation as repulsive and embarrassing. Now, pregnant women are encouraged to enjoy the physicality of their pregnancy—in fact, to embrace the beauty of pregnancy by dressing (and undressing) to show off "the bump."

This is a sea change.

Histories of mothering situated in the Western world highlight the strange mix of horror, fascination, and reverence with which pregnancy has long been treated in the popular culture of each period. Such histories also almost uniformly stress that, at least for white and middle- to upper-middle-class women, motherhood was constructed as part of the realm of the domestic, the private. If they were to be seen out in public, pregnant

FIGURE 1.1 Demi Moore's pathbreaking cover for *Vanity Fair*. Photo by: Annie Leibovitz

women were expected to be "demure and modest."[2] Francus notes that in British fiction of the eighteenth century, women who were not able to be appropriately domestic and maternal were vilified and suspect. Popular literature from the period abounds with tales of infanticide, evil stepmothers, and self-centered women—clearly the antitheses of mothers who met the norms of domestic and modest, nurturing and self-abdicating. Such women were idealized, and domesticity and motherhood were seen as the pinnacle of a white woman's potential development. These women were also relegated to the private realm—the home—outside of the gaze of the public sphere. In some regards, their proper domesticity and maternity depended upon women's invisibility.

These attitudes travelled easily to the United States and very much informed the sociocultural politics surrounding motherhood in the colonial period and well beyond. While women of color and lower-class white women were indeed in the labor force, white women of the mercantile class in the United States were relegated to private life.[3] These mothering women were expected to manage the private sphere and remain outside of the public one; their pregnancies were self-managed and self-regulated, with the help of other women in secret. Pregnancy, an indicator that sex has taken place, was simply considered too risqué for polite company. Contemporary media coverage of female celebrities who highlight their pregnancy in form-fitting dresses on the red carpet at awards shows could not have been imagined a century ago, when "a concern with physical appearance during pregnancy [was seen as] incongruent with the image of the ideal mother figure."[4]

Nor could contemporary representations of celebrity pregnancy have been imagined even as recently as 1950, when Lucille Ball was the first woman to be acknowledged to "be expecting" on television, though the Federal Communications Commission considered the word "pregnant" lewd enough to censor.[5] And they could not have been imagined even in 1970, when Cleveland junior high school teacher Jo Carol LaFleur was placed on mandatory leave in her second trimester, because school administrators worried that her pregnant body would alternately disgust, concern, fascinate, and embarrass her students.

Yet now, twenty-five years after the Demi Moore cover, more than a hundred years of cultural norms seem to have shifted. Some women's pregnant bodies can be seen as acceptable, even desirable. In the years from 1970 to 2000, popular culture became more open to performances of pregnancy; once kept secret and articulated as private, pregnancy became "public." At the same time, the U.S. Supreme Court reached decisions that had the potential to give women a greater measure of control over their reproductive capacity, both while pregnant and while seeking to avoid pregnancy, by articulating a tenuous right to privacy. This is an interesting juxtaposition: women have sought and gained rights to privacy in reproduction, just as they have also sought and received the freedom to be public with their pregnancies.

Popular culture and jurisprudence have facilitated steps toward equality and freedom for women, to be sure. However, the relationship between popular culture and jurisprudence in the period is an interesting and complex one; it is a history of openings and closings, steps forward and back. While part of the story is progressive, a second narrative emerges; it is a neoliberal story in which popular culture and jurisprudence work together to make women more responsible for their pregnancies and the general public more invested in these performances of pregnancy.

The contemporary history of reproductive rights in the United States, from both feminist and legal standpoints and especially as it covers the formative years leading up to and after *Roe v. Wade,* is well told and well known.[6] Much of that history has focused on the momentous Supreme Court decisions and cultural shifts permitting women access to contraception and abortion—the growing right, in other words, to be *private* in one's decision making surrounding reproduction and to make choices to avoid and terminate pregnancy. There is also a well-established body of scholarship illuminating the legal holdings, regulatory practices, and forms of cultural production that enabled women to be *public* with reproductive decision making[7] and to make choices in support of their pregnancies: to retain employment, access benefits, and claim public space, even while sporting a "bump." This chapter draws on these sources to identify key moments between 1970 and 2000—it brings us right up to the era of the baby bump's media dominance—and provides analytical snapshots of the jurisprudence and popular culture of women's reproductive lives in the United States, to help us understand and contextualize the contemporary mania for the baby bump as a sociolegal moment.

The existing scholarship on state control of women's reproductive capacity illustrates that governance serves multiple purposes in the politics of state formation. Rhetorics surrounding motherhood and policies attempting to control women's reproduction served the purposes of nation building in colonialism, into industrialization, and through the contemporary period. In all of its manifestations, those who governed women and their behavior agreed that one of femininity's main functions was to produce citizens and workers. Solinger writes, "In the struggle over who controls women's reproductive capacity, the state has created laws and policies that use female fertility to solve social problems and to sustain traditional roles for women."[8] In a project of nation building and social control via reproduction, the state has had to decide who is "fit" to reproduce, and slavery, genocide, and eugenics all offered ways to determine just who was, indeed, fit to birth and parent.

The history of reproductive politics in the United States has been a history of state and social control over all women's reproductive capacity.[9] Though reproduction was private, it was obstructed, incentivized, and forced in ways that served the purported public interest. The reasons for state control over women's reproduction have shifted over time, and from actor to actor, as have the techniques of this control. And the relationships between hiding—or keeping private—and using—or making public—women's bodies are constitutive and interrelated. Women's reproduction has been constructed as *both* private and requiring secrecy, as well as public and requiring regulation; such construction has often been inconsistent and in tension with other state goals and needs. For example, the argument that women's pregnancies are private was used to disempower women in many realms in the early period of this country's history, by keeping some women out of the paid workforce. The same argument, that women's pregnancies are private, has more recently been used by feminists and progressives to secure some measure of reproductive autonomy for some women. The idea that women are breeders was used by Progressives in the early 1900s to enact far-reaching worker protection laws for women; it was used by slave owners, however, a mere fifty years prior, to justify the rape and forced breeding of women held in slavery.

Yet understanding these relationships sheds light on the popularity of contemporary press coverage of celebrity baby bumps and helps us understand the limitations of, and problems associated with, such coverage. Popular culture, legal, medical, and psychological representations of motherhood, Bassin writes, "tap and shape our complex feelings about motherhood."[10] We must go a step further and see that representations of pregnancy and motherhood in these arenas not only shape personal feeling about and understandings of motherhood, they constitute each other—public policy, medicine, and doctrine are shaped by public representations of what is possible and appropriate in pregnancy. We cannot untangle the complex web of doctrine, legislation, and representation surrounding pregnancy and mothering since 1970, so much as make the strands of that web more readily visible. The 1970s were perhaps the most influential decade, jurisprudentially, for women's reproductive lives. They set the stage for openness to the bump, and pregnancy, that we have today; they also set the stage for the increased surveillance of pregnant women overall and demands for increased self-discipline of their pregnancies.

That 70s Show: Path-Breaking Jurisprudence on Pregnancy

In the 1970s, as women claimed more sexual freedom for themselves and were mothers and were wage earners, many insisted that the meaning of pregnancy itself had to be legally challenged.

—Rickie Solinger, *Pregnancy and Power*[11]

Jo Carol LaFleur and Ann Elizabeth Nelson taught junior high in Cleveland, Ohio, and both were pregnant during 1970–1971 academic year. The Cleveland Board of Education had a policy dating from 1952 that required women to take unpaid maternity leave beginning in the fourth month of pregnancy and to remain out from work "until the beginning of the first semester falling at least three months after they had given birth, and then only with written approval from a physician."[12] The policy in essence required mothers to take a minimum of eight months unpaid leave. Depending on the timing of the pregnancy and birth, this mandated, unpaid leave could be as long as thirteen months, if a woman gave birth at the beginning of December and remained ineligible to reenter the classroom until fall semester, or September. The board's policy was predicated on many traditional and stereotypical beliefs about pregnancy and motherhood. The board's policy also likely seemed pretty safe jurisprudentially.

The Supreme Court had previously affirmed the idea that motherhood and paid employment did not, or should not, mix. One of the most famous examples of these cases came from a challenge to Oregon's 1903 protective legislation focusing on women working in laundries. The Oregon law mandated that laundry owners could not force women to work more than ten hours per day, six days per week. Employer Muller challenged the law on substantive due process grounds, arguing that women should have the right to freely contract and determine their own terms of employment. Attorney Louis Brandeis argued on behalf of the state that in order to be healthy mothers who bore vigorous offspring, women must have their work hours constrained by the state. Brandeis was certain: the state needed to protect women, as they are "at a disadvantage in the struggle for subsistence" when pregnant and mothering.[13]

In reviewing and approving the law, the Court adopted the attitude of positive eugenicists who argued for the state's role in encouraging and creating "better babies and fitter families."[14] Oregon had a legitimate state interest in women's reproduction, the Court concluded, not because *workers* needed protection from capital exploitation, but rather because of the importance of healthy women for "breeding" healthy future citizens. In fact, the Court wrote, such legislation was vital "to the future well-being of the race."[15] *Muller's* rendering of women's rights contextualized in a reproductive role enabled the decision to be consonant with previous rulings that closed aspects of the workforce to women, like the one in *Bradwell v. Illinois* (1873),[16] where the Court justified Bradwell's exclusion from the legal profession on the grounds that, as a woman, her paramount destiny was as a wife and a mother.

As a direct result of *Muller*, states passed and maintained protective legislation for women working in a range of fields. In addition, these laws constructed many areas of employment as ill suited for women at all, and pregnant women in general were barred from several places of employment. By the early 1950s, every state defined pregnant women as unable to work *and* as ineligible for unemployment benefits.[17] The denial of these benefits makes sense only if we assume that women are not the primary breadwinners in the home, or if we assume at the least that women's income is not essential to the household budget. Women were thought to work only for "pin money," the money they would save up to buy small baubles and luxuries. If they worked to support a family, the Cleveland Board of Education might well have wondered how the teachers in that city could afford eight to thirteen months of unpaid leave.

Before the Court, lawyers for the Cleveland Board of Education argued that pregnant women were "less fit to handle the rigors of teaching and disciplining urban high school students" and, returning to ground trod in *Muller v. Oregon*, stressed the "delicate" nature of pregnant women.[18] In the brief they submitted on behalf of their policy, the Board of Education's lawyers wrote that high school students, "nurtured, as the evidence shows, by the violence of television programs and their reactions to the world around them, must be taught by able-bodied, vigorous teachers."[19]

The Board of Education's brief goes on to elaborate its view that pregnant women are not able bodied or vigorous; rather, they are "delicate" and "fearful." A pregnant schoolteacher, according to the Board: "experiences the three classic fears of pregnancy: miscarriage, agony in labor, and a deformed child. Her pregnancy in the environment in which she finds herself, full of active, demanding, disrespectful and, indeed, sometimes jeering young people, affects her ability to teach. . . . She is no longer able-bodied in the classroom."[20]

The mandatory leave policy was defended further on grounds more specific to the "state" of pregnancy itself and in ways that render "the baby bump" as a grotesquery. The board relied on cultural discomfort with pregnancy—the taboo against "showing"—that students would bring to the classrooms, to claim that students would mock LaFleur, make her a laughingstock, and refute her claims to authority—all because she had visible proof of her pregnancy.

The Supreme Court disagreed, and in his ruling for a seven-member majority, Justice Potter Stewart declared the board's policy a violation of due process guarantees.[21] However, rather than take the school board to task for its archaic and Victorian views of pregnancy, Stewart's opinion stressed that the bright lines drawn by the policy were overly broad and restrictive, as "the ability of any particular pregnant woman to continue at work past any fixed time in her pregnancy is very much an individual matter." Justice Douglas's concurrence does hint, though, at his personal distaste for the board's reasoning. He wrote:

> The record . . . suggest[s] that the maternity leave regulations may have originally been inspired by other, less weighty, considerations. For example,

Dr. Mark C. Schinnerer, who served as Superintendent of Schools in Cleveland at the time the leave rule was adopted, testified in the District Court that the rule had been adopted in part to save pregnant teachers from embarrassment at the hands of giggling schoolchildren; the cutoff date at the end of the fourth month was chosen because this was when the teacher "began to show."

Similarly, at least several members of the Chesterfield County School Board thought a mandatory leave rule was justified in order to insulate schoolchildren from the sight of conspicuously pregnant women. One member of the school board thought that it was "not good for the school system" for students to view pregnant teachers, "because some of the kids say, my teacher swallowed a watermelon, things like that."

He concluded: "Whatever may have been the reaction in Queen Victoria's time, pregnancy is no longer a dirty word."[22]

Newly appointed Justice Rehnquist would have upheld the policy. His dissent focused clearly on the states' prerogative in using a rational basis upon which to draw lines around issues relating to employment termination and leave. Rehnquist indicated he would prefer that the Court had not, in *LaFleur*, offered due process protection to those women who became, and remained, pregnant.

Rehnquist was soon able to consolidate a conservative majority on the Court around these issues, and subsequent decisions retrenched the small gains women were beginning to make—in terms of rights to privacy and termination as well as rights to pregnancy. In fact, *LaFleur* was decided in a very unique and particular context; in the years leading up to and just prior to *LaFleur*, the Court was working out a jurisprudence of privacy that would impact women's rights regarding the decision to terminate a pregnancy and render a series of decisions that would become lightning rods for social conservatives.

The key cases in this thread of jurisprudence are *Griswold v. Connecticut* (1965),[23] *Eisenstadt v. Baird* (1972),[24] and *Roe v. Wade* (1973).[25] Until 1965 and the Supreme Court's holding in *Griswold v. Connecticut*, states could prohibit married couples (and all others) from gaining access to prescribed birth control. Griswold, who was Planned Parenthood's executive director in Connecticut, sued on his own behalf, as well as that of an unnamed physician working for

Planned Parenthood in the state, after they were convicted under the law for providing information about birth control, as well as birth control itself, to married couples seeking to avoid pregnancy. Writing for seven members of the Court, Justice Douglas reversed their convictions, which had been upheld by both lower courts and held that the Connecticut law violated a "right to marital privacy." A good deal of the Court's decision in Griswold rests on the assumed penumbral right of privacy within a normative marriage, when the couple, in consultation with their physician, decides together to avoid the "consequences" of heterosexual, monogamous, marital, sexual relationships.

The question of whether such a right to privacy in medical decision making could accrue to single women, who had no marital privacy to maintain, was raised and settled by the Court seven years later in *Eisenstadt v. Baird*. At issue in *Eisenstadt* was a Massachusetts law that feloniously prohibited the provision of birth control to any unmarried individuals, male or female. William Baird, a population control activist and proponent of birth control, gave contraceptive foam to patrons following a public lecture in Boston; he was convicted of violating the state statute that prohibited such provision and he challenged his conviction in the federal courts. Justice Brennan's rationale in striking the Massachusetts law for the Court did not extend the right of privacy argument broached in *Griswold;* rather, Brennan argued that there was no rational basis for the distinction made between "married" and "unmarried" people in the state law and no rational basis for denying access to contraception for those who were unmarried.

Close on the heels of *Eisenstadt,* which allowed single women and men some measure of freedom regarding their reproductive capacity, came *Roe v. Wade*, one of the most controversial and important cases in Supreme Court history. In *Roe*, the Court heard a successful challenge to a Texas law that outlawed all abortion, with the exception of those determined medically necessary in order to save the life of the mother. In a decision that split the Court seven to two, Justice Blackmun's majority opinion struck the Texas law as overly broad.

In the absence of federal law standardizing access to termination, the Court instituted a legal test based on the medical theory of viability as measured by the trimester system of pregnancy. In the first trimester, Justice Blackmun wrote for the majority, states had little legitimate interest in abortion and could not ban the procedure. In the third and final trimester, states had much greater interest in the termination of pregnancy and could legislate to limit access to it on behalf of the fetus. In the liminal space of the second trimester, where fetal viability was less assured, the states' interests in regulation and prohibition of abortion would have to be weighted with a woman's legitimate interests in privacy and the decision to terminate.

The backlash to the rights articulated in *Roe* was swift, long lasting, and multipronged. The Court in *Roe* had attempted to weigh the state's interests in maternal rights and health as potentially antagonistic to fetal rights and health, and several states passed laws elaborating on the idea of a malicious or ill-informed mother who sought to terminate; they revitalized the past century's myth of an "inadvertent murderess" who selfishly terminated without understanding the consequences of her actions.[26] Almost immediately, state legislatures began to pass laws regulating women's access to abortion after the first trimester. In *Planned Parenthood of Central Missouri v. Danforth*,[27] a *per curium* Court upheld Missouri's requirement for "informed consent" of women seeking termination, but struck the state's legislation requiring a husband's consent to the procedure, as well as those requiring parental consent for minors seeking abortion, absent a judicial bypass option. In *Danforth*, the Court's majority reinscribed norms of marriage that place the woman in the home and the man at the head of the household. Though he struck the spousal notification requirement, Blackmun wrote, "We are not unaware of the deep and proper concern and interest that a devoted and protective husband has in his wife's pregnancy," while also imagining equity in the relationship: "ideally, the decision to terminate a pregnancy should be one concurred in by both the wife and her husband."

But These are *Happy Days!*

Even as state legislatures and federal courts worked out the boundaries around women's access to abortion services, narratives about the procedure, and the choice, were quite absent in the popular culture of the period. Featured characters and stars did not have, nor talk about, abortions. The *Mary Tyler Moore Show*, for instance, a long-running and popular sitcom featuring feminist themes and strong women, avoided abortion as a topic completely, causing cultural critics Munford and Waters to write that the show portrayed "media-friendly feminism," that privileged "lifestyle and identity over politics."[28] One exception to the televised silence regarding abortion was the comedy *Maude,* a highly ranked spin-off of *All in the Family* that featured Bea Arthur in the title role. Maude was a "limousine liberal" and an avowed feminist. In the show's first season (1971–1972), when it enjoyed a series-high Nielsen ranking at number four, Maude procured a legal abortion in New York after a late-life pregnancy that she felt, at 47, "too old" to carry.[29]

As time went on, top dramas and comedies like *Three's Company, M.A.S.H.,* and *All in the Family* mirrored the controversies brewing in cultural politics of the era, and offered counternarratives regarding gender, war, and race. But popular culture in the 1970s, for the most part, reinforced gender norms and traditional values. Though daytime soap operas had mature themes, and shows like *Dallas* and *Knots Landing* were gaining market shares, the most watched nighttime dramas and comedies of the decade (with the exception of the acerbic *M.A.S.H.*) were gentle: *Little House on the Prairie, The Waltons, The Brady Bunch,* and *Happy Days.*[30]

With abortion largely absent as a plot line, one would imagine that pregnancy would be present in television shows that had female characters. After all, if women weren't terminating their pregnancies, they had to be giving birth to babies. Yet television continued its decades-long struggle with how it would portray marital intimacy and pregnancy. Separate beds were the rule for parenting couples in other family-friendly shows in subsequent decades like *The Brady Bunch* (1969–1974) and *Eight Is Enough* (1977–1981). Even as their marriages and procreative capacity were acknowledged, women's bodies were hidden under voluminous nightgowns, hairnets, and even face masks; marital intimacy was assiduously avoided.

The sexuality of "single girls" as portrayed in popular culture was even more threatening for public consumption than prime-time examples of married couples. As Katherine Lehman's study of film and television representations of women in the 1960s and 70s demonstrates, these women offered both promise and risk to the viewing public at that time. Trading on ideas of "independence, sexuality, and career ambition," single girls both tantalized and frightened those who viewed them.[31] Even when the public, through the purchase of books like *Fear of Flying* (1973) and *The Hite Report* (1976),[32] showed they might be ready to consider the lives of more sexualized women, the film and television censors continued to demand amendments to scripts to retain the "moral purity" of female characters.[33] Many of the most popular films of this era were set in the 1920s and served to contribute to a revival of the sex panic of "white slavery."[34] This panic, Lawrence Friedman has persuasively argued, had the effect of putting the lid on social mobility for women of ill repute, who might otherwise be able to "move up" through marriage and relationships with men.[35] This theme of moral panic—revitalized from the 20s, just as women were achieving suffrage—reappeared in the 60s and 70s, just as women appeared poised to achieve recognition of their equal rights, their ability to control their reproductive capacity, and the means to mobilize their increasing consumer and employment power.[36]

In an era when birth control was becoming more commonplace and abortion was available, pregnancy was no longer threat enough to dissuade women from premarital sex. So in order to reinforce a status quo that was rapidly changing, media makers offered story lines of "girls" who gave in to the desire for sex to be at risk of being raped and assaulted, even killed. In a confusing paradox, these forms of cultural production were also full of warnings that career women, as distinct from "single girls," became bitter and vengeful, neurotic and controlling—either frigid professional virgins or hypermasculine sexual creatures. In this way, career women were already being positioned as poor mothers in the popular culture, while both the Supreme Court and employers were showing increased ambivalence about the rights of those women who "chose" to carry pregnancies to term. On the one hand, as Cushman puts it, employers argued that pregnancy and childbirth were temporarily disabling and inhibited women from working. On the other hand, they refused to insure women against lost wages or other job setbacks resulting from the "disability."[37]

Despite 1972 EEOC guidelines regarding pregnancy which stated that employers and the government should treat pregnancy just like any other "temporary disability,"[38] women who were pregnant were routinely treated in a disparate and discriminatory fashion. Several states, for instance, routinely denied disability and unemployment insurance to women who were pregnant, even if the cause of their need for coverage was not the pregnancy.

Remarkably, when these policies were challenged, the federal courts— including the Supreme Court—delivered decisions rendered in language that divorced reproduction from gender and ignored the fact that women are the ones who carry pregnancies to term. Part of the reason for this comes from feminist jurisprudence; some feminist theorists were grounding claims for equality of women in the workplace based on their fundamental *similarities* to men. Pregnancy was a difference that this jurisprudence had difficulty reconciling. However, another part of the reason the Court treated pregnancy as separate from gender is simply that the members of the Court had no lived experience of pregnancy, and they were crafting discrimination jurisprudence in a context that saw pregnancy as a genderless "choice," simply one option among many.

As a result, the Court's jurisprudence in this area was at times nonsensical. The conservative Burger Court adopted some of the liberal rationale of *Roe,* namely the idea that motherhood could be "voluntary" (or avoided). This allowed conservatives on the Court to argue, therefore, that women who were pregnant "wanted to be" and were thus ineligible for accommodations in the workplace.

A challenge to California's disability policy made it to the Supreme Court in 1974, in the case *Geduldig v. Aiello,* with several plaintiffs making claims against the California law. Among them were Augustina (Sally) Armendariz, who was denied temporary disability insurance by the state of California after a 1972 car crash that caused her to have a miscarriage. Any other injuries would have been covered, California policy stated, but because the miscarriage occurred as a result of pregnancy, it wasn't covered.[39] Carolyn Aiello, Jane Jaramillo, and Elizabeth Johnson were also named plaintiffs; each of these women had sought disability coverage from California for various reasons relating to their pregnancies and had been denied.

Rather than relying on the due process protections that had afforded Jo Carol LaFleur a victory, lawyers for Aiello challenged California's rejection of her pregnancy-related disability claims on equal protection grounds, arguing that because only women can become pregnant, only women suffer from such policies, which causes gender inequity. In a six-to-three decision, the Court firmly rejected the equal protection claim, with Potter Stewart applying the rational basis test to California's law, and finding it was rationally supported by the state's desire to operate efficiently and save money. Stewart did not entertain the arguments of Aiello's attorneys, that refusing to cover pregnancy was gender discrimination. He wrote simply: "There is no evidence in the record that the selection of the risks insured by the program worked to discriminate against any definable group or class in terms of the aggregate risk protection derived by that group or class from the program. There is no risk from which men are protected and women are not. Likewise, there is no risk from which women are protected and men are not." Policies regarding pregnancy simply made distinctions between "pregnant" or "not pregnant" people. Though the category "pregnant people" always included women, some "not pregnant people" were *also* women; therefore, the Court held, policies that harmed "pregnant people" were not policies that harmed "women."[40]

In response, Justices Brennan, Douglas, and Marshall offered a dissent— one that understood pregnancy discrimination as gender discrimination and therefore impermissible. Brennan makes his position clear:

> In my view, by singling out for less favorable treatment a gender-linked disability peculiar to women, the State has created a double standard for disability compensation: a limitation is imposed upon the disabilities for which women workers may recover, while men receive full compensation for all disabilities suffered, including those that affect only or primarily their sex, such as prostatectomies, circumcision, hemophilia, and gout. In effect, one set of rules is applied to females and another to males. Such dissimilar treatment of men and women, on the basis of physical characteristics inextricably linked to one sex, inevitably constitutes sex discrimination.[41]

Two short years later, in *General Electric Co. v. Gilbert*,[42] Justice Rehnquist would take on Brennan's *Aiello* dissent and elaborate on Stewart's theory of pregnancy. Rehnquist's opinion made it clear that he, and a majority of the Court, viewed pregnancy as something that could (theoretically) happen to anyone, that discrimination against pregnant women was not suspect, and that potentially discriminatory policies should not be given heightened scrutiny because policies relating to pregnancy were not policies specific to a gender.

At issue in *GE v. Gilbert* was the company's policy that denied women access to any nonoccupational sickness and disability benefits provided under their otherwise comprehensive plan. General Electric claimed, and the Rehnquist Court agreed, that pregnancy was not a "sickness." It was, rather "a voluntarily induced condition," for which women should not receive special treatment.

Pregnancy, we might imagine, from the Court's decision, is a choice; a wart, a broken foot, or a case of pneumonia is not.

Congress responded to the ruling of the 1970s rather decisively, by passing the Pregnancy Discrimination Act of 1978, which amended Title VII of the Civil Rights Act of 1964 and served to protect pregnant women from employment discrimination. Congress's quick action, in Strebeigh's words, "state[d] the obvious: discriminating against the pregnant *was* discriminating against women."[43]

Still, by the close of the 1970s, it was clear, in jurisprudence and popular culture, that abortion and pregnancy were constructed as "choices" women could make. They were choices, we would soon learn, that women could make *only* when they could comfortably afford them and only when the state did not "unduly burden" their access to them.[44] Indeed, if jurisprudence and feminist politics in the 1970s were about articulating and delimiting an expanded set of reproductive rights, the 1980s were about forcing women to be responsible for their ability to exercise them. The Court's rulings worked in concert with neoliberal agendas and began the process of unrealistically responsibilizing pregnancy and motherhood,[45] while also attempting to move the nation toward a nostalgic "traditional" set of values. Neoliberalism merged early with this traditionalism, and the results for women's reproduction—on screen, in the Courts, and in the realm of politics—were harrowing.

The 80s: Fantasy, Nostalgia, and Backlash

It is disturbing and frightening to think how certain conceptions of motherhood and family today perpetrated and commodified by the Reagan era are a return to the values of the fifties—a neotraditionalism.

—Artist Barbara Kruger, in conversation with
Therese Lichtenstein, "Images of the Maternal"[46]

Indeed, the years of my childhood were spent in front of the television, learning about being female from a strange mix of weak-willed women who lived to please men and stronger, more independent, characters like Christine Cagney and Mary Beth Lacey. Indeed, *Cagney and Lacey*, which ran from 1982–1988, was an anomaly among television shows of the decade; its first season closed with the episode "Better Than Equal," wherein the show's title characters are put in charge of protecting an "extremist feminist" whose views have made her the target of hatred. Such hatred of women's "extreme feminism," was, as early as the 1980s, a significant part of the general backlash against women fomented by foot soldiers in the "culture wars" that took stances against the Equal Rights Amendment, gay liberation, and women's equality.

Given the nascent backlash, it might not be odd to notice that there were very few representations of women's liberation on television or in the films of the 1980s;[47] a perusal of the lists of most popular television shows and films of the 80s shows them to be confectionary and escapist more than political or nuanced; this is especially true of television marketed to a female audience. With the exceptions of *Cagney and Lacey,* "Diane" on *Cheers,* and *Hill Street Blues'* public defender Joyce Davenport, which did emerge as popular, though controversial,[48] renderings of feminist characters, the most popular TV series of the decade had female lead characters that were decidedly un- (if not actively anti-) feminist. *Love Boat, Beauty and the Beast, Bay Watch, The Golden Girls, The Cosby Show, Full House,* and *Cheers* all studiously avoided most mentions of women's liberation—except when they poked fun at characters like bookish, strident Diane *(Cheers)* or Lisa Huxtable's mostly gentle, teenaged feminist rebellions on *The Cosby Show.*

In hugely popular movies like *The Breakfast Club, The Princess Bride, Ferris Bueller's Day Off, Top Gun, Goonies, Ghostbusters,* and *Back to the Future,* popular culture seemed blissfully unaware of both feminism's progress and the backlash that was soon to be raging against women's emancipation. The neotraditional values of the era were portrayed via nostalgic glances backward, teenaged fantasy, and harmless romance. These same nostalgic values merged with neoliberal regulatory, economic, and judicial politics and were articulated as backlash in politics, popular culture, and policies that demonized strong women.[49]

This backlash first appeared in the political realm with the defeat, in 1982, of the Equal Rights Amendment. During the battle over the amendment, opponents like Phyllis Schlafly constructed a rhetoric around it that made "equal rights," as Lehman reminds us, "the sole concern of antifamily, unfeminine activists who would deny women their natural prerogative to be homemakers and mothers."[50] Such backlash was also evident, as Frances Olsen notes, in the popular rhetoric about "working mothers and 'two-career' families," which were constructed rhetorically as "special problems" for society. Olsen argues that the rhetoric of the 1980s made it seem as though "nurturant families and women's equality may be hopelessly incompatible goals."[51]

In 1984, Nancy Rubin published *The Mother Mirror*, a prescient text that began with a retrospective look at mothering in the 1970s and an examination of how trends in that era were influencing a new way of mothering that was developing in the 1980s. Rubin noted that since the 70s, increasing numbers of women had entered the workforce and were (privately, secretly) challenging conventional wisdom about women's "natural instincts" in parenting and responding to children and babies. She was pleased with the fact that mothers in the early 1980s had become, in her observation, "managers," their children "junior partners," and the household a "corporate endeavor."[52]

Popular culture was replete with images of these junior partners and managerial mothers—often seen failing, rather comically, in their attempts to "have it all." Elizabeth McGovern's character in the Kevin Bacon star vehicle *She's Having a Baby*, stops taking birth control without her husband's knowledge—and upends their lives (but his especially), when she reproduces. There is the unnamed and largely absent managerial mother, who abandons her baby with three bachelors—portrayed by Tom Selleck, Steve Guttenberg, and Ted Danson—in the 1988 comedy *Three Men and a Baby*. One of the most popular movies of the period, *Look Who's Talking*, features a talking baby being raised by a harried, abandoned, careerist single mom, played by Kirstie Alley. None of the women in these movies strikes the proper balance; none of them manage to . . . manage. And, for all the fun and games the movies provide, they have an undertone; by poking fun at the failures, popular culture enables a discourse to emerge, wherein we see a "breakdown of family values" in a culture that had long made women responsible for their maintenance.

While President Reagan had demonized "welfare queens" along racial lines, mainstream popular culture focused on portrayals of white women—demonizing strong, adulterous and sexualized single women, like "bunny killing" pathologized by Glenn Close's character Alex, in 1987's *Fatal Attraction* and Sigourney Weaver's thieving and conniving boss as against Melanie Griffith's gentle "working girl," in the 1988 Mike Nichols movie of the same name. Abortion was not a present story line, with the exception of the film *Dirty Dancing*, which premiered in 1987 with an abortion subplot that stands in stark contrast to the long-held chastity of the main character, Baby, in her relationships with men.[53]

Solinger argues that the view of white single mothers became one that pathologized them: "As Freudian theory began to shape the ways that social services were delivered to agency clients, white single mothers were, for the first time, diagnosed as psychologically disturbed on the basis of their non-marital childbearing. Unwed pregnancy was constituted as evidence that they were unfit to be mothers."[54] Single mothers—even (perhaps especially) wage-earning, white, single mothers—challenged patriarchy at its core.[55] By the late 1980s, the conservative right had begun to use "family values" as a code phrase that captured, in Karpin's words, "the anxiety generated as a result of a feminist agenda that ha[d] destabilized the foundational status of the 'naturalness' of patriarchy, heterosexuality, and white supremacy."[56] Even though the conservative political movement quickly saw significant success, especially in the realm of abortion law and politics,[57] the anxiety remained high. No single popular culture persona was as important in shaping, mediating, and arguing against these anxieties than television's careerist, ambitious, and *liberal* Murphy Brown. The eponymous series, which began its decade-long run in 1987, was an immediate hit—but it did not ignite a firestorm until 1991, when the unmarried Ms. Brown had a baby.

Birthing Neoliberalism:
Jurisprudence and Popular Culture Converge, 1991–1992

The run of the television show *Murphy Brown* spanned the end of the Reagan presidency, the entirety of George H. W. Bush's, and the first Clinton term. Creator and producer Diane English crafted, with the help of a talented ensemble cast, a critically acclaimed and extraordinarily popular television show that was intentionally and expressly feminist. On *Murphy Brown* men and women worked side by side in a workplace that was "more egalitarian than any other on TV at the time."[58] The title character, Murphy Brown, played by Candace Bergen, was a brash and witty investigative journalist on a weekly televised news magazine much like the popular and long-running *60 Minutes*. The story lines of the series often dovetailed with current events and politics, and Murphy's own progressive feminism frequently worked its way into the dialogue and plots. With eighteen Emmy wins over ten seasons, the show was critically acclaimed.[59] It was also highly rated, staying in the top five of comedy series for almost its entire run. Its popularity (and controversy) hit a high point on the evening in May of 1992 when Brown delivered her son, Avery. That night, the series reached thirty-eight million viewers; it was watched in nearly 25 percent of American households.[60]

Murphy's fictional decision to carry her pregnancy to term alone, after a short-lived and ultimately failed reunion with her ex-husband, drew the ire of social conservatives and became an integral part of the culture wars.[61] Vice President Dan Quayle gave a speech in which he accused Brown, the actress who portrayed her, and the show's writers and producers, of "mocking the importance of fathers." As popular culture and feminist author Andi Zeisler puts it, Murphy Brown's pregnancy and single parenting played an "inadvertent role in making 'family values' the major political buzzword of the early 1990s."[62] As popular culture liberalized, in other words, a reactionary politics grew to ensure that public policy remained regressive.

While many recall that Quayle's speech included approbation of Murphy Brown's privileged and managerial motherhood construed as a "lifestyle choice," much more of the text of that speech dealt with a different kind of single mother: black women living in poverty. Beginning with a racially tone-deaf discussion of the Los Angeles riots in the aftermath of the Rodney King verdict, Quayle's speech moves, before discussion about Murphy Brown, into territory well trod by the Reagan presidency of years earlier. Saying that he is concerned about the "single mother raising her children in the ghetto" who must worry about "gang violence," Quayle tells his listeners that "84 percent of the crimes committed [in 1990] were crimes committed by blacks against blacks."[63] He insinuates that "black poverty" in the 1960s was a better type of poverty than that suffered in the 1990s, because it was poverty endured by married couples:

> Let me share with you a few statistics on the difference. . . . [I]n 1967, 68 percent of black families were headed by married couples. In 1991, only 48 percent of black families were headed by both a husband and a wife. In 1965, the illegitimacy rate among black families was 28 percent. In 1989, 65 percent, two-thirds of all black children were born with never-married

mothers. In 1951, 9 percent of black youths between 16 and 19 were unemployed. In 1965, it was 23 percent. In 1980, it was 35 percent. By 1989, the number had declined slightly, but it was still 32 percent. The leading cause of death of young black males today is homicide.

He concludes this portion of his speech in this way: "Children need love and discipline; they need mothers and fathers. A welfare check is not a husband, the state is not a father. It is from parents that children learn how to behave in society. . . . [F]or those who are concerned about children growing up in poverty, we should know this—*marriage is probably the best anti-poverty program of all.*"[64]

In the short term, this kind of thought, wherein "race and class politics work together," provided the justification for coercive birth control policies and the stepped-up policing of women's bodies.[65] The time that President Reagan was in office was a particularly difficult time for women of color, but the Reagan years served merely as a jumping off point for increased coercion and control of women of color's reproduction. Welfare recipients—white and black, but publicly coded "black"—were coerced to adopt long-lasting birth control methods like Norplant and Depo-Provera, though little attention was paid to women who manifested life-altering side effects on these drugs. In this period there was also an explosion of charges against women for "prenatal crime," like the use of drugs while pregnant: this policing disproportionately impacted black women and women living in poverty.[66] Roberts reports, "between 1985 and 1995 at least 200 women in 30 states were charged with maternal drug use."[67] Her analysis is cogent: "The prosecution of drug-addicted mothers is part of an alarming trend toward greater state intervention into the lives of pregnant women under the rationale of protecting the fetus from harm." As we could have anticipated, given the way the Supreme Court approached abortion and pregnancy in its jurisprudence on these policies, "*the interests of the fetus [we]re [increasingly] pitted against those of the mother.*"[68]

In Quayle's speech, we see his concern that, absent a responsible father, the state must intervene to coerce women to be responsible mothers. Paradoxically, the case that fully consolidated this position was one that was initially viewed as a victory for women's rights and a correction to discriminatory wage and hiring practices. In *United Automobile Workers v. Johnson Controls Inc.,*[69] the Supreme Court ruled on behalf of the union and unanimously struck down as unconstitutionally discriminatory all workplace fetal protection policies instituted at Johnson Controls, Inc. These policies had banned all women of reproductive age (ages sixteen to sixty), from jobs at the plant that risked their exposure to high levels of lead. In addition to increasing the potential for exposure to lead, which could negatively impact fetal development, these jobs also tended to pay better and offer increased potential for advancement. Further, only women were barred from the jobs, even though men's reproductive capacity was also potentially diminished by working in these hazardous environments, and birth defects for children born to men working in those positions were also common.

In what was heralded as a victory for women, Justice Blackmun held these policies to constitute sex discrimination and wrote that such discrimination, even when well intentioned, violated Title VII of the Civil Rights Act as well as the equal protection clause of the 14th Amendment. For Blackmun and the Court, the fetal protection policy was obviously discriminatory, both "because it treated fertile men and fertile women differently and because it discriminated on the basis of pregnancy."[70] The Court mandated that the jobs be opened to women, regardless of their plans for reproduction; women, the Court reasoned, could make decisions about their work and how it could impact their pregnancies. Nowhere in the decision does the Court suggest that Johnson Controls create a safer, less toxic work environment for its employees—the duty of the business is merely to provide equal access to potentially toxic jobs.

Certainly this was a victory for women's rights, defined as rights to equal access. But the *Johnson Controls* decision consolidated a decades-long shift in the burden on women in their pursuit of healthy pregnancies: if women wanted better-paying jobs, they had to be willing to accept the poor consequences for pregnancies that might result. And they accepted those poor consequences under the watchful eye of a potentially retributive state. Just as Vice President Quayle articulated marriage as one of the obligations women had toward the fetus, the Court in *Johnson Controls* saw biological fetal protection as part of a woman's duty. Further, the Court refused to construct a duty for the employer in policing or changing workplaces that could be toxic to reproduction. If they wanted control over their reproductive capacities, women were to be responsible for the outcomes of their pregnancies: *UAW v. Johnson Controls* constitutes a clear moment in the consolidation of that expectation. If Murphy Brown birthed a neoliberal culture war in 1992 by becoming a single mother on prime time, the Supreme Court birthed the biopolitical neoliberal responsibilization of mothers in the *Johnson Controls* decision. With it, women were exhorted to regulate themselves, to police their own pregnancies, to take control of their bodies as workers and mothers, and to bear the brunt of the consequences caused by actions that were called "choices" but which were made in a context of decreasing economic freedom and increasing social control.

When *Roe,* in 1973, acknowledged women's right to terminate their pregnancies, it was also constructed to give them obligations surrounding those pregnancies they chose not to terminate. By the late 1980s, the government was no longer the active policing agent for working women as they attained and carried through with pregnancy: women were expected to police themselves. The Court had declared that pregnancy was not a gendered issue and that access to termination was not related to socioeconomic status. Deregulation had taken hold, and industry was largely unfettered. But the culture wars continued, in different locales and with different arsenal, and continued to catch pregnant women in their crossfire. The federal government, beginning with the Reagan presidency, devolved the control of pregnancy and reproduction to the states and the lower courts—a clear consequence of the ruling in *Roe* combined with organizational techniques of the right to go grassroots and begin to control local school boards, zoning commissions, and small-town judgeships. At the same time, we began to see the manifestations theorized by Foucault of the end of the disciplinary state and the rise of the state of social control. In this era, while doctrine still purported to leave open the possibility of pregnancy termination, we saw the public shaming of those who have had abortions, allegations that those women would become much more depressed than women making other reproductive choices, violence and protests at clinics, and the publication of lists of abortion-providing doctors' names and home addresses, thereby allowing nonstate actors to effectively target them for harassment and, in some cases, murder.

Through the late 1990s and early part of the new millennium, popular culture turned to the frontier of gay rights, which were normalized and ho mogenized in shows like *Ellen* and *Will & Grace*. The rights-expanding jurisprudence of the period was also more interested in gay rights (and stopping gay rights) and same-sex marriage than in women's reproducing bodies. Perhaps popular culture makers and courts felt comfortable in looking away, as women had rather easily been convinced of their necessary role in self- and other-surveillance of those among them who might abort, or work in a toxic environment, or take toxic substances while pregnant.

As we entered the twenty-first century, pregnant women were certainly more visible, and popular culture attitudes toward pregnancy had certainly shifted. Emblematic of this shift is the multiple ways that the popular television show *Friends* incorporated several pregnancy story lines into its run:[71] Phoebe carried triplets as a surrogate for friends—delivering the babies on the show's one hundredth episode; Rachel gave birth to baby Emma at the end of season eight; Monica and Chandler struggled with infertility and adopted twins in the final season. Davis-Floyd notes, "Today, we see pregnant women everywhere, from the classroom to the executive office, from the night club to the formal dinner, and it is only the few die-hards who mutter under their breath about unseemly display."[72] The pregnant female body had gone from being an embarrassing reminder that women had sex and therefore a private state of being to being considered both public property for regulation and commercial property to be celebrated as a sexy. Pregnant bodies now could sell, as Demi Moore's *Vanity Fair* cover made clear, a wide range of pop culture products.

This shift might indeed be lauded as emancipatory; women are now enabled to be much more public in their pregnancies than they were mere decades ago. We might give pause, though, to observe that the growing obsession with idealized representations of celebrity pregnancy in the early part of this century provide us an insight into imperatives for the self-management of pregnant and mothering women. The managerial mother of the 1970s and 80s became the *managed* and *self-managing mother* of the 1990s and 2000s and, in large part, that management has been self-induced and internalized, with help from the media as well as the state.

The pregnant body was losing the stigma and shame with which it had been treated prior to 1970; women were gaining some measure of control over their reproductive capacity via access to abortion and birth control; and women were able to be pregnant and remain in the workforce. In the midst of all of these openings, though, the pregnant body also became the site of increasingly strict and harsh regulation, regulation conducted both by state policies and, increasingly, the judgmental gazes of ordinary citizens. The pregnant body became a powerful site of the neoliberal approach to governing: self-governance for "responsible," "disciplined," and "autonomous" citizens; unremitting state punishment for "irresponsible," "undisciplined," and "heteronomous" citizens. We see this clearly in what is perhaps a unique and surprising place: the bodies of pregnant celebrities.

CHAPTER 2

CELEBRITY BUMPS, BOOBS, AND BOOTIES

APPEARING ON *THE DAILY SHOW* in late October 2011, CNN journalist Campbell Brown patted her belly and said with pride, "I've got the bump!" Then, in an aside to the audience she added, "I'm pregnant." Wearing a body-skimming turquoise knit dress, Brown didn't look heavy, or pregnant—but she was quick to clarify that any additional curves on her body were the result of pregnancy, not self-indulgence.

Brown's statement about her bump is to be expected; the current media mania for the pregnant celebrity body takes the form of an overwhelming obsession about the beginnings, growth, and loss of the "baby bump"—the primary visual indicator of a woman's pregnancy. Stand in the checkout line of any grocery store or browse online entertainment sites, and you will see speculation: "Is that a Bump, Julia?" certainty: "Jennifer [Garner] confirmed . . . that she isn't just unfortunately bloated . . . she's expecting" and praise: "Jennifer [Love Hewitt's] bump is so CUTE!"

Pictures of pregnant celebrities clad in form-fitting, belly-revealing, and stylish clothing abound. The bump is, indeed, the hottest accessory a woman can have. Through and with them, women are encouraged to look after their physical bodies and indulge in vanity and care with their looks when pregnant; and they are told they can do so without being termed "bad mothers" for it. No longer required to be only or primarily demure and modest, women have begun to "reject the asexualisation of the body during pregnancy."[1]

Images of celebrities enjoying their sensual bodies reinforce the message that pregnant women (and by extension, perhaps, moms in general) are still sexual beings. While in previous years, law and norms required that these sexualized pregnant bodies be hidden and covered, there is now "a proliferation of images and texts that suggest that if you are pregnant you no longer have to be dowdy.. . . . [I]t is now possible to be pregnant and fashionable; pregnant and sexy; pregnant and a corporate manager; pregnant and sporty."[2] Indeed, it is now possible to be pregnant and a celebrity. What, though, are we learning from these celebrity bodies?

Embodiment, Performance, Representation, and Celebrity

With the advent of movies and television, the rules for femininity have come to be culturally transmitted more and more through standardized visual images. . . . We are no longer given verbal descriptions or exemplars of what a lady is or of what femininity consists. Rather, we learn the rules directly through bodily discourse: through images that tell us what clothes, body shape, facial expression, movements, and behavior are required.

—Susan Bordo, "The Body and the Reproduction of Femininity"[3]

Images of pregnant celebrities are important cultural artifacts. As performers of both femininity and maternity, these women give "regular" women cues about appropriate (and inappropriate) deportment during pregnancy. As Angela McRobbie has noted, "fragments of 'info' [provided in popular magazines] about favorite pop stars, films stars and TV celebrities are now the raw material of fantasy."[4] Political theorists like Jodi Dean are concerned with the opiating impact of such fantasies, in terms of their effects on mass mobilization; I am concerned with the rules these that fantasies transmit, the norms and ideals they pose for women.

Media coverage of sexy, powerful, and creative women as expectant mothers *can* offer new and positive models for parenthood and highlight the creative potentials of corporeal femininity. Some of these images certainly appear liberatory, and many of them give sexual and relational agency to women in a way that reimagines the pregnant female. But the majority of media representations of pregnant celebrities trot out tired clichés that serve only to reinforce limiting and constructed gender norms.

In her Foucauldian analysis of "the modernization of patriarchal power," Bartkey asks, "Who is the disciplinarian? Who makes women act in disciplined forms?" Her answer is that discipline is not merely institutionalized and bounded; for women it is "*unbound*, anonymous, widely dispersed, everywhere and nowhere, internalized."[5] Images such as those routinely consumed by readers of fashion and gossip magazines constitute a disciplinary technique; they facilitate the internalization of gendered norms constructed in a system of patriarchy, white supremacy, and neoliberal capital. A close look at the coverage of representative celebrity pregnancies reveals several disciplinary practices inscribed on the body of the mother-to-be and mother-as-she-parents. These practices include an imperative to slimness and self-discipline, a complex system of meanings by which "good" and "bad" mothering is embodied by particular women, rhetorics that sexualize women of color celebrities in ways reminiscent of colonial race relations, and terms for sexualized white women that give them rather limited roles. Law is ever-present, though sometimes latent: regulation is ready to step in where self-regulation fails.

This chapter develops a theory of embodiment that I arrive at via an examination of the normative idealization of femininity and pregnancy offered in mass media coverage of the celebrity baby bump.[6] Embodiment is an important topic of critical theory, which emphasizes "discourses, practices, and material conditions,"[7] and can show how these conditions impact how bodies are understood, experienced, and constructed. Embodiment, with its twin emphasis on performance and experience, is a particularly fruitful subject for feminist analysis.[8] When we understand that culture comes to be embodied via lived experience, we can see that concepts like age, illness, and pregnancy are *both* biological and culturally constructed. In her work on aging, Margaret Morganroth Gullette notes, "We both *have* a body . . . and *perform* our body."[9] A perspective from embodiment also understands that humans are not *only* limited by structural, institutional, biological, and ideological constraints; they also replicate, recreate, and rebel against them.

Certainly, women's bodies have been key elements in the way individuals and societies understand, and treat, pregnancy; policy and rhetoric surrounding pregnancy centers on the bodies of women—though often these policies and rhetorics have attempted to naturalize pregnancy, to make it a matter of biology, rather than social construction. "Age," Gullette argues, is more about "culture" than "chromosomes."[10] Embodiment helps us understand that "something as apparently 'natural' as appetite or sexuality turns out to be a product of culture: the body is progressively trained and constrained by social norms."[11]

Pregnancy is both a natural and biological state, and a cultural practice or performance. It is a practice and performance constrained by institutions, structures, and ideologies. Pregnancy is performed by everyone who experiences it, not just celebrities. The ways that women experience pregnancy—pathologize it, love it, hate it, live with it—*these are cultural.* We should not concern ourselves *that* these celebrities are pregnant, but rather *how* they are pregnant—and how average, contemporary women, who have long been accustomed to practices that use female celebrities as "vehicles to encourage female spectators to become consumers," experience and evaluate celebrity pregnancies as part of the daily process of navigating the "contested terrains of competing discourses of femininity."[12] In popular culture treatments of them, some celebrity pregnancies become representations of what is both normal and ideal for other pregnant women to achieve; others become instructive narratives for what to avoid and detest. These categories open further windows onto surveillance and regulation of women by creating norms and ideals, and deviations from them.

Normalization and Idealization

When we normalize something—an attitude, a body type, an ideology—we naturalize it and set it as an expectation. "Normalization," writes Iris Marion Young, "consists in a set of social processes that elevate the experience and capacities of some social segments into standards used to judge everyone."[13] These processes give us our "default" bodies[14] and tell us what "should" be. Normalization establishes our habitual ways of doing or thinking about things; it routinizes and structures our lived experience.[15] It also structures institutions and policies.

Focusing on disability and embodiment, Young shows normalization to be a "process of injustice produced by social structures" upon bodies of those not deemed "normal."[16] Injustice occurs when society refuses to adapt, or neglects to see the need to do so, when the bodies of some of its members fail to meet the norm. For example, "Many workplaces and other public institutions such as schools . . . assume[d] that the bodies populating them never menstruate, are pregnant, or lactate."[17] They have assumed, in other words, that not-being-pregnant was the normal state for most workers; institutions and structures then were built without instituting policies that would address, let alone embrace, deviations from that norm, and pregnant women suffered discrimination.

Idealization, distinct from but related to normalization, results from processes that work to objectify and reify ways of being. Idealization gives us goals to strive for, habits and attitudes to adopt on the way to the idealized form. As chapter one has elaborated, in the past the idealized pregnant or maternal woman was "passive, self-negating," and "obedient."[18] Motherhood was seen as intensely private, while simultaneously the height of women's moral perfection. Current cultural representations of idealized pregnancies are often a far cry from these old standards and offer different ideals of beauty, sensuality, and power.

Media coverage of contemporary celebrity pregnancy offers normalization and idealization as a biopolitical discipline.[19] Consumption of media about these celebrity pregnancies normalizes particular celebrity bodies, attitudes, and actions. In fact, as Bordo notes, a primary feature of visual media is that it enables our self-discipline by providing examples we are meant to follow, bodies we are meant to emulate and adore, attitudes and poses we are meant to strike and hold. To the extent that average women fall short of that normalized form, celebrity pregnancies also become the ideal: the goal that pregnant women are encouraged and coerced to strive to emulate. What norms, then, are operating to discipline women's behaviors in and of pregnancy? What ideals are crafted through contemporary coverage of the celebrity baby bump?

Bump Size: Valorizing Self-Disciplined, Docile Bodies

The obsession with the bump, and the appropriateness of its size—Brown's declaration that her larger belly is a "bump," a "baby,"—is not surprising, given the cultural imperatives to slimness under which North American women operate. Significant social and psychological research has shown that "the preference in Western cultures for slim female bodies serves both to discipline women's diets, and to create guilt when they fall short of the slim ideal."[20] Ussher argues that imperatives to slenderness "underpin feminine body management,"[21] and feminists have long written about the performance of gender as it relates to body size and femininity.

Given that weight gain in pregnancy is both unavoidable and advisable, some psychologists have argued that pregnancy is the one time women are allowed and even encouraged to have a large body[22] and that they experience that allowance as liberating. However, in her study of female embodiment in the workplace Brewis found that "showing" one's pregnancy can be a double-edged sword: it opens women to discrimination and retaliation, while also legitimizing their newly claimed physical space.[23] Recent ethnographic work from social scientists has convincingly demonstrated that to a great extent women are comfortable with their weight gain in pregnancy precisely because they know it is *temporary* and socially acceptable.

In her interviews with female subjects regarding their experiences of pregnancy, Sarah Earle finds that the distinction between pregnancy and "fatness" emerges very early in pregnancy. Of her interview subjects, Earle writes, "The majority . . . were keen to demonstrate that pregnancy was 'responsible' for changes to body size, weight, and shape."[24] Acknowledging that women take up more space when they are pregnant than when they are not, many of the women she interviewed preferred to justify the additional space they claimed, with clear reference to their pregnancy. Lucy Bailey's work on women's embodied experiences of pregnancy provides similar findings and focuses on how pregnancy impacts feelings of femininity and womanhood. Like Earle, she notes that, for her respondents, "Appearance was not insignificant: they were pleased when the pregnancy progressed to the point where they were clearly pregnant, rather than 'fat.'"[25]

Pregnant women therefore covet the bump not only for its outward manifestation of a desired pregnancy, but for the public confirmation that their weight gain is not from overindulging. Rather, as one of Earle's respondents told her, the bump is "all baby."[26] Interviewing dozens of women about physical changes associated with pregnancy, Bailey found four main themes in respondents' talk about their pregnant bodies: womanhood, sensuality, shape, and space. She writes, "Many of the women saw their pregnancies as a confirmation of adult womanhood. They described themselves as feeling more womanly as their bodies changed."[27] With this increased sense of femininity—which was empowering for some women—came increasing vulnerability. Bailey notes that during pregnancy, "the women's body boundaries could also appear less distinct." Women who are pregnant become accustomed to strangers touching them, asking intrusive questions, and offering advice about their behaviors. Therefore, and perhaps paradoxically, Bailey writes, "at the same time as they were permitted greater public space, many [pregnant women] felt an erosion or invasion of their personal space as they experienced a dissolution of social boundaries from both within and beyond their bodies."[28]

In a Western cultural context, media obsession with pregnant celebrity bodies may actually be dangerous for women. This is true for women generally, whether or not they are pregnant. As Bordo has written, "popular representations [of female bodies] . . . may forcefully employ the rhetoric and symbolism of empowerment, personal freedom, 'having it all.' Yet female bodies, pursuing these ideals, may find themselves distracted, depressed, and physically ill."[29] Pregnant women appear even more at risk of distress, however, when their bodies fall short of idealizations.[30]

So, while women might enjoy the openings provided by the pregnant celebrity body—the chance to be pregnant and sexy, pregnant and powerful, pregnant and athletic, and so forth—they are also being assaulted by images of (usually) ultrathin celebrities with a (usually) manageably sized "bump." Average women are simultaneously privy to the shaming of celebrities who don't perform their pregnancies well, those who gain "too much weight," and those who don't lose it quickly enough. Well-managed celebrity pregnancies are upheld as both ideal examples and as normal practices for women to mimic. Overabundant bumps—such as Kim Kardashian's, Jessica Simpson's, or Bryce Dallas Howard's—are seen as shameful and indulgent, not to be emulated. Photos of Kardashian, Simpson, and Howard routinely carry captions that shame those women, rather than celebrate them. Of Jessica Simpson, *Life and Style* magazine wrote, "Pregnancy is supposed to be a beautiful time in a woman's life, and while it certainly was for Jessica Simpson, it also came with its downfalls. . . . 'I was so insecure,'" the magazine quotes her, "'I couldn't even believe what I weighed.'"[31] The celebrity gossip website *TMZ* noted, shortly after her second child was born, that her "fat days are numbered."

FIGURE 2.1 Jessica Simpson on *The Tonight Show*, March 2012. Photo credit: NBC-NCBU Photo Bank/Getty Images

When Simpson appeared on *The Tonight Show* with Jay Leno, *everything* about her seemed voluptuous and over the top, from her hair to her bump to her shoes. *Huffington Post* covered the height of her heels (six inches) and wrote that the "ever growing" Simpson "looks ready to pop."[32] Commenters on that site opined that she had "gained too much weight" and would "need the best trainers in Hollywood to bounce back." Additional photos of Simpson on multiple celebrity-watching websites carried captions that indicated she was "very, very pregnant," "bulging at the seams," and "enormous."[33]

While Perez Hilton said Kim Kardashian's "baby belly" was "beautiful," most other gossip sites and magazines were less kind. Responding to the criticism, Los Angeles artist Daniel Edwards made a sculpture of Kardashian's pregnant body titled "L.A. Fertility." In his artist's statement Edwards wrote, "The lifesize sculpture features lactiferous breasts and a voluminous belly to entice visitors to give a respectful rub for good luck and success."[34] Aware of the press surrounding her pregnancy, Kardashian showed up for the unveiling of the sculpture; months later, Kardashian told Jay Leno that the rude comments about her pregnant body "hurt my soul."[35]

Significantly, photos of Simpson, Kardashian, Carey, and others were often juxtaposed with slimmer famous women, pregnant at the same time: Jessica Alba, the Duchess of Windsor, Jennifer Garner, and Megan Fox. Photo editorials paired the stars in fat-slim dyads, with the slimmer pregnant woman obviously favored by popular press coverage. Often, the slimmer star was portrayed as the one most able to police her desires to eat and grow large, and the press valorizes the women most able to exhibit self-control while pregnant.

One photo editorial on *TMZ*, preceded by pages of commentary on the size of Kim's bump, notes that "*slim* sister Khloe [Kardashian]" was set to announce the sex of Kim and Kanye's baby on the next episode of their reality show.[36] Another features a photo of Kate Middleton, Duchess of Cambridge, with the headline "Not All Famous Preggo Chicks Have to Be HUGE."[37] And *The Superficial* pairs a photo essay of Hillary Duff, whose body, according to the site, "has never fully recovered" from pregnancy, with photos of a "stunning" Beyoncé Knowles.[38] The message is clear: thin women with small bumps who get back into shape quickly after birth are doing something right.

However, though the popular media may focus on the health and radiance of many slimmer pregnant actresses, some—while still admired—are also worried over. The press casts these women as virtuous in their self-denial, but also in need of protection in the way that they take that self-discipline to extremes. Though motherhood (and divorce) gave the press reason to portray Katie Holmes and Nicole Kidman as women of style and substance,treatment of their pregnancies and postbaby bodies highlighted their self-discipline and self-control in ways that infantilized and patronized both women.

One of the most remarkable features about the coverage of Nicole Kidman's pregnancy was the concern voiced by members of the media and online commentators about the seemingly small size of her bump. Many captions point out that her bump seems unnaturally and perhaps unhealthily small; several of them note that her bump was only "slowly growing." One reporter wondered if Kidman's baby bump was "big enough" to be healthy, and the *Daily Mail* reported that in photos where she held onto her belly, like several taken at the Academy of Country Music Awards, the "slender actress" was "trying to make her bump as big as possible."[39] Her pose was both demure and protective; it also accentuated the bump.

Commenters on *JustJared* agonized over Kidman's bump, wondering if the pregnancy is "fake," because the bump is "so small." "Bob" wrote, "She's due in a month? She's not very big. My wife is due in 2 months, and her belly is MUCH bigger than Nicole's. I hope her baby is allright [sic]. My guess is that it's goign [sic] to be extremely underweight due to Nicole's age."[40] Not constructed as healthy or natural, Kidman's body during pregnancy was portrayed as the site of denial, a denial that may or may not have negative consequences for her child.

Very few paparazzi photos of Katie Holmes were taken while she was pregnant. In those that do exist, her slight frame has a nearly covert posture; she is often covered in a large coat, with her eyes shielded by enormous sunglasses. Self-discipline and docility are written on her material body. Given the nearly constant presence of paparazzi, Holmes's desire to stay out of the limelight is understandable; and her marriage, now dissolved, to one of Hollywood's most powerful men afforded her privacy unavailable to many other celebrities.[41] However, in the absence of photos, the press wrote its own narrative—one of Katie Holmes as a cloistered, closeted woman in need of liberation from a controlling spouse and held hostage to cultish religious beliefs. Conspiracy theories proliferated, focusing on the "miniscule" bump as proof that Holmes

FIGURE 2.2 Nicole Kidman at the Academy of Country Music Awards. Photo by: Charley Gallay/Getty Images

was faking her pregnancy as part of a contractual arrangement with Cruise.[42] Stories about the birth plan, allegedly influenced by the tenets of Scientology and envisioning a drug-free, "peaceful," or "quiet" birth, were widely distributed with panicked captions. As Suri's due date approached, the media were concerned, and headlines screamed: "Katie won't be allowed to speak!" "She won't have access to drugs!"

Between the time of Suri's birth and the TomKat divorce, the image of Holmes as a cloistered and secretive woman continued, though she was much more frequently photographed. In these photos she still wears huge dark sunglasses, cardigans or blazers over her primary outfit, and she seldom looks at the camera head on. Almost always, there is speculation that she might be pregnant again. A July 2008 entry on the *TomCruiseWatch* website features a photo of Holmes in a cable-knit sweater and jeans, with a wool pea coat covering her; a sliver of belly is exposed and the blogger has circled that sliver in red. The copy read:

> This could be nothing more than the way the angle was shot and how she was walking. It could be a small bump from "that time of the month" or even a baby. We all know she isn't gaining weight, this chic [sic] eats salads. But look at her skin, her eyes are dark but she's also glowing at the same time. In this photo it looks like she has a secret to hide but she isn't telling, but she's hoping the world will know by the slight tiny bump in her shirt that is also showing her belly.[43]

Twenty pages of speculative comments follow.

Feminist theorists Katie Conby and her coeditors, in their introduction to *Writing on the Body: Female Embodiment and Feminist Theory*, cite Foucault's *Discipline and Punish* when they write, "To make the transition from nature to culture, woman must deny her potentially 'dangerous' appetites and continuously shape what Foucault calls a non-threatening 'docile' body."[44] The coverage of Katie Holmes's and Nicole Kidman's pregnancies and postpartum bodies stresses both their docility and their incredible abilities to discipline their "dangerous appetites." While worried over, however, both actresses are seen as closer to nature than culture—wilder and in need of taming and regulation. This changes, as the two grow into mothers. Holmes's move to a short, sophisticated haircut and frequent appearances alongside style maven and celebrity mom Posh Spice/Victoria Beckham (both in svelte haute couture) changed the way the press reported on her. She became known as a fashionista, a style maven, *and* a mom. Kidman's public comments about pregnancy and how her husband protects and stands up for her may serve to reinforce the image of a helpless pregnant woman; however, recent articles have also tried to recapture some of her image as an Aussie interested in wilderness and nature by focusing on her gardening pursuits and part-time life on a horse ranch. While their pregnancies were worried over, motherhood (and divorce) have allowed the press to see both Katie and Nicole as possessing style and substance, as though having grown into womanhood through their self-sacrifice and maternal roles. Kidman and Holmes are both marked as "good women," the kind of moms we aspire to be, in the kinds of bodies we aspire to have—even as we understand that is impossible.

Good Girls, Bad Girls, and Hot Sexy Mamas

Julia Roberts, the second most bankable star in Hollywood from 1990 to 2008 (second only to Arnold Schwarzenegger in the same period),[45] is an excellent example of a celebrity mom typed as a "good girl." Roberts is undeniably a celebrity and iconic figure: "indisputably the period's most valuable female screen asset."[46] Much of her appeal comes from the fact that she is seen via the characters she portrays, as well as the image she projects, as "feisty" yet sweet. Ben Brantley of *The New York Times* observed, "Her range onscreen runs from feisty but vulnerable . . . to vulnerable but feisty. . . . Kind, amiable, friendly, considerate, pleasant and delightful, while equally determined, strong-willed, brave, energetic, and (politely) aggressive."[47] Brantley expands, "her strength . . . is in her sameness, which magnifies everyday human traits to a level of radioactive intensity, and a feral beauty that is too unusual to be called pretty . . . [she is a] down-home Garbo."[48] The key to Roberts, McDonald insists, is that everyone can relate to her.[49] She is the ultimate "good girl," the classic "girl next door."

Roberts has been pregnant in the public eye twice in the past fifteen years, after famously, finally, finding love with a regular working-class guy (a cameraman–cinematographer). Though she got some negative press for dating and marrying a man who was married to someone else when their relationship began, approbation of the relationship never reached a fevered pitch in the press. Roberts and her husband, Danny Moder, have three children: twins Phinneas and Hazel (born in 2004) and son Henry (born in 2007). Press surrounding Roberts's pregnancies stressed her "radiance" and her "naturalness." The website *Moono* reported in March 2004, "Julia Roberts was radiant as can be at the Oscars. But was that a maternal glow?" The site continues, saying that the *New York Daily News* had reported Roberts to be "more buxom than usual." It also noted, "Julia's brown roots were peeking through her lightened locks;" the blogger explained that "some pregnant women stop dying their hair, although it's as much a fashion statement as a health choice these days."[50]

Indeed, press coverage of Roberts as a maternal figure increasingly identified her as an environmentally aware parent—a prototypical "earth mother" whose image was burnished by her role in the proenvironmental film *Erin Brockovich. Us Weekly* magazine copy notes that Roberts is "naturally gorgeous" and "fresh-faced," and comments on the fact that she's carrying the book *Organic Crafts: 75 Earth-Friendly Activities.*[51] The magazine, in a separate article, also praises "Roberts' newfound domesticity" as "a long way from her swingin' single days" and notes that now, "Roberts' first love is her family."[52] Roberts publicly joins environmentalism to traditional values associated with parenting and takes them both on as a celebrity and mother. As a consequence, the media and commentators highlight her "natural" and "easygoing" style and point to her as a "healthy" role model. In the representations of her pregnant body as a site of environmental consciousness and her mothering style as responsible environmental citizenship, Roberts embodies the nuevo-hippie ideal of the generous, compassionate, overflowingly abundant earth mother.

Similarly, Jennifer Garner is lauded in magazines and on celebrity-watching websites for being a "friendly," "simple," and "traditional" "girl next door." Garner even received praise from the website *Celebitchy* for eschewing "trendy Hollywood baby names" in favor of "more traditional names."[53] And it turns out that she even cooks traditionally; *Celebitchy* breathlessly reports "Garner let us get a glimpse of her shopping list, which includes organic hotdogs, wheat germ, chicken, and chocolate." What could be more American than hot dogs—even if they are organic? Part of the allure of the girl next door, after all, is that she plays by the rules, follows tradition, and plays it safe.

Like Roberts, Garner is portrayed as a devoted, down-to-earth mom. Magazines call her "supermom," "an engaged parent," and a "mama bear"— all of the articles praise her hands-on approach to her children, while publishing photos of her family at the park, on the beach, and at the ice skating rink. Under a photo of Garner carrying her pigtailed daughter Violet, *OK!* magazine opines: "Caring mother Jennifer Garner, 36, holds 2-year-old Violet close to her hip while having an educational day."[54] Her public appearances played up a wholesome image, and "fresh-faced" beauty and her "cuteness" seem to make her an ideal mother.

Garner and her partner, Ben Affleck, announced their plans to divorce in summer 2015. It will be interesting to see if the press continues to portray her as a "good girl" in the years to come; it will also be interesting to see if her popularity among "average" moms continues to be strong. And she is quite popular. On one celebrity-watching website, "Colormesticky" wrote about Garner, "She's so cute. She could have 12 kids one right after another and I wouldn't pick on her for it." "Caligirl1201" added "I would love for someone as nice and beautiful as Jennifer G. to have more kids."[55] Many blog commentors contrast Garner with Britney Spears in a way similar to "Colormesticky's" post: "Britney, on the other hand, needs to stop breeding now."[56]

Bad Girls—Redeemed (or Not) by Motherhood

Pop sensation turned mother of two, Britney Spears is one of the most famous pregnant and parenting celebrities of the last decade. With her troubled personal life and tarnished image, the media coverage of Britney Spears as a mother has, until very recently, presented an image of a prototypical "bad girl." Vilified in the press and in online blogs, Britney is the archetypal girl gone wild and portrayed nearly everywhere as a tragically unfit mother. Her out-of-control antics included flashing her unclothed crotch at onlookers, shaving her head, pairing with unacceptable men, and reportedly attempting suicide multiple times. Where other celebrities received glowing copy about their pregnant bodies, Britney's body was mocked as fat, flabby, and wasted. Even though she is quite wealthy, Britney is often referred to as "trailer trash" and "trashy," in sharp distinction to the pregnancies of girls next door Garner and Roberts. Spears did not perform her pregnancy and parenting in ways expected of wealthy white women; rather, she enabled the media to typify her behavior as "white trash" and "ghetto."

Though it is likely that addiction and depression were at the root of much of her behavior, Britney got no sympathy in the press. Spears did not engage in the "rigorous body management and adherence to medical discipline [that] are the unquestioned tasks of the pregnant and birthing woman." As Ussher predicts of any woman, Spears's "failure to adhere to these practices is positioned as a negation of the needs of the unborn child, a sign of a 'bad mother.'"[57]

And yet, superficially, much of the bad press surrounding Spears's pregnancies and mothering focused on her lack of bodily discipline; much of the negativity centers on her physical body. As the site *Bumpshack* (a site devoted to celebrity bumps) puts it, "Pregnancy Not Always Pretty for Britney Spears."[58] Her bad mom persona is marked through her fashion specifically, her "trailer park" style featuring short-short denim skirts, midriff-baring tops, and low-cut blouses that strain buttons across her chest. Online comments posted to *The Superficial,* alongside a photo of Britney heading to the gym in a midriff-baring top and baggy sweatpants, are uniformly critical. "Pat" writes, "just what this world need [sic] is another trailer trash baby from a trailer trash mama . . . that's the last thing this stupid bitch needs."[59] The comments get even more mean spirited. "Cate" writes "for the sake of our entertainment, I pray to God she's pregnant."

Britney is mocked in the press even when she looks good and presents a more sophisticated image. *Harper's Bazaar* featured Spears in 2006, pregnant with her second child, in a striking series of photographs. Nude save for jewels, Spears takes rather modest poses.

The public response was more approbation than approval; gossip website *Backseat Cuddler* posted one image from the magazine, adding the comment: "Oops, did she do it again? Reproduce that is." It goes on to announce that if Britney was indeed pregnant, it was likely because she was jealous of the attention her pregnant (unwed, and teenaged) sister had gotten. Her later cover for Q magazine traded on that bad-girl image.

A large part of Britney's presumed bad-mother persona also rested on her postbaby antics, many of which did indeed seem to be attention grabbing, and most of which were made evident on her body. Her tattoos, shaved head, and panty-less poses were, according to the press, physical manifestations

FIGURE 2.3 Britney Spears cover for *Harper's Bazaar*, August 2006. Photo by: Alexi Lubomirksi

FIGURE 2.4 Britney Spears cover for Q, November 2006. Photo by: James Dimmock

of erratic behavior (and possible postpartum psychosis) and thus signaled Spears as unfit for parenthood. Sympathy is clearly lacking from most conversations about Britney's body, babies, and mothering. Also missing is responsible discussion of possible mental illness, emotional distress, medication side effects, or that Britney might have needed help instead of bad-girl blame. Instead, the media flocked to stories of Britney as a vagina-flashing, head-shaving crazy. As two commenters on *The Superficial* noted, "Bipolar meds cause weight gain, reduce mania & depression . . . The result: Crazy, thin, vagina-flashing, head-shaving, Adnan-dating Britney is gone, replaced by slightly chubby, maternal, productive, level-mooded Britney" (posted by "sla"). And "Anne's" painfully honest note:

> One of the drugs she was reportedly taking after being committed was an anti-psychotic. They are used for bi-polar, Post partum Depression, schizophrenia among other mental disorders. Problem is they cause horrible weight gain. They are fabulous drugs for helping with the disorder, but the weight gain is usually why people go off of them. I was on the same drug she was reported to be on for postpartum depression and gained 60 pounds in 3 months. Still trying to lose that.[60]

Truthful discussions of postpartum depression and psychosis could help millions of women; the opportunity was lost in press obsession with Britney's admittedly wacky behavior and fluctuations in weight. Pregnancy has not helped this "bad girl"—and the press did her no favors either. Pregnancy and early motherhood failed to redeem Spears's image; rather, she became even more vilified as a trashy girl and unfit mother.

Whether her performances of motherhood were influenced by postpartum illness and addiction, were reflecting narcissistic behavior, or were intentional and purposive statements against normative images of mothering, Britney Spears was either unwilling or unable to adopt a style admired by the popular press. The message to the public reinforced a good-mom/bad-mom dualism and served as a clear semiotic warning to other women.

In contrast, former "bad girl" Angelina Jolie serves as a model redemptive mother. The press allows, and even encourages, Jolie to speak about her own mental and physical health as well as to speak in a proxy for women and children worldwide in her role as a philanthropist and "celebrity diplomat."[61]

FIGURE 2.5 Angelina Jolie at the Davos World Economic Forum. Photo credit: Time, Inc.

In that role, Jolie has been frequently photographed in suits and twinset sweaters that solidify a remade image. She is a working professional woman whose pregnancy is not the focus of the photo or the work.

Indeed, Jolie's formerly fraught image has been improved by pregnancy and presentation of herself as maternal. Her chic style, wealth, and philanthropy have helped her seem transformed and redeemed by pregnancy and motherhood.

Jolie used to be prone, as the *New York Times* reports, "to provocative statements about blood, tattoos, and bisexuality."[62] Formerly married to oddball actor Billy Bob Thornton, who left his wife, Laura Dern, for her, and now partnered with Brad Pitt, after his divorce from popular "girl next door" Jennifer Aniston, Jolie early developed a reputation for home wrecking and an insatiable sexuality.[63] Her fashion choices, which once relied heavily on tight black leather and Goth-inspired creations, reinforced her bad-girl image, as did her badass, butt-kicking performances as Lara Croft in the *Tomb Raider* films, and her oddly sexualized relationship with her brother as it played out on red carpets in the early 2000s.

Jolie now parents with Pitt, and the two have six children: three biological and three adopted. And the image Jolie has portrayed since partnering with Pitt and becoming a mother is markedly different from her previous persona. Though she still emphasizes her sexuality, Jolie currently delivers an image that emphasizes wealth, comfort, and luxury, combined with a message of empathy, compassion, and activism on behalf of women and children. While pregnant and since giving birth, she has stepped out in body- and bump-conscious, though comfortable-looking, gowns. She wears richly hued silk with plunging necklines and little makeup. She appears voluptuous and sexy, yet subdued.

Aside from awards ceremonies, Jolie is often photographed in airports and shopping malls, a child in one arm, the other five holding onto her hands, skirt, and bags. Her six children represent a multicultural crew. From Shiloh's blonde curls to Maddox's Cambodian heritage, the Pitt-Jolie family presents the embodiment of a multicultural America, and Jolie is consistently in the public eye as its maternal head. Even Jolie's most recent tattoos are motherly tributes that nod to multiculturalism. Rather than dragons or lotus flowers, her newest documented tattoos feature the latitude and longitude of each child's birthplace written on her body in blue ink.

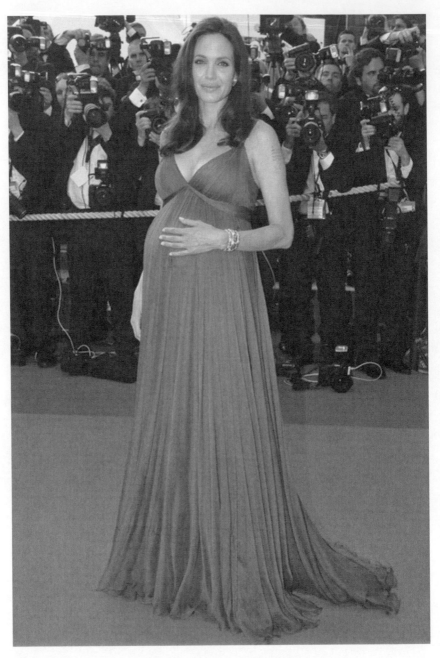

FIGURE 2.6 Angelina Jolie at Cannes. Photo credit: PA Photos

Though she will never be "the girl next door," nor "America's sweetheart,"[64] Jolie has become a woman redeemed through her embodied commitment to her children and performed in her role as UNICEF ambassador, as well as her outspoken advocacy for women's rights in making health care decisions. In this role, Jolie has been a public and vocal advocate for refugees and has taken on humanitarian causes as pet projects. In 2009, she spoke at the Davos World Economic Forum on the maternal problems associated with poverty and the need for the United States to sign the UN Convention on the Rights of the Child. As Andrew Cooper notes, "In the same mold as Audrey Hepburn, Angelina Jolie has rebranded the definition of a celebrity diplomat."[65]

Jolie's 2013 editorial in the *New York Times* about her decision to have a double mastectomy when she found she was carrying the BRCA1 gene, which dramatically increases her chances of breast and ovarian cancer, is the latest in a line of public stances she has taken in regard to women's health. Hailed by many women as a brave telling of a complex health care story, Jolie's editorial urges public health intervention. She writes:

> It has got to be a priority to ensure that more women can access gene testing and lifesaving preventive treatment, whatever their means and background, wherever they live. The cost of testing for BRCA1 and BRCA2—at more than $3,000 in the United States, remains an obstacle for many women. I choose not to keep my story private because there are many women who do not know that they might be living under the shadow of cancer. It is my hope that they, too, will be able to get gene tested, and that if they have a high risk they, too, will know that they have strong options.[66]

Additionally, Jolie's editorial stressed that she made these medical decisions in large part on behalf of her desire to parent her children longer into their lives than her mother lived in hers. She writes, "I wanted to write this to tell other women that the decision to have a mastectomy was not easy. But it is one I am very happy that I made. My chances of developing breast cancer have dropped from 87 percent to under 5 percent. I can tell my children that they don't need to fear they will lose me to breast cancer." Before this revelation she was open as well about her choice to breastfeed her biological children, Jolie had previously granted an interview to the *New York Times* in which she stressed that her kids are with "Mommy and Daddy every day for every meal" before telling the reporter that she might need to take a break to pump breast milk for the twins. Discussing breasts as both markers of femininity and nourishment, Jolie disrupts ideas about her body that are constructed by the action hero sex objects she portrays.[67]

Also key to her redeemed image, "Mommy and Daddy" are a uniquely present feature of press coverage surrounding the Pitt-Jolie family. Nancy Chodorow is certainly correct that "the current organization of parenting separates children and men."[68] Though single mothers are generally suspect, press coverage of pregnant and paired celebrities or celebrities with their children almost never features a father, let alone the family in its totality. The photos are almost always of the unaccompanied pregnant female (or a pregnant woman out with her "girlfriends," usually shopping) or of the mother and her child. This is true, even when the father is every bit as famous as the mother. Interestingly, though, for Angelina Jolie, the press coverage often does include Pitt, in a way that reinforces her rehabilitated image, in part by her association with her partner.

Some remain unconvinced by Jolie's transformation—web boards always have "haters"—but by many accounts, Jolie's retooled image has been quite successful. In a *US Weekly* magazine poll from August 2008, 64 percent of respondents said that from a list of celebrity tots, they would most like their children to play with Shiloh Jolie-Pitt.[69] As one reader explained, "Shiloh's family seems the most normal." Of course, the Jolie-Pitts are not normal or average in any palpable way; they are extremely wealthy and incredibly famous. Indeed, wealth and fame allow them to achieve the image of normalcy and family life that so fascinates the media. In contrast, that same poll reported that only 6 percent of respondents would want their children to play with bad-girl Britney Spears's son, Sean Federline. Britney and her struggles are perhaps too normal, too real, for *Us!* to fantasize about.

Hot, Sexy Mamas

Jennifer Garner, Julia Roberts, and Angelina Jolie, along with so many other celebrities, are stylized as sexy women who are also mothers. Yet their sexiness is secured and made safe by virtue of their heteronormative marriages, sophisticated fashion sense, entrepreneurial or humanitarian spirits, and displays of concern for their children. Often these celebrities are portrayed as settling comfortably, if a bit unconventionally, into domestic bliss. Their sexiness often takes a backseat to maternity, comfort, and domesticity. Particularly interesting is a recent photo spread of a postpartum Julia Roberts frolicking on the beach with her children, wearing a tropical print bikini. As a "good girl–girl next door" and a mother celebrated for her presumed parenting skills, to have Roberts appear publicly in a bikini disrupts the notion that pregnant women, newly postpartum women, or mothers in general should cover up because their bodies are somehow "unseemly and improper."[70] People identifying as women commented en masse on the websites that published these photos, defending Roberts's mature (yet svelte) physique against those who found her thirty-nine-year-old body too "old" and "maternal" to be sexy.

This is decidedly different coverage from that received by the sexy women of color whose "bumps and boobs" are covered lasciviously by the mainstream press. Even as pundits tout the idea that we have become a "postracial nation," Wojcik argues that Hollywood has drawn even firmer lines around issues of race, gender, and class and that celebrities replicate status quo identity norms, rather than trouble them. She writes, "In today's seeming diversity, the actor is defined *increasingly* by physical appearance, race, body type, age, gender, and sex. . . . In the interests of upholding shifting conceptions of realism, Hollywood has proliferated rather than blurred the lines."[71] And, while Jane Ussher is correct that pregnancy generally "represents feminine excess at its most extreme, the boundless . . . bulging body standing as the epitome of unruly fecundity,"[72] it is notable that the press coverage of pregnant celebrities of color focuses *more* on how difficult it is to control them, how likely they are to "pop" or "burst," and how "hot"—rather than radiant, or glowing—they are.

Four celebrities in particular—Salma Hayek, Jennifer Lopez, Beyoncé Knowles, and Halle Berry—have received significant press attention that hypersexualizes their mommy bodies. Though they could just as easily be portrayed as "good" or "bad" girls, the media coverage of the pregnancies of these women of color celebrities has almost uniformly highlighted their "exotic" and "sexy" bodies. They are all constructed by the media as "mamas!" who's very hotness is "smokin'" and in need of our control; captioned photos of Halle Berry like the one here repeatedly use the line: "Whoa mama!"

FIGURE 2.7 Halle Berry at the London Film Festival, 2007. Photo by: Claire Greenway/ Getty Images. Sourced at: JustJared.com

Berry, who was voted "Coolest 1st Time Mom this Year," by readers of *OK!* magazine, was also named *Esquire* magazine's "Sexiest Woman Alive!" in 2008. *OK!* documents Berry's pregnancy in more than twenty-five photographic slides accompanying the online article, which is titled "Sexy Mama!"[73] A paparazzi photo of her at nine months pregnant includes the caption, "Whoa Mama! Halle Berry, Still Hot as Ever, Looks Like She's About to Explode." Another photo of a casually dressed Berry tooling around town reads, "Whoa Momma! Halle Berry May Be About to Bust, but That Doesn't Mean She Can't Be Smokin' Hot!" Accompanying a third photo of Berry, in a plunging V-neck dress of lavender silk is the caption, "Whoa, Mama! Halle Berry Was Busting Out (in a Good Way) . . . Pregnancy Is Good for Her!"[74]

Salma Hayek, too, was often touted as a "sexy mama" during her pregnancy. It was a status she seemed to embrace. One much-seen photo shows Hayek in a flowing black skirt with a black cap-sleeved T-shirt covering three-fourths of a protruding belly. The writing on her shirt read, "Stylish. Sexy. Pregnant." One online commenter continued in this vein by commenting on Hayek's baby's name (Valentina Paloma Pinault), "Ooh! Sexy name!"[75] The sexiness is apparently congenital.

For Hayek, though, as well as for Berry, an incredible amount of media focused not only on her bump, but on her breasts. *Bumpshack* posted pictures of Hayek in a spaghetti-strapped dress and labeled her breasts, "Milk Factory #1" and "Milk Factory #2." In May 2007, on the gossip site *CelebWarship*, "Noni" commented on a picture of Hayek, "Those boobs look pretty knocked up too. I mean, Christ . . . they're out of control!" On another site, her breasts were crudely labeled "Leche" and "Shit." Certainly, both women possess bodies that are conventionally beautiful according to dominant aesthetic norms; these are bodies that are both envied and desired. But they are also bodies that are "curiously and uniquely unreliable" in their propensity to "burst" and "explode" with child.[76] This is very different from coverage given to white celebrities.[77]

Jodi Dean has noted that our consumption of images of abundance and excess are key to neoliberal capital's unquestioned expansion.[78] Photos of pregnant Kate Winslet's dinners out and continent hopping from Heathrow airport are examples of acceptable expansion and abundance. However, such abundance and excess, when "enjoyed" by the "wrong" people, becomes cast as threatening to the populace. Women of color's abundance is presented as "dangerously volatile . . . out of control. . . . Their bodies threaten to uncontrollably spill, leak, or seep."[79]

This paranoia is clear in the writing about celebrity women of color that focuses on their bumps and boobs. It is also clear in the attention paid to these women's backsides. As Julia Jordan-Zachery argues, the "script" of the black booty (in her terms, "the black ass") is a powerful and prevalent one in mainstream representations of these women, used to reduce black women to "a piece of ass" outside of the realm of political and social belonging and power. Coverage of pregnant Jennifer Lopez and Beyoncé, in particular, obsesses on their "booties." One website for African American moms and moms-to-be (Cafemom.com) profiled the editor's five favorite booties, all possessed by women of color; J. Lo's was described as "big and juicy," Beyoncé's as having "delicious jiggle."

Mary Beltran has argued that press coverage of J. Lo's prebaby booty was emancipatory and powerful. She wrote:

> It is possible to view Jennifer Lopez not as another victim constructed in a still-racist society as an ethnic sexual object (although there are no doubt elements of this dynamic in the representations of Lopez in late 1998), but as empowered and empowering through asserting qualities such as intelligence, assertiveness, and power, while also proudly displaying her non-normative body and declaring it beautiful.[80]

Beltran acknowledges that women of color have "historically . . . been viewed as more 'bodily' than whites," and that:

> Latinas historically have been enslaved, raped, and otherwise constructed similarly through narratives of colonization as available and accessible sex objects. These constructions subsequently became emblems that came to represent Latinas as a whole to many European-descended Americans . . . as exotic, sexual, and available, and as more in touch with their bodies and motivated by physical and sexual pleasure than white women.[81]

Yet she suggests that media representations of J. Lo are emancipatory— showing Lopez as powerful and in charge of her body and sexuality, thereby in control of her image. I disagree that this is the case.

Rather, I am persuaded by the work of Dorothy Roberts, Susan Bordo, and Julia Jordan-Zachery, all of whom point to the hypersexualization of black women through physicality as flash points for their continued oppression, not liberation. Bordo wrote that representations of black female bodies (and, I would argue, Latina bodies as well) as "inviting," with "overly exaggerated genitalia and rear ends," contribute "to notions of black women as fair game for sexual conquest."[82] It is no accident that Beyoncé, J. Lo, Halle Berry, and Salma Hayek are eroticized in wildlike ways, evoking an out-of control primal sexuality.[83] Rather, this exoticization painfully recalls and perpetuates a particular sexual objectification and sexual use of women of color in American history, replicated often in pop culture media, which has a long history of sexualizing women of color in particularly animalistic ways.

The construction of women of color as exotically sexy during pregnancy follows a dubious theme of envisioning them as available, fertile, robust vessels. It also recalls their construction as devious, lying, and not particularly trustworthy. Beyoncé's much-anticipated pregnancy, following on the heels of a fairy-tale wedding to media mogul and hip hop artist Jay Z, seemed almost too good to be true. Some media even reported that she was faking her bump. In November 2011—three months before she gave birth—*Us Weekly* magazine reproduced publicity photos of the singer and announced, "her bump is bona fide."[84] It isn't clear what about this photo convinced reporters, but her pose certainly makes the bump prominent.

The media constructs these women's public images as less constrained, demure, trustworthy, and docile than white women's. Salma Hayek and Halle Berry may be famous women to be admired, but in the hands of tabloid media their admiration hinges on their status as "sexy Other." Women of color can attain status and attention—but as the sexy seductress, not the good girl. That (still limiting) option remains largely closed, available only to those pure, sophisticated, and stylish white girls. While it is a recent cultural phenomenon, and possibly liberatory, to acknowledge pregnant bodies as potentially erotic and mothers as sexual beings, the treatment of these particular pregnancies focuses the sexualized gaze on the unreliability of the bodies and their seemingly unconstrained growth and voluptuousness. It does so in ways that objectify particular body parts, while denying the humanity of the person embodying them.

FIGURE 2.8 Beyoncé Knowles at New York City's Roseland Ballroom, 2011. Photo credit: Jim Spellman/WireImages

Stardom does not operate absent whiteness and structural inequality tied to race and class. As Redmond notes: "Stardom and whiteness have a special relationship with one another, connected by the mythic trope that stars and whiteness are simultaneously extraordinary and ordinary, present and absent phenomena. . . . When the signifying systems of *idealized* whiteness and stardom come together, an *extraordinarily* powerful representation emerges that ontologically privileges and secures this form of whiteness (white 'stardom') as the highest ideal available to man/woman."[85] American patriarchy has long idealized *motherhood* as the highest ideal available to women. Similarly, celebrity motherhood, inscribed via whiteness, normalizes and idealizes particular performances of pregnancy, while it troubles others as disruptive.

Redmond continues, "On the one hand, it is all to do with absence, abstinence, repression, purity, and perfection. Idealized white stars are supposedly above and beyond their own (and everybody else's) sexual desires, greed, and vices. They are 'holy' vessels, embodiments of all that is good and virtuous about (super) human kind."[86]

Britney Spears, the unredeemed bad girl, loses her racial privilege by becoming "white trash" and "ghetto." She lets go of her whiteness by being unruly, and her body becomes racially coded by a proxy of derision related to her purported socioeconomic class—her middle- to lower-class "roots." Good girls and redeemed bad girls, in contrast, are constructed in the press as "embodiments of all that is good and virtuous," and the docile and disciplined bodies of Katie Holmes and Nicole Kidman are made salient through the special class of celebrity pregnancy notable for its extreme self-denial. All of this coverage stands in stark contrast to a final category of celebrity maternity, embodied in the cool, removed, and controlled sexuality of the MILFs and yummy mummies.

Yummy Mummies and MILFs

The term MILF (an acronym for mother I'd like to fuck) was popularized by the films in the *American Pie* series[87] and has come to denote women of a certain age who are painted as nearly predatory in their sexual desire, mature in their tastes, and rather icy in their ability to control their responses to their own passions. Much like the Mrs. Robinson of a previous generation, these women are in control of their sexuality and are used to seeing their beauty as a form of power. Gwyneth Paltrow, who famously wore a succession of miniskirts in decreasing lengths at each separate premiere of her film *Iron Man,* which showed off long, toned, and tanned legs, is cast in the popular media as an acceptable version of the MILF. Paltrow's website, *Goop,* an "eminent lifestyle publication" and e-commerce shop extends the actress's brand with ties to high-end designers, "clean" eating, and spiritual musings; her entrepreneurial presence extends the image of Paltrow as a powerful, elite, and sexual woman.[88]

Photo essays of Paltrow, and accompanying interview and copy text, insinuate that she has a particular kind of sexuality: mature, experienced, controlled. This image was perpetuated recently by the announced divorce of Paltrow and her husband of eleven years, Coldplay lead singer Chris Martin. The popular press reported unconfirmed rumors of Paltrow's numerous affairs,[89] the couple's "open marriage," and a broken-hearted Martin who was "devastated" by the split. In the popular lexicon, yummy mummy refers to either, according to the popular culture bibles Wikipedia and Urban Dictionary, a "General Mills monster-themed breakfast cereal," or a "sexually attractive mother." Urban Dictionary further elaborates:

> There is an important age distinction between a yummy mummy and a MILF. Yummy mummys are younger than 30, while MILFs are older than 30. . . . [A Yummy Mummy is an] attractive, healthy, and very sexy mother! Usually a young woman or sometimes a really gorgeous and hot middle aged mother. Yummy mummies usually wear trendy clothes, have great hairstyles and always look fabulous.[90]

The yummy mummy moniker comes from a 2006 book written by Polly Williams, a London-based writer for *In Style* magazine, who consciously channeled "Gwennie-and-Apple" (Gwyneth Paltrow's daughter's name is Apple) when writing the novel *The Rise and Fall of a Yummy Mummy.* Perhaps satirical, certainly funny, the novel argues that parenthood can take a woman from self-centered to other-centered, as well as from slim to frumpy. It is also overtly and frankly sexual, as when, six months postpartum the lead character, Amy, decides to become more "yummy" than "mummy" and recapture her husband's attention.

Importantly, the sexualized postbaby bodies of MILFs and yummy mummies are different from those possessed and enacted by hot sexy mamas in part because they are parenting bodies, not pregnant bodies—but primarily because they are white, controlled, and disciplined bodies. They are bodies, presumably, that we need not worry about, though we may not want to leave our husbands or sons alone with them.

And yet, as Jane Ussher notes, "the fecund female body," the one both pregnant and mothering, "stands at the centre of surveillance and policing of femininity—both externally, and from within."[91] The fecund celebrity body presents women with idealized and normalized versions of femininity against which to measure themselves. While pregnant celebrities do usefully trouble the "familiar, pervasive cultural dichotomy between motherhood and sexuality,"[92] they are still allowed only a limited range of roles and identities in which to perform their pregnancies. Idealized and normalized pregnant bodies not only reinforce gender norms, they reinforce racial and ethnic stereotypes in the exoticization of "sexy" women of color and obfuscate the role of wealth and access to resources in obtaining perfect "bumps," babies, and postpartum bodies. Coverage of pregnant celebrities tends to rely on familiar stereotypes reiterated in the themes I've presented here:

Good Girls, Bad Girls, and Hot Sexy Mamas

The Docile, Disciplined Body

The M[others] I['d] L[ike] [to] F[uck] and the Yummy Mummy

These themes, read in context of the legal and cultural history of pregnancy in America presented in chapter one, remind me, usefully and sadly, of Andrea Dworkin's words regarding beauty and womanhood. Dworkin wrote, in her essay titled *Women Hating:* "Standards of beauty describe in precise terms the relationship that an individual will have to her own body. They prescribe her motility, spontaneity, posture, gait, the uses to which she can put her body. They define precisely the dimensions of her physical freedom. And of course, the relationship between physical freedom and psychological development, intellectual possibility, and creative potential is *an umbilical one.*"[93] The constraints on performances of pregnancy by celebrity women modeled as ideal and normal for women in general certainly show the continued constraints on women's "motility, spontaneity, . . . physical freedom, . . .

intellectual possibility, and creative potential." It seems that all women, by virtue of their pregnancies or ability to become pregnant, remain the objects of legal and social gazes that continue to discipline and normalize them. The next two chapters turn to an examination of those techniques of discipline, surveillance, and regulation.

CHAPTER 3

WANTING THE BUMP

NEW YORK TIMES editorial writer Molly Jong-Fast put it this way in 2003: "It seems as if babies are the new Birkin bag." Jong-Fast was referring to the famous, coveted, and insanely expensive Hermes leather bag named for model Jane Birkin. The Birkin is a celebrity "must-have" item just like, she intimated, a baby or perhaps a baby bump. Her critical statement got picked up, rather uncritically, five years later by Billy Joel's wife, Katie Lee, when she told *E!*, "I'm always thinking about cute [baby] names. I always say that babies are the new Birkin. They're the hottest accessory right now. Everybody has to have one."[1]

In fact, the bump may be *better* than a Birkin; it might be the new Oscar statuette. Celebrity-watching website *TMZ* announced the news of Scarlett Johansson's pregnancy the morning after she was a runner-up at the 2014 awards ceremony, with a headline that read, "Forget the Oscar, Scarlett Johansson has an even bigger award on the way."[2] Johansson's reproductive labor is all the more valuable, we can assume from this coverage, than her creative and professional labor. A baby bump trumps an award any day! The awards season lasts only eight weeks, from Golden Globes to Oscars. But a celebrity's baby bump brings nine months (and more!) of traffic to websites and readers to a magazine's glossy pages.[3]

Of course, Katie Lee Joel is not going to run out and buy a baby. She isn't saying she could *purchase* a bump. And Scarlett Johansson likely hopes for an

Oscar in her professional future, as well as a healthy child. But the rhetoric of the bump as a fashion accessory—as something to acquire and show off—is played out again and again in popular culture treatment of celebrity pregnancy, and the idea of a baby—or at least a baby's image—as a marketable item is ever-present in discussions of celebrity families.

Much as the average woman might look forward to the presence of the bump in midpregnancy to show the world she is carrying a child, so too do celebrity watchers devote incredible time and space to the "bump watch." Writers of blogs, articles in celebrity magazines, and comments on celebrity websites all speculate over photos that seem to indicate a bump, praise the size and shape and stylishness of the proof of pregnancy, and coo over celebrity women's styling of their bump. And, much as women are expected to "lean in" and create meaningful and lucrative careers,[4] they must also remember their other roles: the production of children and the consumption of goods and products in the service of maternity. The precarious balance, when a woman is pregnant and mothering, between consuming, producing, and working, is one we can pay attention to in part by paying attention to how celebrities seem to render the juggling act possible. To do so, we must pay attention to the commodification of the bump, the baby, the postbaby body, and the accoutrements needed to achieve an effortless "look."

At the same time that celebrities' bumps and babies are constructed as marketable—they sell magazines and generate web traffic—these women and their babies are styled as consummate consumers whose appetites and purchases we should emulate. The superstars' tastes are watched and reported on, then distilled to those of us with the pocketbooks of mere mortals, in the form of "how-to" articles for getting celebrity style on a working woman's paycheck. Under conditions of neoliberalism, consumption is an act of citizenship; and pregnancy, with all of its new market-based needs, is an opportune time to prepare to birth a new citizen, while exercising economic options. Consumption of celebrity pregnancy and infant-related products becomes another biopolitics of control over women's bodies.

In what follows, I take Katie Lee Joel seriously and discuss the commodification of the bodies related to pregnancy—bumped and pregnant bodies, fetal and infant bodies, and postbaby mommy bodies—as they relate to celebrity. And I elaborate on the construction of citizens as consumers in a neoliberal context that casts consumer activity as political. As the chapter closes, I examine the need for the consumer to be regulated and surveilled, which opens the analysis I undertake in chapter four about "watching" the pregnant celebrity body—and by extension—watching ourselves.

Celebrity's Role in Constructing Commodities

Celebrity, and the mythical "close relationship" we imagine we have with the stars, is an extremely important part of the affective economy of late neoliberal capitalism.[5] More than mere symbols, individual celebrities become branded exemplars of how ordinary people can and should live.[6] Marketing these lifestyles for emulation requires identifiable star brands, as well as consumers that are "easy to categorize and therefore easy to track consumption and market to."[7] Through the use of celebrity as a general category, and individual celebrities in particular, the media help to sell a particular lifestyle and set of products and services to niche markets of categorized consumers. The woman who watches Julia Roberts's movies will, by extension, be interested in what hair care products she uses; Keira Knightley's female fans will certainly look closely at the maternity dresses she wears on the red carpet and to fashion week. Celebrity helps to fulfill a necessary homogenizing function, channeling consumer desire toward the quotidian rendered extraordinary via celebrity.

Media coverage of celebrity pregnancies performs an important role in helping to craft practices of consumption for noncelebrity women. As Sternheimer puts it, "celebrities have served as representatives of the link between status and consumption throughout at least the last century,"[8] and particularly in the Reagan era, when "celebrity culture glamorized massive wealth." It is not coincidental that interest in celebrity lifestyles has reached high points in the 1930s, 1980s, and 2010s—all times of recession and economic downturn in the United States. During each period:

> Celebrity stories helped prop up the illusion that a glamorous lifestyle was not only possible, but moral, despite the counterculture movement's calls for reduced consumption and finding meaning outside of materialism. Articles regularly revealed dollar amounts of big paydays and described the lush lifestyles of the rich and famous.[9]

In the 1930s and 1980s this glamorization was accomplished through lavish magazine spreads of stars' homes and getaways—think Robin Leach's *Lifestyles of the Rich and Famous,* but in print. Now, the glamorization of wealth—and its distillation to regular people—happens in magazine articles that tell consumers how to get stars' "looks for less," as well as in social media and through paparazzi shots. They are so effective at this work because they seem to give average people access to celebrities' private lives. Sternheimer argues that paparazzi photos of celebrities "promote a consumption-based lifestyle highlighting their expensive clothes, cars, and vacations. Many . . . magazines filled with paparazzi shots of [celebrities'] daily lives are little more than catalogues of advertised goods that we might buy."[10] Paparazzi shots of pregnant celebrities are catalogues of the ways that we can mother— and the products we need to do that work well.

In addition to the role of celebrity in channeling general patterns of consumption, celebrity has long been put to use in the construction of females as consumers in particular. Using oral histories collected from British women who came of age in the 1940s and 50s, Jackie Stacey's research notes "a clear link between formations of female subjectivity and processes of self-commodification through consumption."[11] She argues, "female stars offer . . . spectators ideals of feminine desirability which, through the purchase of certain commodities, they tried to recreate for themselves."[12] We have seen in chapter two that a focus on a particular size, shape, and styling of a star's bump is part of the normative gaze employed on pregnant women—part of how they learn how to perform pregnancy. Here, I argue that the commodities pregnant celebrities buy, sell, and use are also important parts of that normative gaze; we can fruitfully ask what commodities pregnant women are being taught to desire when they indulge in media about pregnant celebrities.

Pregnant women are seen, from the first trimester on, as important new marketing opportunities. Moms, and moms-to-be, buy new and different groceries and are, as Swigat notes, target markets for the clothing industry and toy manufacturers.[13] Once pregnant, women embark on a path of consumption unrivaled by many other social identities. Because women's consumption patterns have long been important constitutive "component[s] of hegemonic femininity,"[14] women know that they must track and note the purchases of pregnant celebrities in order to learn how to be not only feminine, but how to be good mothers. It is clear, as they are constructed in the coverage of celebrity pregnancies, that good mothers buy good (expensive, name-brand) things for their children. From dressing the bump to undressing the postbaby bikini-worthy body, and all the steps in between, moms are consumers, and they have plenty of celebrity models to emulate.

Dressing the Pregnant Body

As interest in celebrity pregnancy has grown, so have apparel lines associated with pregnancy and motherhood. Maternity wear is a big business; IBIS reports that maternity wear is a two-billion-dollar industry, employing more than seventeen thousand people.[15] Mass marketers Walmart and Target, which are consistently ranked first and second, respectively, in terms of retail revenue on apparel, both have dedicated maternity lines. Target Corporation partnered with fashion designer Liz Lange in 2002, just a few years after she created what the retailer markets call the "first designer maternity wear line." Lange published a book in 2003—*Liz Lange's Maternity Style: How to Look Fabulous During the Most Fashion-Challenged Time*—and continues as creative director of the Liz Lange line at Target, even after Cherokee Inc. purchased the brand in 2012, for $14 million.

Other key players in the mass market maternity apparel field come from Gap Corporation, which owns the Banana Republic, Gap, Old Navy, Piperlime, Athleta, and Intermix brands. Both Gap and Old Navy have maternity lines, though it is interesting to note their relatively late arrival to the field. Gap Inc. launched Gap Kids in 1986 and babyGap in 1990, but did not move into the maternity wear marketplace until much later (2000), and then only on its online Gap store, not via dedicated floor space in retail locations.[16] Though some Old Navy retail locations provide maternity clothes on site, the online retail space offers the widest and most reliable selection.

The maternity wear market is most deeply saturated, though, by the corporation Destination Motherhood—which is the parent company to four distinct brands: Motherhood, A Pea in the Pod, Destination Maternity, and Edamame Maternity Spa. Started in 1982 by twenty-eight-year-old Rebecca Mathias, who, according to the Destination Maternity website, "had difficulty finding appropriate maternity apparel for the office," Destination

Motherhood was, by 2013, "the world's leading maternity apparel retailer," with over "$500 million in annual sales" and more than 40 percent of the maternity apparel market share.[17] The company operates 1,923 retail locations worldwide, from stand-alone stores and websites, to a licensing agreement that gives it rack space at Kohls Inc. to retail the Oh Baby line, to a licensing agreement with Macy's department stores (Destination Macy's) and Destination Maternity lines sold in Sears and Kmart. The retail centers employ women almost exclusively, though the entire executive board of this publicly traded company is composed of men.

Destination Maternity quickly caught on to the celebrity pregnancy buzz, partnering with Nicole Ritchie in 2008 to create a "capsule collection" for A Pea in the Pod. That collection, according to the corporate website, "was designed to be bohemian and free-spirited, which emulates Nicole's signature style, and tailored to fit mothers-to-be." Since then, Heidi Klum has designed two "unique" capsule lines for "fashion savvy" mothers-to-be, and Destination Maternity has partnered with Jessica Simpson and Jennifer Love Hewitt to design or lend their names to capsule collections.

A Pea in the Pod's website markets "looks" that have been worn by celebrity moms; you can click on a link to "shop the look" worn by Emily Blunt or "shop the jeans" worn by Jennifer Love Hewitt. The same page on that site offers "CONGRATS!" to celebrity moms on the births of their children, featuring the name and birth date of each child. A second sidebar on the celebrity page for A Pea in the Pod features "Spotlight[s] On" particular stars and their pregnancy style, with signed headshots of the actresses and direct quotes extolling the virtues of the A Pea in the Pod brand. Motherhood's site doesn't market celebrity lifestyle as overtly, but it does market products bearing celebrity names, such as "Jessica Simpson's Seamless Clip Down Nursing Bra" (for $28), which you can link to for purchase from the Destination Maternity blog.

Part of the maternity wear craze relates to the dressing of the "royal bumps," first of Princess Diana and most recently of Princess Kate. Though the internet had not yet made possible the kinds of bump watching of Princess Diana that Kate has undergone, there was—from the moment her pregnancy was announced—obsession with Diana's pregnancy. Through both of her pregnancies, royal watchers observed Diana's smile, her bump, her fashion choices—and that attention has continued with Kate's pregnancies as well. Both Diana and Kate were touted in the press as "one of us"—both "commoners" who married princes and struggled with morning sickness and overbearing mothers-in-law; their pregnancy styles were shown as accessible glamour: high-end yet modest.[18] London-based Seraphin maternity trades on that association, labeling itself as "the clothes brand of choice for A-list celebrities . . . loved by Hollywood Royalty and Actual Royalty." On its website you can click on any outfit featured—all with the tagline "WORN BY . . ." an array of famous folks, from Jessica Alba, Halle Berry, and Kate Winslet—to the Duchess of Cambridge (Princess Kate) herself. The About Us page of the company's website notes, "We are proud to have dressed some very glamorous bumps."[19]

Some stars bypass the licensing agreements altogether, dressing their glamorous bumps in clothes of their own design. Ska rocker and California girl extraordinaire Gwen Stefani is a prime example of a celebrity who has made dressing women—even pregnant and mothering women and their children—a large part of her financial success and public image. Stefani and her husband Gavin Rossdale have three sons (Kingston, Zuma, and Apollo); her image as a successful entrepreneur and designer relies for its success on the commodification of family life. Alluding to the fact that Stefani has her own fashion line, with maternity and kids' clothes integral to it, *Glamour* magazine wrote, when announcing Stefani's third pregnancy, "Expect [to see] some seriously cool maternity wear."[20] In fact, much of the coverage of Stefani's pregnancies discusses her fashion sense, "edgy" style, and pregnancy-defying body. As a writer for the fashion section of *The Telegraph* put it: "Call us creepy, but we took a vested interest in the pop star's pregnancy. The Hollaback Girl framed her burgeoning baby bump in a catalogue of natty camo coats, jumpsuits and tasseled dresses, and never even contemplated stepping out without heels on. Her selfie in a slinky black dress and leather trousers at nine months pregnant universally shamed mothers who had succumbed to the stretchy pants lifestyle."[21] Perhaps because her band, *No Doubt!*, has been on hiatus frequently during her pregnancies, most of the coverage of Stefani while pregnant focuses on her style in ways that capitalizes on her *image* as a rock star, rather than engages her in *performances* as a rock star.[22] *People, US Weekly,* and *Bazaar* note, variously, that she has a "bold" pregnancy style, is "California cool" while pregnant, and is "never one to blend in with the crowd." Significantly, many of the eye-catching designs that Stefani wears are from her own collection: L.A.M.B., which she started more than a decade ago "in [her] kitchen."[23] Featuring sleeveless sweaters retailing for $298 and black satin zippered jumpsuits for $498, L.A.M.B. offers a rock star look with a slightly affordable price point. When Stefani is taking her kids to school, attending Christmas Eve services, or "running errands" in Los Angeles, she is not only a rock star mom being snapped by the paparazzi, she is an entrepreneur helping to drum up business for her clothing line. Stefani seamlessly portrays her lifestyle as something that can be purchased and very clearly connects motherhood to consumerism in the process.

To be sure, part of the explosive growth in pregnancy retailing is less about dressing princesses and celebrities and more about the actual needs of pregnant women as they play an expanded set of roles in society. Pregnant women—now allowed to be public with their pregnancy—do need appropriate work clothes. Pregnant women are now able to engage in physical activities like yoga and biking without as much social or medical disapproval as they faced in previous years: they will necessarily need workout gear and clothes for the gym.

As a contemporary woman's body changes with pregnancy, she has wardrobe needs that she might not have anticipated, especially if she wants to avoid falling into the "shameful" trap of "stretchy pants." In tandem with maternity retailers, celebrity-watching websites have those needs covered: PopSugar helpfully lists the "top" or "most chic" celebrity maternity styles every year, and features articles like "Best Dressed Pregnant Celebs: Get Their Looks For Less." The first paragraph tells readers: "The threat of swollen ankles and morning sickness doesn't seem to have anything on Hollywood's most stylish moms-to-be, who make looking great, right up until delivery day, seem like a breeze. . . . Throwing on a great dress is the easiest way to wardrobe an expanding baby bump. To get the look of your favorite famous expectant mamas, without breaking the bank, check out these fab finds . . . for a whole lot less than their designer counterparts."[24] Because a significant part of the growth in the pregnancy and postpregnancy market is the celebration of celebrity spending and consumption patterns, marketed to those who don't have the financial means to reproduce that consumption, articles like "Looks for Less" are often shared, and they feature links to the more reasonably priced clothing that average women can click and buy. This is just more reinforcement, of course, of the idea that mothers are consumers.

But pregnant women and new mothers need to buy much more than clothing. Good moms buy lots of things, for themselves and for their children. If we watch the press coverage, we notice that celebrity good moms, almost more than anything, are good consumers.

Good Mommies Buy (Lots of) Things for Their Babies

In the 1960s and 70s, the growing consumer power of women very quickly translated in television ads, branding, and imperatives that focused on shaping women's desires and consumption. Women, by and large, purchase household products and grocery items, and women buy clothes for the entire family. At all ends of the financial spectrum, women are the family's financial decision makers. Recent market research shows that the average "multitasking, carpool-driving, Starbucks-hopping, grocery-shopping mom" is an active consumer. "She uses debit and credit cards about twice a day and more than 40 times a month. She tends to shop most at a few establishments, five to 10 places that are 20 minutes from her home."[25] Pregnant and mothering women are incredibly valuable consumers for the secondary market as well; as a measure of their power for capital exchanges, sociologist Janet Vertesi notes, "the average person's marketing data is worth 10 cents; a pregnant woman's data skyrockets to $1.50."[26]

American Express, Chase Bank, and Bank of America are all wooing the maternal consumer—offering Amex EveryDay cards, BankAmericard, and Chase's Freedom Card—cards with rewards based on the number of purchases made in a given time period, rather than the amount spent. AmEx upped the ante by securing celebrity mom Tina Fey as the spokeswoman for the EveryDay card in spring 2014. Print ads feature Ms. Fey sitting like a cross-legged yogi in an astoundingly messy—but well-outfitted—kitchen, various accoutrements of contemporary life littered around her: an iPhone, a MacBook Air, a Starbucks coffee—one child clutching her, the other cuddling a puppy. Both televised and print ads show a tally of her AmEx purchases, "everywhere from the drugstore (for chin acne cream) to the street food truck (waffles) to the dry cleaner . . . to the grocery store," purchasing milk like there's no tomorrow.[27] This celebrity mom is the ultimate consumer—she has massive disposable income and a savvy sense of style, a busy lifestyle, and a posse to dress and feed. If only Fey were pregnant in the ads! Then she would need to add prenatal vitamins, maternity clothing, and nursery furniture to her shopping list.

In the construction of celebrity pregnancy, contemporary media put tremendous emphasis on what the stars buy and where they make their purchases. Many of the paparazzi shots of expecting celebrities are taken of them while shopping. Typical of the coverage is an article titled "Halle Berry and Her Bump Go Shopping," accompanied by photos of Berry at Trader Joe's, the LA Bakery, and other food retailers. Several websites ran photos of Mila Kunis shopping in the final weeks of pregnancy; a writer for the *Daily Mail* opined, "And while the 31-year-old may boast a big bank balance, she's not above shopping at budget chain Target." The article on the shopping trip also noted that Kunis was dressed "casually."[28] An "unnamed source" told *People* magazine, "Mila seems very low-key when it comes to buying things for the baby. She doesn't want a cluttered nursery with unnecessary items."[29] Insofar as celebrity moms are styled as good girls and good moms, their purchases gain legitimacy as the goods that good moms buy. In fact, just as in neoliberal discourse being a "good consumer" is tantamount to being a "good citizen," being a "good consumer" is also a way to be a "good mom."

The secondary products associated with pregnancy, birth, and raising an infant—breast pads and pumps, bottles and bottle washers, diaper genies, high-end strollers, bathtubs—are not incidental markets. From "The Perfect Diaper Bags for Our Favorite Celebrity Moms-to-be,"[30] we learn that Dolce and Gabbana diaper bags can run more than $800; the most reasonably priced bag shown is more than $145. Parents are exhorted to "BuyBuy Baby"[31]—to purchase toys and computers to help their infant learn various languages, even CDs you can play for them in utero to help them develop early and quickly.[32] Margaret Morganroth Gullette dismays: "Americans are simply being 'readied' at earlier ages for whatever the dominant system requires us to face . . . [providing us with] the pre-professional child. Adult eyes—including those of working-class parents—have learned to see in the toddler . . . a future New Economy worker."[33] The message from the media as it covers celebrity pregnancy and parenting is clear: good moms have an obligation to grow good babies—smart, self-reliant, neoliberal subjects with purchasing power.

Baby's First Pictures

No one is going to pay me $5 million for my son's baby pictures—even though he was super cute. But his grandparents do expect regular photos, and I (over?) share about his achievements on Facebook, after snapping Instagrams of them. Technology allows us to keep in touch with far-flung friends and family. It also enables us to portray a particular—managed—image, and to selectively curate the slide show that represents important moments in our life. Within the realm of celebrity, the management of the child—via that child's image—is most certainly a commodified arena, and (unlike those of my son) the first published images of the babies of celebrities are extraordinarily expensive items.

According to *Forbes* reporter Lacey Rose, who compiles that publication's list of the most expensive celebrity photos, *People* magazine paid $6 million for first rights to the baby pictures of J. Lo's twins.[34] The magazine paid Brad Pitt and Angelina Jolie $15 million for rights to publish the first photos of Knox Leon and Vivienne Marcheline Jolie-Pitt in a nineteen-page "family album." *People* paid just over $4 million for the first pictures of the Jolie-Pitts' daughter Shiloh and $2 million for photos of Pax Thien. Rose notes that "Brangelina, as the celebrity media has dubbed the A-list couple, scored big buzz—and an even bigger price tag—for the first glimpse of its brood's latest additions." Rose writes this about the Shiloh photos: "The first biological offspring of two of Hollywood's hottest stars became a (pricey) must-see for the masses."[35]

There is much to unpack in the Jolie-Pitt photo prices alone. The clearly higher value paid for a "biological daughter" over an adopted son reifies particular biological understandings of "family" and implies that the value of a white infant is somehow higher than the value of an Asian toddler. Shiloh is somehow more real, more authentic (and therefore more valuable) than Pax. The Jolie-Pitts, Jennifer Lopez, and others have made public statements defending the high price they demand (they also disclose that they donate the fee, usually to a charity associated with children). They argue that by releasing the photos taken in a controlled environment, photos snapped by paparazzi on the sly will be less profitable and the demand for them reduced. This, the stars hope, will help their children lead more normal childhoods, not hounded by the rogue press for candid shots. From the point of view of supply and demand, this logic makes a certain sense.

In response to the same perceived problem, Beyoncé and Jay-Z took a different track, releasing the first pictures of their daughter Blue Ivy on Tumblr. In doing so, they avoided the question of purchase price altogether and took a path away from the "bidding wars" associated with the celebrity baby pictures. Beyoncé has continued to release Instagram shots of herself and Blue Ivy, often obscuring the toddler's face—with a hat or in a photo of the back of her head or of her feet. This earns her praise from *Huffington Post* bloggers, who write copy like "Beyoncé Shares Blue Ivy Photo, Still Manages to Keep Her from Prying Eyes," and "Though Blue's face is often photographed by the paparazzi when she's out in public with her parents, it seems Beyoncé made the decision to shield her daughter's face in personal photos she shares on social media. This way, she can share photos of her child with her adoring fans and still retain a sense of privacy for baby Blue."[36]

Other stars reportedly refusing to sell photos include Sarah Jessica Parker and Matthew Broderick, Jennifer Garner and Ben Affleck, and Halle Berry.[37] Kim Kardashian and Kanye West have also refused to sell photos of their daughter, declining $3 million offers for first pictures of North.[38] They provided Kardashian's 23.2 million Instagram followers with photos of the baby instead. Later Instagram photos show toddler North in an almost laughably opulent setting; one artistic shot from November 2014 shows the little girl in a black fur coat and ballet flats embedded with crystals, standing on the front step of one of the family's homes.

Refusals to sell are becoming more and more common, and the proliferation of social media has made the sale of baby images less necessary, as stars can control, to a somewhat greater degree, the public's access to images of their lives and the lives of their children. They can certainly attempt to curate an image of the child and their family life. However, paparazzi still stalk the stars, and adorable photos of famous toddlers on the streets of New York command big prices; so do embarrassing—and titillating—photos of post-baby celebrities in bikinis.

The Hot, Rockin' Postbaby Body

In summer 2013, actress Kristen Bell appeared on the cover of *Redbook* magazine in a photo taken eleven weeks after giving birth to her daughter. She wore a bold-colored top in a forgiving cut, and the brightly patterned slim slacks of the season. She looked healthy—not emaciated. In the interview, Bell seemed to speak frankly about the enormous interest paid to the postbaby body and how quickly stars can return to their "pre-pregnancy selves." She told the magazine that she refused to lose baby weight on a timeline expedited by Hollywood, saying: "I refused to worry about something I could not change, and I still refuse. Look, I'm like any other woman. All this evolved b.s. that I'm telling you is my mantra: It's not something I practice naturally. I had to surrender to not worrying about the way I looked, how much I weighed, because that's just part of the journey of having a baby. I am not a woman whose self-worth comes from her dress size."[39]

The *Redbook* cover made news in the media; it trended on Twitter, and bloggers wrote about it—approvingly. The magazine's editor in chief, Jill Herzig, blogged about the Bell cover, asking, "How did we get to this ridiculous place, where losing the baby weight is a competitive sport followed by millions?" She went on to acknowledge, "Magazines certainly haven't helped, with their covers of celebrities in bikinis, all smiles and hipbones, showing off how thin they've gotten just a few months—or even weeks—after giving birth. As the editor of *Redbook*, I'll admit I've sometimes been part of the problem." The fact that women have to announce that they are taking time to lose baby-related weight, and that magazine editors feel a responsibility to apologize for their coverage, shows just how powerful the desire for a slim postbaby body is. Kristin Bell appearing on a magazine cover, postpartum, without a stick-thin mommy body seems almost as revolutionary now as Demi Moore appearing pregnant and nude twenty years ago.

And of course, the slim postbaby body has always been a subtext of the coverage of the celebrity baby bump. In fact, the fabulous postbaby body is an obsessively desired possession. If we read any popular media, we likely know that J. Lo trained for and competed in a triathlon (to benefit charity) within months of giving birth to twins. Though "sexy" was not the word most often used to describe Jennifer Lopez's pregnant body, it was used often in descriptions of her amazingly quick return to her prepregnancy body.

FIGURE 3.1 Kristen Bell cover for *Redbook*. Photo credit: Brian Bowen Smith for Redbook

Magazine captions nearly always remark upon how sexy she looks, and so "quickly after babies!" Angelina Jolie famously mourns the loss of her bump and the voluptuousness of pregnancy but steps out stylishly svelte within months of giving birth and is public about her breast reconstruction surgery postmastectomy, for the way her famous curves help to keep her feeling feminine. And then there is Gwyneth Paltrow, mother of two young children, who dresses to show off her lean physique and runs her own blog ("Goop") dedicated to healthy (and skinny) living.

Paltrow is a lightning rod personality among media-watching moms. Some vilify her. They point to her sappy (and some say insipid) "unconscious coupling" essay about divorce from Chris Martin in 2014 and her tone-deaf statement to the press that finding work-life balance was harder for her than "regular moms," because time on set was more variable than those of us who had "regular jobs."[40] She is praised by others, who point out that she had the good sense and kindness to stress, in other interviews, that she returned to prebaby weight in large part because her job as a movie star requires it of her. She also points out that she is supported by staff and money in the ability to devote four hours per day to her workout regimen.

The vast majority of new mothers not only don't have the necessity of making their body their business, they also don't have the time or the money to pay the help that would provide the time to spend those long hours in the gym. The celebrity postbaby body is far from reality for the majority of "regular" moms. Yet unrealistic as it is, second only to the bump, the postbaby body is a coveted possession. The "rockin' hot" postbaby body is something to possess. And it is yet another physical manifestation of how we judge mothers and how they judge themselves. Did they gain enough weight: 20–35 pounds? In the right places: that bump or those boobs? And did they lose it quickly enough: within three to four months?[41]

Even as "regular" women eye celebrity bumps while measuring their own, they are told in nearly every article on celebrity pregnancy that each star already has a plan to get back to her prebaby body. The insinuation, of course, is that they should, too. This imperative to slimness is irresponsibly reinforced by the obsessive focus on how soon stars are able to return to their prebaby body, while such coverage neglects the extreme work, self-negation, and expense associated with such a return. The press coverage also neglects the fact that celebrity moms' livelihoods and careers depend upon such a return—while ours, arguably, do not. And yet the media, and we with it, obsessively follow the loss of the baby weight and judge celebrities harshly for taking "too long" to lose the extra pounds. Mainstream magazines feature postpartum workout routines of the stars; the tabloids find postpartum celebrities on vacation and publish flattering (and not) swimsuit photos.

Images of celebrity bodies, postbaby, reinscribe norms of whiteness, body size, and socioeconomic class in ways that can almost only shame those gazing at them. Further, fixation on the celebrity baby bump and postbaby bodies runs the risk of exploiting women at a time of already distorted body image. Research shows that pregnant women view their bodies as disproportionately large at even higher rates than do women suffering from anorexia and bulimia, and viewing fashion magazines and images of superthin women has the documented effect of exacerbating those body distortions. A constant diet of celebrity baby bump images reinforces unrealistic expectations for women when they are pregnant. Women want "the bump" as a marker that their weight gain is appropriate to pregnancy; they also want that bump to be perfectly sized and sexy—and they want it to disappear almost immediately after giving birth. As Sue MacDonald, the head of education and research at Great Britain's Royal College of Midwives, told the UK's *Daily Mail*, "Many women feel the pressure to get back on their feet soon after childbirth. And seeing celebrities like Amanda Holden looking fantastic just weeks after almost dying during childbirth must be very, very frustrating."[42] Read the popular press and we learn that Heidi Klum "walk[ed] the Victoria's Secret runway less than six weeks after giving birth to her fourth child," and Miranda Kerr "g[o]t back to work for Victoria's Secret," wearing a string bikini for print ads, just three months after the birth of her first son.[43]

We know that the photos are airbrushed and that the stars may be starving themselves—but on a certain level, it doesn't matter: we hold ourselves to an impossible standard. Western middle-class women often hold on to an "emphatic belief in agency."[44] They believe they are able to do the hard work necessary in order to mold their dreams into reality—or their bodies into slim sizes. When they fail or find it difficult, their frustration is most often with themselves, rather than the expectation or norm. Indeed, with all of the attention to *how* stars achieve their postbaby body, such a physique seems to be something that we *can* possess, *if only we try hard enough.* Just as middle-class and working-class folks are told that we can emulate the luxurious lifestyles of celebrities by buying the right products, we are told that another set of products will help us emulate their bodies. There is no shortage of advice for women seeking to become "trim, taut, and terrific," as Robyn Longhurst puts it in her cogent analysis of women's athleticism during pregnancy.[45]

Health magazine recently published a list of the thirteen "fastest celebrity post-baby slimdowns," lauding the likes of Jennifer Lopez, Gwyneth Paltrow, and Beyoncé. Author Amanda McMillan noted, "While some stars may resort to surgery or dangerous cleanses, most simply diet and exercise."[46] Though the article purports to care that women lose their baby weight in a "healthy" way, to present that statement alongside photos of Posh Spice/Victoria Beckham, with glowing copy about her dramatic slimness, sends a decidedly mixed message. Of Beckham, the website notes, "The *Daily Mail* reported that the mom of four was following the Five Hands Diet—which involves eating only five handfuls of food a day—so she could slim down in time for New York's Fashion Week in September." I cannot imagine a way that eating five handfuls of food a day is "healthy." But I am a mere mortal.

Those stars who were widely criticized for being overly voluptuous during pregnancy have an increasingly high-stakes return to a better-than-ever post-baby body. Jessica Simpson signed a $3 million deal with Weight Watchers to be a spokeswoman as she worked hard to lose her baby weight. Mariah Carey signed on as a Jenny Craig spokeswoman after giving birth to twins via C-section and rather quickly lost eighty pounds. *Health* magazine's medical expert offered this assessment: "'Assuming some of that weight was indeed due to water retention, Carey's stunning loss is not only healthy; it's actually doable,' says [Dr.] DeFazio. Two pounds a week, 10 pounds a month, is safe, and you can do that without starving yourself or working out for hours every day."[47] After highlighting radical weight loss by celebrity moms, *Health* magazine runs a sidebar article titled "What's Normal?" The paragraph dedicated to normal weight loss for average women recommends an 1,800-calorie a day diet for breastfeeding moms and notes that women will be quite tired in their new roles as moms. The article ends with this wisdom: "Every new mom can get back to her pre-baby body, but the best way to do that is to figure out how to make it work for your own life and to listen to your own body."

With the promise that everyone woman can eventually be her own version of a stylish "yummy mummy" come product lines with that very moniker. Newly postpartum women can buy a T-shirt for their infant, created and marketed by the clothing company *No Added Sugar*, that read "My Mummy is a Yummy Mummy." There is even a YummyMummy Lifestyle System, a weight loss aid that provides, according to the internet ads on mothering websites, "Everything you need to get your body back."

But self-denial and self-discipline are only parts of what enables stars to possess spectacular postbaby bodies, and those character traits may be the cheapest part of the weight loss plan. Celebrities can also afford to take more than six weeks off, unpaid, from their multimillion-dollar silver screen jobs, a fact that makes the physical and emotional recovery from labor and transition into motherhood potentially much easier. After reportedly gaining forty-two pounds due to pregnancy, Kelly Preston (actress and wife of actor John Travolta) took an entire year off, to mother and lift weights. McMillan reports, for *Health* magazine, "The actress lost [the weight] and got back to her high-school jeans size 14 months after the birth of her son in November, 2010." Presumably, Preston also paid those she hired to watch her infant a better-than-living wage. Nor could Jennifer Lopez and Gwenyth Paltrow achieve their marketable postpregnancy bodies without a team of personal trainers, nannies, and cooks. Even though it was reported in both *Huffington Post* and *Health* that "losing the baby weight after the birth of her second child in 2006 was 'by far the hardest thing [she had] ever done,' Paltrow opined that women shouldn't use excuses to avoid the work of returning to their prior shape and size, 'Every woman can make time—every woman—and you can do it with your baby in the room,' she said. 'There have been countless times where I've worked out with my kids crawling all over the place.'"[48]

In her book *How to Look Great in a Minivan* former editor in chief of *Us Weekly*, Janice Min, writes that though she recognizes the limits we have on our ability to look like superstars postpartum, "I profoundly believe that every mother has the (very attainable) dream of radically upping her game," and becoming, like Min herself did after her pregnancies, their "*own* version of a chic mom—someone polished and put together, if also a little sleep-deprived."[49] You may never get your "old" body back, she assures us; rather, with proper guidance, you can be, postpartum "a thinner, better-looking, and even sexier mom."[50]

In other words, no one is off the hook.

A woman who is unable to reach the normative idealized version of the postbaby body, perhaps because she is working outside the home and lacks additional resources, knows that she is somehow failing in the essentialized role she's been assigned: body maintenance of herself and her child. Over-reliance on celebrity models of mothering and body management puts even the "menial" labor of bodily maintenance outside of the control of the average woman,[51] who can never hope to have the resources necessary to adequately manage her body or her child's.

One thing is clear, though: how-to articles *sell* magazines. Janice Min tells her readers, "When I was working at *Us,* it was a sure bet that anytime we ran a 'post-baby body' story (and accompanying photo) on our website, it would instantly become a top draw."[52] Amazingly, these stories of transformation are often publicized as a form of empowerment. In fact, Min—just like hundreds of others trumpeting the power of the postpartum makeover—offers a version of feminism that sees polish and self-disciplined chicness as anti-dotes to the martyring mother of their childhoods. Taking time for a facial, a manicure, or a haircut at "an expensive salon" is touted as an act of feminism because it is caretaking of the self and (moderated) expression of individuality. Min tells us that "being a 'hot mom'—or even just a presentable one—is really about achieving one's potential," winning in a cutthroat world.[53] In this view, being a "hot mom"—or even "just a presentable one," is somehow an act of feminism. This is feminism coopted by the project of capital.[54]

Consumptive Citizenship and Fashionable Feminism: A Biopolitics of Branding

"Feminism" that is actually just a focus on commodification further posi-tions the body as something to work on, to improve upon, to possess. The body becomes, in this way, property. Celebrity pregnancy and postbaby body stories allow and encourage the growth and expansion of neoliberal-ism through the construction of citizen-consumers, whose bodies (and the bodies of their children) are properties to be improved upon; this, when we call it self-care and empowerment, sells. In fact, we become responsible for the maintenance of our bodies-as-property, for their upkeep and upgrading; we are responsible for finding ways to buy and use the products meant to aid us in this endeavor.

Zillah Eisenstein anticipated this responsibilization of women's self-care and its marriage to consumerism. As she put it almost thirty years ago, the "backlash today" against women in general, and feminism in particular, "is deep and profound." It is a backlash that "transform[s] the militancy of this feminist individualism into a privatized consumerism. . . . *Feminism becomes redefined as an individualized consumer self-help market;* and the politics surrounding the struggle for equality drops out the bottom."[55]

Mid-1990s work on law and social change posited that it was the intervention of legal means into radical social movements that caused them to become more moderate and incrementalist. Radical ideas like women's equality and equal rights for people of color as collectivities were turned into more moderate claims for individual rights that could be litigated over—individually—slowly and over time. Eisenstein and many others argue that the moderating feature at play in neoliberalism is less law than the market. Redefining political and legal goals as goods in a marketplace casts social movement actors and citizens as consumers, not activists, not even rights-bearing individuals. Just as we would expect in neoliberalism, in many regards law has ceded its power to control and channel behavior to the market. Of course, because we can't all afford to be good consumers, law remains a necessary governing force.

But to a large degree the moderation and commercialization of feminism gives us women who are hard-working and seemingly authentic self-governing subjects. The neoliberal marketplace conflates bodies with property, consumers with citizens, and markets with politics. Neoliberal entities use branding as a biopolitics in the construction of a docile, disciplined, self-denying body politic and treat that body as a perpetual work in progress, always open to change and improvement. Much of that constructive improvement is expected, in particular, of the female body—pregnant or not.

We can see this imperative toward self-improvement marketed at women clearly in the branding practices of lululemon yoga wear. In their analysis of the brand, Christine Lavrence and Kristin Lozanski show clearly that lululemon constructs ideal citizen-consumers through a particularly disciplined female body. The brand very famously caters only to specific body types and offers its clothing in a very limited range of sizes (2–12). The largest waistline measurement offered by the brand reaches a mere 32.5 inches, and the largest hip size is 40 inches. Lululemon does *not* sell to pregnant women, but the language and images lululemon uses to sell its clothing are similar to the texts and photos accompanying pregnant celebrities. Both focus on self-actualization, consumer behavior, and beauty; both offer idealized images for regular people to emulate. And both offer advice to women. Lululemon usually features photos of lone yogis (or a very well-organized class), with tag lines that tell women, variously, to "do one thing a day that scares you," "sweat once a day to regenerate your skin," and avoid stress because "stress is related to 99% of all illness." Despite its expense,[56] the widely publicized judgmental statements of its former CEO, and its limited sizes and availability, the brand has become exceptionally successful. Between 2010 and 2012, lululemon raised its earnings by 40.6 percent, accounting for nearly $1 billion worldwide.[57]

Lululemon's branding practices, according to Lavrence and Lozanski's analysis, "appropriate yogic practice into a consumerist model of discipline and self-care." As a brand, lululemon markets "seemingly incongruent themes of social responsibility and self-optimization," folding "discourses of empowerment into consumerism," and illustrating "how discourses of choice and self-care reinforce the responsibilized self, that is, the foundation of contemporary neoliberal societies."[58] Lululemon links women's self-care with both beauty *and* health—an important nexus in neoliberal risk management, because in neoliberalism, "the promotion of the goal of healthy bodies is no longer the exclusive domain of the state, because the state can now assume that good citizen subjects desire to be healthy and are actively working to this end."[59]

Just as "hotness" became the imperative of women, "health" as a form of self-care becomes the responsibility of the citizen. In this way, health and wellness are expected of citizens, and citizens become responsible for their success. But there is more: in neoliberalism, "the optimal self is a perpetual project," a "personal and moral achievement" in and of itself. The ideal neoliberal subject not only self-polices, she is "healthy . . . predictable . . . governable."[60] In neoliberalism, "wellness," Lavrence and Lozanski argue, "is seen as the result of good choices made by morally autonomous and efficacious citizens, and is the central site of moral transformation and civic participation."[61] Within this matrix, medical care becomes a paramount consumer product, and the maternity care afforded the stars becomes an important conversation topic among moms-to-be.

I'll have a Water Birth to Go, Please

Though much of the branding and commodification associated with celebrity pregnancies involves fashion, diet, and luxury consumer goods, there are also important conversations around celebrity pregnancy that deal with norms of good mothering as they are constructed in expectations for behavior and outcomes surrounding labor and delivery and pre- and postnatal care. The contemporary shift to biopolitical power via consumerism in the realm of health care is well remarked upon. Although "medical practice has always had a place within the commercial network . . . these commercial sites were [until recently] marginal to the main focus of the medical profession, which [previously] maintained its distance from the commercial world."[62] Contemporary Americans, however, have now become accustomed to the idea that they "shop" for health care and insurance in "the marketplace" as a matter of course. And, we know that health care is a big business, accounting for over 15 percent of the nation's domestic national product.[63]

In fact, in their fascinating history of the architecture and design of American hospitals, *Medicine Moves to the Mall,* David and Beverlie Sloane note that an important conceptual shift occurred when patients were reframed as "consumers" and clients. They call this part of a movement to "humanize" hospitals, to make them more user-friendly and patient-centered. This move has taken place across hospital arenas—from cancer centers to orthopedic and sports centers. But as Sloane and Sloane argue, "perhaps no hospital unit better illustrates the movement to humanize the hospital than the labor and delivery suite."[64]

Historically, they note, "maternity units were designed to attract middle- and upper-class women to the hospital while still offering services to those women in need of charity care."[65] Early consumers within the upper and middle class placed a premium on cleanliness and an antiseptic and scientific environment. Now, middle- and upper-class families seek comfortable, homey, and even luxurious environments for birth. The World Health Organization and UNICEF designate hospitals "Baby-Friendly" when they meet specific health-related criteria related to breastfeeding, safety, and good outcomes. In the United States, according to press associated with the initiative, "181 U.S. hospitals and birthing centers in 43 states and the District of Columbia—or, the sites of less than 3% of births in 2009—hold the Baby-Friendly designation."[66] Healthy babies are luxuries, as are comfortable and woman-centered birth experiences. It is not accidental that media watchers learn that Julia Roberts had a water birth in a birth center associated with a hospital in Los Angeles, that Angelina Jolie gave birth in an incongruously luxurious birthing suite in Africa, and that Victoria Beckham scheduled her C-sections around husband David Beckham's soccer schedule.

I examine the surveillance technologies associated with medical models of birth in chapter four; for now, we need only recall that popular culture knowledge of celebrity birth practices and choices is in keeping with the fact that women's rights to keep and terminate pregnancies have long been rendered public via commercialization. Decisions to terminate and keep pregnancies have been rendered as consumer choices, rather than political acts. Students in my reproductive law and politics course are often shocked to see 1940s-era advertisements of Lysol disinfectant spray as a "douche" for feminine cleansing and an abortifacient; they are shocked to see birth control advertised to middle-class women in the Sears and Roebuck catalog. Growing up in a small town in the late 1970s and early 80s, I always knew there was something vaguely and residually "dirty" about the Five & Dime downtown. There were some aisles that we simply knew to avoid. I assumed these to be the candy aisles, but realize now that they were the aisles where women could purchase feminine products—including access to unscientific and unsafe means of birth control and abortion.

The reality of those aisles in the Five & Dime was brought home to me while reading Senator Orrin Hatch's reasoning for limiting poor women's access to abortion after *Roe*. Arguing on behalf of a federal amendment that would ban the use of federal funds to help poor women seeking elective abortions, Hatch, in Solinger's analysis, tried to make those women "into consumers, just like other women. 'Imagine the abortion-seeking woman as a potential spender who could, if careful, stash away a 'five' or a 'ten' every couple of days,' Hatch said. 'There is nothing to prevent [a poor woman] . . . from either exercising increased self-restraint, or from sacrificing on some item or other for a month or two to afford [her] own abortion.'"[67] The Supreme Court cases regarding access to abortion accept Hatch's analysis and assume a market in the service.

In this framing, termination of pregnancy is a commodity, not a right. Access to dignity in labor and delivery, however women define that, is increasingly framed in the same way. Women's rights to bodily autonomy and care in reproductive decision making are now little different from commodities that can be saved for and purchased—luxury goods like lululemon yoga pants and venti nonfat sugar-free caramel lattes.

CHAPTER 4

SURVEILLING THE STARS

OF THE THOUSANDS OF IMAGES I viewed while doing research for this project, one occasionally still keeps me up at night. I've been unable to forget it, and the sense of urgency that it evokes in me has stayed with me throughout the writing of this book. It is a photo of Jennifer Garner, newly pregnant with her second child. She is wearing a pale pink cardigan sweater and a casual black skirt and has been out shopping in Brentwood, on what seems to be a sunny Southern California day. In the photo, she's peering into the window of her SUV, with a look of real concern on her face. Her two-year-old daughter, Violet, has gotten into the vehicle, with the keys, and locked her mom out. The paparazzi were there to capture the moment, and both the *Daily Mail* and *Celebitchy* covered the event as though it were news.[1]

What parent hasn't had the dark fantasy, the nagging worry, of leaving her keys and her baby in the locked car on a warm day? Of leaving, in a different version of the same anxiety, the coffee—or, worse, the car seat—on the roof of the minivan? And here is Garner, in a situation that parents dread, while also being cornered by men with cameras.

It is an embarrassing situation to be sure, and also a vulnerable one. What might be a worrisome hassle for a regular mom becomes magnified under the gaze of the ever-present paparazzi cameraman. In a second shot, looking up from the window, Garner's open-mouthed half-smile–half-shout at the camera speaks volumes: she is uncomfortable, unhappy, and worried. Yet she's trying to be a good sport about the whole thing.

The first time I viewed that photo, a voice in my head muttered, "They're stalking her. She's under surveillance." I saw the immediate parallels to hundreds of other women who have embarrassing moments while pregnant or mothering and to the ways those moments lead to increased surveillance and intervention by others or the state. I thought of women who battle various addictions and who are judged for drinking a frappuccino, smoking a cigarette, or taking crystal meth. I thought of women living with intimate partner violence, whose bruised arms and face allow us to judge them unfit to mother. I thought of women with "geriatric" pregnancies—those of us pregnant over thirty-five, who are told that amniocentesis, Doppler imaging, and genetic testing of the fetus are "the norm."

Of course, celebrities often want to be watched. Their profession requires and depends upon it. And women want healthy babies; amnios and genetic testing can help catch problems early and sometimes offer methods by which medicine can intervene. But in the coverage of celebrity pregnancy, there is a convergence of multiple trends within neoliberal governance. In her elaboration of a theory of communicative capitalism, Jodi Dean argues "celebrity is that mode of subjectivization in which individuals *present themselves as content*."[2] She continues, "when communication makes everything potentially public, everyone is potentially a celebrity."[3] That potential for celebrity seems to make *everyone* ready to be watched for the moment that celebrity might take place.

Our desire to become celebrities—or at least to become *like* them—necessitates our watching of them and facilitates our own desire to be watched. We become content, but not for the television audience; rather, our lives are content readable by the state, the corporation, and the stranger on the street. It is therefore the contemporary context within which the surveillance takes place and the purposes to which it is fashioned—commodification and control—that should give us pause.

Surveillance: Paparazzi Pics and Privacy

I argued in chapter two that pregnant celebrity bodies are variously adored, judged, and emulated, and in chapter three that they are used to accomplish goals related to commodification and capital. Here, I argue that these bodies are also *stalked* and *surveilled* in ways that serve the needs of neoliberal capitalism in the control of fertile female bodies.

In large part, we could argue, the paparazzi and public obsession with celebrity pregnancies is a job hazard: by becoming famous, in part for their performances, these women are expected to perform their pregnancies in the public eye as well. And not all paparazzi photos are stolen. Indeed, some are staged to accomplish particular goals necessary to the celebrity: one might show a famous couple out and about, for instance, to quell relationship-on-the-rocks rumors; photos of a celebrity mom with her kids might counter party girl photos.[4] Yet the staged photos share qualities with those that are stolen. They are made to look accidental; they are made to look as though stars are somehow being "caught in the act" of living. Our consumption of tabloid surveillance of stars allows all of us to enter the private space of those stars, often against their will.

Though the photo of Garner hits a particularly strong nerve with me, I found it incredibly disturbing to view most of the images of pregnant celebrities posted on websites and published in magazines. Certainly, I was troubled by the unrealistic standards of beauty celebrated by the images, but even more so by the sheer hauntedness in the eyes and posture of these women. They are nearly always wearing dark glasses or shielding their eyes; if they have already had their child, they are clutching that child closely. Their posture appears hurried, furtive—they glance to the left or right; they appear ready to take flight. Sometimes these celebrity moms appear exasperated, even angry at the unhelpful intrusion of the camera. A second chilling shot of Garner, entered into the congressional record in California as she and other celebrities worked on legislation to stop publication of paparazzi shots of their children, shows a burly man with a large camera standing in front of Garner's car. She is facing him, a small woman, holding an iPhone, taking his picture as he snaps hers (while another camera person takes a picture of them both). It's not a comical photo; it's a frustrated and frustrating one.[5]

And yet in other shots, the celebrity mom appears so serene that the viewer realizes that she was likely unaware she was being photographed. You can see Sarah Jessica Parker pushing a stroller in Central Park and earlier in the same day walking an older child to school.[6] Paparazzi used telephoto lenses to capture shots of Simon Crowell and his pregnant partner Lauren

FIGURE 4.1 Jennifer Garner taking a photo of a photographer. Photo credit: PHDLA.
Sourced at: eonline.com

Silverman on a yacht in the south of France,[7] Jennifer Lopez and her new-borns on the water in Spain,[8] Julia Roberts playing beach ball on vacation with her kids. Not even small-town Iowa is safe from the paparazzi, where photos of Ashton Kutcher and Mila Kunis were captured when they went home to visit his family shortly after Kunis announced her pregnancy.[9]

In 2013, celebrity couples Jennifer Garner and Ben Affleck, Dax Shepherd and Kristen Bell, and Halle Berry and Oliver Martinez helped to move an interesting piece of legislation very quickly through the California state house. Senate Bill 606 amends the California Penal Code and makes the intentional harassment of a "child or ward of any other person because of that person's employment" a misdemeanor punishable by up to six months in county jail or a $1,000 fine for a first offense, with increasing penalties for subsequent offenses.[10] The bill further defines "harassment" as:

> Knowing and willful conduct directed at a specific child or ward that seri-ously alarms, annoys, torments, or terrorizes the child or ward, and that serves no legitimate purpose, including, but not limited to, that conduct occurring during the course of any actual or attempted recording of the child's or ward's image or voice without the written consent of the child's or ward's parent or legal guardian, by following the child's or ward's activi-ties, or by lying in wait.

California had a previous law on the books that defended the rights of children from their images being captured. That law (AB 3592) made it il-legal to harass children because of their parents' employment. Importantly, it was "meant to specifically address the increased harassment faced by the children of health care facility employees where abortion procedures were performed."[11] The amendment to the bill originally gained momentum after law enforcement officials were targeted by gunman Christopher Dorner, which highlighted the vulnerability of their families. As it moved toward its third reading, the focus turned to celebrity families and became, according to the Committee on Judiciary, an effort "to curb the behavior of overly ag-gressive paparazzi that seek to profit from the public's seemingly inexhaust-ible fascination with celebrity."[12] In what the *New York Daily News* called "emotional" testimony before the Assembly Committee hearing the bill for the final time, Jennifer Garner said that "she and her children were followed everywhere they go."[13] Doctors who performed abortion—those who helped women gain a modicum of control over their reproductive lives—used to be the targets; now, celebrities—those who teach us how to be pregnant and maternal in the public eye—are stalked, surveilled, photographed, and haunted.

In their press appearances since the passage of the bill, Dax Shepard and Kristin Bell have taken the analysis a step further. They call the photographers who continue to stalk and harass their family "pedarazzis"—clearly alleging an illicit sexualized pleasure in the photos and hoping to shame magazines from publishing them.[14] The couple has called for a boycott of magazines that do publish those photos and argues that the consumer who purchases these magazines is participating in "disengaged voyeurism."[15] Their references to voyeurism and pedophilia bring us full circle to the kinds of moral panic experienced and fomented in the 1920s, and again in the 1960s, when women gained political suffrage and, later, some modicum of equality and sexual liberation. But Shepherd and Bell turn the moral panic argument on its head—advocating for a return to privacy of images and decision making and a retreat from the public eye; they indict those who seek to control them by controlling their images.

A Biopolitics of Surveillance in a Technological Age

As Nikolas Rose has pointed out, in neoliberal societies, "personal practices of consumption" have long had an intricate relationship to "governmentality (the government of conduct)."[16] With technological advances since he first wrote, however, that relationship has gotten more complex and become even more insidious. Communicative capitalism has a technological fetish and casts a net we call the "worldwide web," which allows us to imagine we are somehow "global."[17] Dean writes that combining technology and surveillance with global reach "strengthens the grip of neoliberalism. Our everyday practices of searching and linking, our communicative acts of discussing and disagreeing, performing and posing, intensify our dependence on the information networks crucial to the financial and corporate dominance of neoliberalism."[18] That these same networks become networks of social control via surveillance and the state for purposes of national security is well documented.[19] The domestic use of the surveillance technologies is also tied to capital expansion.

We have already seen how media coverage of pregnant celebrities feeds a desire to consume and commodify. This drive to consumption is also a mode of governance made possible via surveillance, which constructs citizen-subjects as either consumers or criminals.[20]

Sometimes that surveillance is absolutely explicit, as in economist Juliet Schor's chilling narrative of the ethnographic methods used in collecting data about how kids consume. She describes researchers sitting in bathrooms with children as they bathe behind a shower curtain, listening to how they use various products and spend their "alone" time. She describes marketing firms' research strategy of putting headbands on children with cameras embedded and a battery pack in their backpacks to enable researchers to watch the kids make shopping choices unfettered. The camera allows researchers to see what aisles children run down, which ones they skip; it allows researchers to note whether kids go straight to the toys they want or if they browse.

Sometimes the surveillance is less overt. We adults know—but tend to forget—that nearly every click of a mouse on a commercial website will generate data about our spending habits and desires, just as we know that our use of loyalty cards at the supermarket will result in different coupons and "special offers" tailored just for us. We consent to these kinds of surveillance. We agree to let our data be gathered in order for companies to sell us better and more appropriate products. Pop-up ads for the running skirt I looked at yesterday show up on the *New York Times* website today; a new version of a pair of shoes I looked at last week is suddenly on sale in an email "newsletter" I get from a discount retailer.[21]

Think of the "cookies" that are deposited, crumb-like, along the virtual trail of an online shopper and the data collected by Google and other search engines as we surf the web for clothing, shoes, medication, and books. Think as well of the anticipatory purchasing algorithms that allow Amazon.com to preemptively ship the products we will soon be buying—*What to Expect When You're Expecting*, perhaps—based on how long our hand hovers on the mouse. Of these cookies and crumbs and data bytes, Passavant writes, "The technologies that give us pleasure if we are good consumers are . . . the same technologies that the state seeks to utilize to discover potential terrorists and to preempt future terrorist action."[22] The same technologies that give us pleasure as soon-to-be mothers—like algorithms that develop coupons just for us at Target and our local grocery store—are also the technologies that allow corporations to alert single dads to the fact that their teenage daughters are pregnant.[23] This happened in 2012, when Target mailed coupons for maternity wear, formula, and diapers to the home of a single father with a teenage daughter, marketing them for the parents-to-be at the residence. The father went to the store with the coupon book and insisted that no one in his house was pregnant, only to find that computing algorithms of recent purchases and buying patterns correctly indicated that indeed someone in the home was expecting.

These are the same tools that permitted Gmail to know that sociologist Janet Vertesi was engaged before she told anyone and which spawned her most recent research: an attempt to hide her pregnancy from "big data" by restricting her online interactions. She found keeping that secret to be "inconvenient," "expensive," and "*so much work*."[24] In fact, just as we might expect from our knowledge of the consumer-criminal dyad constructed in neoliberalism, Vertesi's attempts to go off grid made her look criminal. She tells an interviewer, "it looks like [I'm] up to no good. Who else is on Tor every day and pulling out cash all over the city and taking out enormous gift cards to buy a stroller? It's the kind of thing, taken in the aggregate, that flags you in law enforcement systems."[25] No one wants to be flagged by law enforcement as a criminal mastermind or political terrorist; even when you know you're innocent, just think of the hassle.

So, sure, it might make me slightly uneasy. But if allowing cookies, data bytes, and the aggregation of my data helps to make my life more convenient, helps me save money, and renders me "normal," why wouldn't I want to be surveilled?

When we follow this line of thinking through to see the logic of surveillance in the benefit of capital and consumption, we can begin to imagine how powerful it is when the logic is applied to medical risks associated with pregnancy. The ultrasound that gives a woman and her partner pleasure in bonding with an unborn child and helps their doctors to detect both gender and potential defects is the same technology that is forced upon women wanting to make autonomous reproductive choices in several state jurisdictions. Why wouldn't an expecting mother consent to far-reaching surveillance of her health and fetal well-being? Why wouldn't she engage in her own surveillance? The medical technologies that give us pleasure as consumer goods and medical services, in other words, enable governance of our reproductive capacities at a microlevel.

The (Often Salutary) Role of Surveillant Medicine in Pregnancy

Pregnancy has become, in Jane Ussher's words, a time of life "signposted by medical checks and controls, women being presented with strict guidelines as to how they should prepare for conception, how they should 'manage' pregnancy and childbirth . . . with dire warnings of danger meted out to those who might resist submitting the passive and docile pregnant body to the all-controlling medical gaze."[26] This gaze begins even prior to pregnancy, when women who anticipate reproducing are told to take a regimen of prenatal vitamins; to avoid cigarettes, caffeine, and alcohol; and to eat certain foods.[27] The medical gaze continues into the surveillant monitoring of both woman and fetus once pregnancy is determined and absolutely reaches an apex during labor and delivery.

The removal of birth from home to hospital began in the early 1900s and was largely complete by the 1950s, with only 2 percent of births nationwide taking place out of hospital. Homebirth has been replaced by scientific, medical, and technocratic models of birth.[28] This movement from the home to the hospital was in large part very beneficial for public health. It brought with it decreased maternal and child mortality rates, improved birth outcomes, and often a high standard of care. Feminists lauded the move, as it offered women access to epidurals and analgesic, giving them the ability to labor and deliver without the pain that previous generations had seen as punishment. Such a movement also, however, devalued women's knowledge and experience, increased the power of medical professionals, increased the rate of unnecessary intervention and emergency cesarean sections, and often removed women's agency in the moments of labor and delivery.

Rather stunningly, the growth of technologies that enabled doctors in hospitals to visualize and hear the fetus developed alongside changing cultural understandings of what the fetus is and the proper place of fetal rights in law and politics. In her history of the ultrasound, Mitchell notes that since the 1950s, "our perceptions of the fetus have changed, and these changes are a result of the interplay between biomedicine, reproductive and gender politics, ethics, law, health care economics and even commercial and entertainment interests."[29] Rather than understand that mothers and their fetus form a complex bioecology and relationship, medical science understands the two as separate, though the mother clearly "hosts" the fetus. The ability to view the

fetus via ultrasound in a seemingly self-contained environment, visually separate from the mother, Mitchell argues, led to disembodied understandings
of birth that denied some essential connective aspects of maternal experience
and hyped others. In particular, contemporary understandings of pregnancy
stress the risks associated with it, especially those risks that might attend
the unborn child.[30] Looking at books about pregnancy and popular guidance given women, Mitchell notes: "within both medical science and popular
wisdom . . . pregnancy is conceptualized as a time of risk and potential danger. . . . [T]hese ideas are organized, institutionalized, perpetuated, and given
authority through a medico-scientific discourse that focuses on risks to the
fetus and that tends to locate the source of those risks in the bodies and be-
haviours of women."[31] The medicalization and mechanization of birth fulfills
the task of mitigating risks associated with the process—risks that are less
than they were a hundred years ago and, paradoxically, often caused by the
technocratic interventions themselves. Many aspects of this medicalization
and mechanization are made manifest in technologies of surveillance.

Surveillant monitoring of pregnant women takes several forms. Indeed,
pregnancy is a time of nearly weekly testing of the woman's body. Prenatal
care in a doctor's office usually focuses on surveillance of a woman's weight;
as with the bump watch of Kim Kardashian and Nicole Kidman, the nurse
seeks to determine whether a woman is gaining "too much" or "too little"
weight at each stage of her pregnancy. Such care also includes routine measurement of the pregnant belly, monitoring for drug abuse and disease via
blood draws and cervical swabs, and monitoring for diabetes and other potential problems via urine analysis. Such monitoring also very frequently
involves amniocentesis and ultrasound technologies and extends to the surveillance of women and the fetus during the birth process itself.

In the 1960s the U.S. military developed Doppler ultrasound technology, which was used first in naval war scenarios and later in electronic fetal
monitors. By 1969, Corometrics Medical Systems had developed an external
"fetoscope," another name for a small-scale, hand-held Doppler ultrasound.
Within five years, Corometrics had a $5 million revenue stream from that
product. The fetoscope was originally intended only for managing high-risk
pregnancies, but it has become "an ever-present surveillant technology during
birth." Block notes that in 2005, 93 percent of laboring mothers had external,

continuous, electronic fetal monitoring as a part of their birth experience.[32] There are multiple locations for and practices of surveillance during birth beyond the fetoscope. Women are usually connected to electronic fetal monitoring during birth and have frequent cervical "checks" during late stages of pregnancy and early stages of labor. During labor, the pressure on time management and the imperative to keep delivery moving[33] only adds to the risk of stepped-up technological interventions during birth, even as these technologies and techniques increase the risk of pathogens leading to infection.

Even though surveillant techniques like the routine use of X rays for pregnant women in the 1950s caused tremendous fetal harm that resulted in severe birth defects,[34] such technologies remain an exceedingly important part of the cultural understandings of and expectations for pregnancy. There is a discourse among professionals that indicates that "seeing the fetus through the ultrasound has certain 'psychological' or 'psycho-social' benefits for women— namely, reduced anxiety about fetal health, and maternal 'bonding' with the fetus."[35] Mitchell argues that women look forward to ultrasound because it will help them identify the fetus as theirs—that it gives the fetus identity.[36]

Reality television shows featuring stars like Snooki, Jessica Simpson, and the Kardashians all include these moments in the life of pregnant women: hearing the fetal heartbeat for the first time, genetic testing and amniocentesis, and the ultrasound procedure. Similarly, on MTV and TLC, television viewers can watch "teenage moms" and "high-risk pregnancies"—all shows reinforcing specific norms that inure women to technological intervention and surveillance while pregnant. We learn through coverage of celebrity pregnancies and "reality" television devoted to labor and delivery that "good mothers" are hypervigilant about the health of their fetus. They engage in amniocentesis and ultrasound as a matter of course. Mitchell writes: "The ultrasound fetus is so emotionally compelling that it has become a source of cultural entertainment. It appears in movies, . . . television shows, and comic strips, as well as in print and electronic advertisements—for example, for computers, cars, . . . telephone companies, and sports cable networks."[37] And the moment of "being shown" the baby is an important ritual in pregnancy— and one that constructs mothers as "good" or "bad" early on. Mitchell's ethnographic work demonstrates that ultrasound technicians "show" more to the women they perceive as nice and good mothers. These techs manage a line between the clinical purposes of the ultrasound (measuring, movement, and so on), the entertainment value of such a demonstration, and the social construction of mothering integral to the display.

Of course, as Mitchell writes, on one level, "simply by having an ultrasound, the woman is demonstrating that she is a 'good mother'—responsible, altruistic, and willing to reduce risks to the fetus."[38] Beyond this construction, there is an additional set of material politics to the use of ultrasound to image the fetus. Mitchell elaborates on the role of the medical community in endorsing and encouraging ultrasound technology—both at the level of the organized lobby and according to individual physician preference. She writes, "part of the history and contemporary practice of fetal imaging involves the competition between radiologists and obstetricians—and, more recently, family practitioners—for resources (patients, equipment, funding, scientific data, medical prestige, selection and training of residents), and also for the authority to produce and interpret ultrasound images."[39] The growth of ultrasound technologies in the 1950s and 60s as part of a professionalization project of obstetricians and radiologists, and in competition for market share and medical hegemony, echoes a similar professionalization project of doctors undertaken around the same time—to have monopoly over the moral and medical claims of women seeking "therapeutic abortion," as documented by Kristin Luker.

Jennifer Block highlights another aspect of neoliberal politics related to ultrasound technology when she notes that external and internal fetal monitoring during birth is defended by medical doctors and their associations, in defense of their fears of malpractice litigation.[40] This is part of a larger platform endorsed by many professional associations, as well as most state Republican parties, encouraging "tort reform" and "damage caps."

As an important part of the cultural imagining of pregnancy, ultrasounds have become an integral part of the ceremony surrounding celebrity moms. The media hungers for ultrasound images, and publishing these images—pictures of pictures of the fetus—magazines both normalize ultrasounds as an integral part of pregnancy and reinforce these underlying maternal politics. As well, they extend the expectation of surveillance from celebrity women to average women.

Some celebrities are more than happy to provide photographic evidence of the fetus. Actress Busy Philipps recently posted her ultrasound photo to her

124,000 followers on Instagram; television star Sarah Drew posted a narrative of her ultrasound experience as part of her blog series for *Oh Baby!* magazine;[41] and the trailer for Beyoncé's HBO biopic documentary *(Life Is but a Dream)* included grainy, low-resolution footage of Blue Ivy's fetal image.[42] Tom Cruise went even further; he reportedly spent $200,000 on an ultrasound machine for his personal use with then-fiancé Katie Holmes; he told reporters that he used it "quite a lot" to see images of the developing fetus.[43]

Not all celebrities willingly make their ultrasound photos public, however. Actress Evan Rachel Wood angrily denounced the *Daily Mail* for publishing a paparazzi-snapped photo of her on the roof of a parking garage outside of her doctor's office, holding a sonogram printout. Wood clearly did not anticipate the paparazzi's surveillant reach. She tweeted "I have never been more violated by a photographer. That's the inside of my body and my child. Would u like my soul too? nothing is sacred."[44]

Surveillance Is Gendered

Ultrasound technology also plays into a desire to see into and exert control over women's reproductive bodies. Democratic theorists and feminists Iris Marion Young and Nancy Fraser have both remarked that surveillance and the security state are quite often patriarchal and gendered.[45] Those who are "protected" via paternalism are simultaneously "subordinated" to patriarchy. Feminists from a wide range of disciplines—from literary theory to sociolegal analysis—agree with and magnify this point. As Francus writes in her analysis of eighteenth-century literature, the female body, because it is "a convenient site for chaos, as it is located between the created and the uncreated,"[46] must be guarded and controlled. Similarly, in her investigation into religious rituals that vilify women's corporeality, Ussher argues that the physical markers of male-female difference found within women's reproductive lives "necessitate . . . containment" because they are threatening.[47]

Mass culture itself is often coded as "female,"[48] as is the gossip generated on the web boards of communicative capital. It stands to reason that surveillance techniques promulgated by mass culture are often incorporated into the everyday lives of females in ways that render them increasingly subject to governance. Kristin Bumiller's contemporary examination of gender and rape and the media vis-à-vis the Central Park jogger case argues clearly, "Incitement of anxieties about women's bodies can justify expanded forms of social control"[49]—these forms of social control are played out on women's bodies, not the bodies of those made anxious by female power. We could medicate and surveil those made anxious by women's reproduction—but we don't. Rather, we medicate and surveil the women who are—or could be— reproducing. Media surveillance of pregnant celebrities comes at a time when women have begun "to assert themselves, to claim their sexuality and attempt to control their reproductive choices."[50] At these times, the media becomes complicit in portraying women as part of a society "out of control."

Some "out-of-control" women are those who will abort, so the use of ultrasound technology became relevant in the abortion debate. Mitchell writes, "by the early 1980s, around the same time that real-time grey-scaled ultrasound was coming into wider use, the terms of the abortion debate had changed significantly."[51] Ultrasound revitalized a pro-life activism that focused on picturing the fetus in the womb and imagining women's bodies as "penetrable social space."[52]

At least one pro-life blogger covers celebrity pregnancy with the explicit hope of marking out a pro-life agenda. She also makes explicit political links from celebrity ultrasound to antiabortion politics. Of Halle Berry's description of her ultrasound on the David Letterman show, this blogger opines: "While unmarried Berry is a poor role model for black women, already in crisis with a 70% illegitimate delivery rate, her baby is a blessing nonetheless. And I'll take her free advertisement of the value ultrasounds bring to reveal the humanity of preborn babies and also enhance parental bonding."[53]

In addition to the politics surrounding abortion that are facilitated via ultrasound technology, the use of technologies to aid in surveilling our pregnancies and an obligation to make good and healthy choices to mitigate risk also make pregnant women seem almost monstrously powerful—and unduly burdened with responsibility. They bear responsibility not only for their own well-being, but also for nearly every aspect of fetal growth and development. Reponsibilizing jurisprudence like the Supreme Court's decision in *Johnson Controls* dovetails with popular culture like an October 2010 *Time* magazine cover story featuring a naked pregnant woman, her body seeming to float in a kind of amniotic space. The woman has long blonde hair, and her eyes are

FIGURE 4.2 *Time* magazine cover, Oct. 4, 2010. Photo credit: Merrick/Morton Columbia

only half open; she is shown in profile and has a very fit body. The magazine's headline reads, "How the first nine months shape the rest of your life: The new science of fetal origins."

In the interior pages, the magazine features a close-up of a pregnant belly with the caption, "The Womb. Your Mother. Yourself. Cancer. Heart disease. Obesity, Depression. Scientists can now trace adult health to the nine months before birth."[54] The article goes on to cite studies that show that an obese mother's children process fats and carbohydrates differently from any children she has delivered after achieving healthy weight loss.[55]

The message is clear: unexpected things, many of which may be beyond your control, may affect the type of life your fetus has, how your children will "turn out." Paul puts it this way: "The kind and quantity of nutrition you received in the womb; the pollutants, drugs and infections you were exposed to during gestation; your mother's health, stress level and state of mind while she was pregnant with you—all these factors shaped you as a baby and child and continue to affect you to this day."[56] Moms are suddenly responsible for so much—including much that is out of their control. It appears reasonable that women's behavior while pregnant should be monitored—and, the media seems to argue, if a woman is not willing to do self-surveil, society is happy to step in. Pregnant women in general, just like pregnant celebrities, become fodder for the gossip mills.

Pregnancy and Gossip

Pictures of pregnant celebrities do not stand alone in the popular press; the reproduction of these images is not done absent commentary. Indeed, often the most telling aspects of the coverage of stars' pregnancies are found in the captions, comments, and text accompanying the photos. These texts are not distributing news; rather, they are distributing gossip. And they are doing so in ways that used to be facilitated in in-person interactions: the conversation over pancakes at the Shrove Tuesday meal about who was and was not pregnant, the dinner table and lunch counter speculation about the quiet trips "away" for young girls in a certain period of history, the rushed update at the photo-copier or the water cooler. Indeed, one of the features of birth prior to the technocratic age of hospitalization as a matter of course that is least remarked upon is the role of the "gossip" in attending the labor and delivery of women prior to the movement into the hospital for birth; much like a modern-day doula, these women would attend the births of other women in a supportive, nonmedical capacity. Unlike contemporary doulas, these gossips would also be responsible for spreading the news of the birth in the community after it had occurred.[57] Social media performs that function for the average woman: we post birth announcements and first pictures to spread news of the birth to our wider community. And we see celebrity media playing that role now, spreading the news of baby bumps and deliveries in the mainstream press.

Gossip is an incredibly important part of celebrity culture.[58] Even when gossip is not indulged in as a leveler, we rely on gossip columns and celebrity interviews to help us "piece together" our "knowledge of the star's 'real' life."[59] And gossip clearly plays a role in the public lives of pregnant celebrities. Much like gossip magazine features devoted to "outing" gay and lesbian celebrities, features like the "bump watch" and publicity devoted to the bump are attempts to take power and control from famous women in the decision about when, how, and whether they tell us that they are pregnant. Mitchell's ethnography of regular, noncelebrity pregnancies notes that the moment of "telling others" is a very significant moment in a pregnancy. She writes, "publicly announcing oneself as pregnant carries tremendous social and symbolic weight and thus needs to be managed."[60] Celebrity women have careers that rely on their physique, as well as images that are tied to particular stories of their relationships; the moment of pregnancy "outing" can have significant ramifications.

Anthropologists have posited gossip as an important way to instantiate an everyday politics, and understanding of morality, into day-to-day in-person interactions. Gossip is a marker of locality—the ability to participate in it marks one as an insider.[61] Gossip via digitized media evokes a global space—and allows participants to feel like "insiders" in realms they've never physically visited. Significantly, though, gossip online may be different from in-person gossip, because people express things online they might not express in public—deep and intimate truths about themselves, as well as negative and officious beliefs.[62] The comments section on any celebrity pregnancy blog bears witness to this.

While we may fantasize about our pregnancies in terms of the celebrity scripts we're receiving, and even feel empathy and sisterhood with celebrities who are pregnant while we are, the truth is that this is a mediated, constructed, and false relationship. It is a relationship based on a conversation between bloggers and commentators, between magazine copywriters and consumers of popular culture; it is not a relationship between or among actual pregnant women. Just as it marks locality and insider status, gossip facilitates a process of othering.[63] Gossip, seen as "a conversation between 'us' and 'us' *about* 'them' [is] distinct from a conversation, or dialogue, *between* 'us' and 'them.'"[64] So not only are celebrities made "other" by this (often incredibly cruel) gossip; women are made "others" to each other and themselves and subtly discouraged from seeking sisterhood and empathy "in real life." Through celebrity magazines and gossip websites, women hungry to learn about others' pregnancies feel entitled, even responsible, to imitate and judge—rather than connect and relate.

Pregnancy: Protection and Approbation

Robbie Davis-Floyd argues that from the moment women learn they are pregnant and announce it to the world, their social identity changes. She hypothesizes pregnancy as a series of moments of transitions, a process of "becoming" that occurs in several domains: personal, public, medical, formally educative, and peer group. She argues that encounters in the public domain are particularly formative for women.[65]

Once publicly pregnant, women are told what to do and not do; they learn to maintain "social hygiene" in order to maintain identity as good moms.[66] If you chat with almost any pregnant woman or new mother, you will hear stories about strangers commenting on her size, asking invasive questions. Pregnant women are often asked, "What are you having?" The question is meant to elicit a fetal gender; my favorite way to respond, when I was pregnant, was to cheerfully reply "We aren't sure—but we're hoping for a bear cub!"

This surveillance often breaches personal space. By the seventh or eighth month of pregnancy, a pregnant woman "probably no longer even flinches when strangers reach out to pat her stomach, having learned and accepted the social reality that her belly is now a part of the public interactional domain."[67] Mitchell writes, "welcomed, reassuring, and helpful though some of it might be, the increased attention" and "watchful gaze" can also be "restrictive."[68]

Strangers will happily tell a pregnant woman what to drink or eat or avoid. I recall a student telling me early on in my pregnancy that drinking a cola was "bad for my baby," though it was the only thing I could get past my gag reflex during that phase of morning sickness. One friend recalls being denied service in a sushi restaurant; another remembers being admonished for riding her bicycle while pregnant. Where the state cannot, or does not, reach, average citizens are happy to surveil and step in.

A pregnant woman can expect to face social censure when she orders a glass of wine, eats lunch meat, or, heaven forbid, smokes a cigarette. And watching the coverage of celebrity pregnancies reinforces this expectation of approbation. Women who Google "what can I eat when I'm pregnant?" will quickly find photos of celebrity moms eating their favorite things or posing with their "cravings," and a visit to babycenter.com provides a slide show of celebrity moms "caught" smoking, complete with disapproving commentary from hundreds of women. Moms-to-be learn from those photos what is acceptable to eat, drink, and inhale—and what is not. They will learn to self-regulate, at least in public, or face backlash, comments, and gossip.

Pregnancy and Self-Surveillance: A Biopolitics of Responsibilization

As we have seen, much of the surveillance of pregnant women focuses on medical risks that they, their doctors, and the general public need to be alert to. This is to be expected in a "risk society"[69] wherein, as Fox puts it, "almost every aspect of life has become filled with perceived dangers: physical, psychological, and moral, from hazardous carbon emissions causing climate change to the hazards of adolescent sexuality." Individuals, Fox warns us, "have to continually assess the risks (the likelihood) of these hazards befalling them."[70] This is true, even though biohazards and risks like mercury levels in fish, pollution in breast milk, and the impact of global climate change are well beyond the control of average women.

More and more, individuals are the focal point of the responsibility. The medical profession provides a set of services, but a person is responsible to avail herself of them. The media provide information and models for pregnancy; a woman is responsible for following the proper examples. This constitutes, as Rose puts it, "the resonsibilisation of life"[71] through which, increasingly, our behavior is seen to be "subject to *self-reflection* and *self-management*" wherein there grows "a moral dimension to bodily behavior, creating a hierarchy between those who choose safe ways to manage their bodies and those who do not."[72] This exhortation to take responsibility often occurs absent an understanding of structural constraints on women's ability to do so.

In this society of risk, women are responsible when they self-surveil and self-castigate. In earlier eras an idealized maternal woman was considered "good" if she was caring, nurturing, self-neglecting;[73] a "good woman" and "good mom" now is all of those things, while also being adept at self-surveillance and body management guised as being healthy and hip. Ethical subjects engage in governmentality: surveillance meant to control, manage, and govern the self[74] and coerce their behavior. Rubin's "managerial mother" has become a managed woman with a managed body.[75]

Fox notes that "self-surveillance and reflection on how a body should conduct itself have become ingrained in contemporary culture."[76] One of the ways that these norms are reinforced and experienced is in surveillance-style photos of pregnant celebrities published in every major celebrity-focus magazine and website, and the gossip-as-text that accompanies them. The camera's gaze disciplines our actions, much as Foucault had theorized it would, in a panoptical setting.[77] Where the camera fails, comments and headlines step in to focus moral and responsible behavior. There is no need to follow a pregnant woman to the grocery store to make sure she purchases the right goods; there are enough photos of pregnant celebrities in the magazine aisles and the checkout line to keep her in check.

However, these imperatives to self- and other-regulation coincide with a contemporary political movement that appears increasingly desperate to engage state actors and doctors in the surveillance and regulation of women's reproducing bodies. This is evident in an increasingly strident legislative call for heightened restrictions on access to birth control and abortion, as well as laws that would criminalize natural events like miscarriage and those that will penalize crimes against pregnant women, on behalf of the fetus. While complex politics are behind the recent return to antiwoman legislation in several states, our popular culture reinforces the idea that ultrasounds, testing, and fetal protection unduly burdening women's autonomy are the "norm," whether or not they have salutary effects on the lives of women and children. Cultural acceptance of them has roots in and synergy with our acceptance of popular culture representation, commodification, and regulation of celebrity pregnancies.

Stalking and Surveilling, Gossiping and Regulating

When, by the way, did it become okay to criticize pregnant women?

—Janice Min, *How to Look Hot in a Minivan*[78]

In her popular culture reference manual *How to Look Hot in a Minivan*, Janice Min normalizes the gossip and surveillance we perpetuate on other women. She tells one story about stalking a friend of a friend's Facebook page to help a group of women determine whether that person had gotten Botox. She tells another: "Recently, I was at a pool party for one of my son's young friends, and my husband and I had a very real and very legitimate (also very private) conversation about whether some of the mothers, based on the way they looked and dressed, had ever worked as professional escorts." Yes, she acknowledges, having such conversations is "lame . . . cheap . . . even mean. But we all do it."[79]

Min apparently disapproves of the mom with too little time to brush her teeth. Though she clearly participates in the perpetuation of a popular culture that critiques mothers, values certain (consumer and self-controlled) behaviors over others, and provides several examples of "bad moms," Min actually asks her readers "When, by the way, did it become okay to criticize *pregnant* women?"[80] The question seems laughable for its hypocrisy, and perhaps can be taken seriously only as a rhetorical query.

However, I do not believe that Min is being disingenuous. Her tone throughout the book indicates that she's trying to be helpful, to give women the tips they need to be sexy, powerful, successful women. She is certainly offering one version of feminism.[81] Yet the answer to the question, "When, by the way, did it become okay to criticize *pregnant* women?"—as we know from any good history of reproductive politics—is that it has almost *always* been okay to criticize pregnant women. In fact, it has been more than okay; the critique of pregnant women and the monitoring of their actions have long been deemed necessary. As Robin Longhurst acknowledges, "pregnant

women are considered to be a public concern [and] . . . the everyday behav-
iours of pregnant women tend to be policed by strangers."[82] Witness pregnant women refused glasses of wine by well-intentioned waitresses or advised
on the dangers of tuna and lunch meat by strangers in the grocery line. With
the stars it is even easier to weigh in on their behavior, as they are under constant surveillance by the press and paparazzi.

CHAPTER 5

GOVERNING THE BODY THROUGH THE BUMP

SUSAN HARMAN was sixty-nine years old when she was arrested in 2010. A political activist living in Northern California, Harman was peacefully protesting the death of Oscar Grant, an unarmed public transit passenger fatally shot by police in the year prior. As a veteran activist, Harman was prepared for the arrest. She had her insulin for her diabetes, a lawyer lined up, and bail money at the ready. She planned to spend the night in jail. She did not plan to be denied access to her insulin, and she certainly did not plan to be forced to submit to a pregnancy test. The same is true for Nancy Macias, also an activist, who was arrested in 2012 and also required to take a pregnancy test as part of her less than twenty-four-hour stay at the Glenn Dyer jail in downtown Oakland.[1] Part of the political action group Code Pink, Macias was appalled and humiliated at being required to undergo the pregnancy test and contacted the American Civil Liberties Union upon her release.[2]

Macias and Harman are not celebrities. Yet they are emblematic of a new trend in "bump watching"—the surveillance of average, everyday women who *might* be pregnant.

Bump Watching and Governmentality

Scholars of law and culture have persuasively argued that governance frequently takes place via what Alan Hunt calls "the moralizing of popular culture"[3] through the proliferation of rules around mundane, everyday cultural moments and texts. In his examination of early modern sumptuary laws regarding what people were (and were not) permitted to wear, Hunt discusses legislative attempts to discipline popular culture and those who partake of it and constitutively produce it. The proliferation of sumptuary laws during early periods of urbanization and industrialization was very clearly tied to the moral panic and a sense of crisis eventuated by that move. Contemporary moments of panic and crisis offer more, though different, opportunities for governance that extends the reach of the state into culture and culture into the state.[4] As Hunt writes of the contemporary period, "I am tempted to conclude that sumptuary law is alive and well in all but name."[5]

When the imperative to good and proper consumer behavior fails to adequately channel citizens' power, surveillance and regulation via "new technologies of governance" become a necessary project.[6] Writing from a feminist perspective on these new politics of governance, Cruikshank notes how the smallest, most mundane, most everyday technologies are used to govern, regulate, and simultaneously construct citizens.[7] This is a vital process in neoliberal governance: the biopolitical responsibilization of life and the devolution of responsibility to the individual in the face of extreme risk. In neoliberalism, citizens must be hypervigilant to risk and be responsible at all times for the safety, health, and integrity of their bodies—even in a period that denies their ability to do so. We cannot guard ourselves against the personal consequences of climate change, of chemical weapons, nor of nuclear meltdowns in other countries—but we are expected to be vigilant enough to try, and responsible enough to mitigate their consequences.

The contemporary state is a state of fear and risk.[8] In order to self-perpetuate, such a project of governance must have a state formation that simultaneously secures its citizenry, applauds and encourages their immense egocentrism, and reifies their accumulation of material goods—then must justify the actions needed to tame those very citizens, empowered by egocentrism and mandated to surveillance.[9] The neoliberal state appears to be in perpetual crisis and seems to need inordinate levels of administration and regulation to maintain control, even as its boosters call for smaller government. Indeed, the neoliberal state is one of greater and greater administrative capacity; neoliberal governance is both administrative and decentralized, dispersed, "widely spread throughout the social body."[10]

The spread of state power in neoliberalism is often made possible through its diffusion via proxies—intermediaries that do this naturalization and reification with panache.[11] These proxies are corporate, private, and social actors—not state actors. Yet state reach in neoliberalism is not limited; rather, by using private proxies, "the state's power has drastically extended its reach."[12] Passavant's focus is the war on terror and its excuse for stepped-up policing of protest, but his point is integral for those interested in understanding the current war on women's bodies, as well as stepped-up surveillance of pregnancy and reproducing females.

Feminist political theorists have long understood that the fertile womb is a site for the surveillance of women—a place from which, and the reason for which, the minute and mundane moments of women's lives can be governed. Pregnant women in particular have long been constructed as inhabiting unreliable bodies. With bodies that balloon in size, waters that "break," labor that—if unmedicated—can be primal, loud, and out of control, pregnant bodies provoke anxiety. Socially constructed as emotional and hormonal, pregnant women are shaky subjects—not stable, not in control, unable to manage the risks and anxieties associated with their pregnancies. There may not be enough products in the world to adequately control pregnant women or enough money in their pockets to purchase those that do exist. The self-controlled and self-disciplined pregnant citizen-consumer is still a shaky subject, one whose importance and femininity make her all the more subject to more direct and authoritarian control.

The inadequately disciplined female body has long been a theme of reproductive law and politics in the United States. Because legal rhetorics around reproductive choices have pitted women against their fetuses, the worry about how women will inhabit, live, and control their own bodies reaches a fever pitch when it concerns decisions about birth control, abortion, and pregnancy.[13] Indeed, the history of reproductive politics in the United States offers ample documentation of the moral panic surrounding women's entry into the workforce, urbanization, and anonymity, as they dovetailed with and facilitated the availability of birth control.[14] In the contemporary period, successful rights claiming by women, as well as by gays and lesbians, has contributed to a triggering of a renewed sense of crisis and panic among members of the population, often—but not exclusively—articulated by the religious right and ultraconservative political movements. But these are not merely partisan politics; Wendy Brown convincingly ties the development of rights and recognition for women to a more general growth in "state and medical control over women's reproductive and sexual conduct," and notes the expanded use of "regulatory discourses" to manage these populations.[15]

The nation-state has slowly devolved power over women's bodies from states to localities to the public at large when we fail to govern ourselves, so that our own freedom and privacy—the things that feel like rights and privileges—are actually ways that we are forced to be responsible for things we cannot always control: the health of our babies, the outcomes of our pregnancies, the variable nature of everyday life.

The Unmediated State

The rate of legal abortion in the United States has been steadily declining since reaching a high point with national decriminalization in the 1970s. In large part thanks to expanded health care coverage and access to sexual health information and contraception, the abortion rate reached an all-time low in 2010 and is expected to continue to decline.[16] There has been very little new jurisprudence in the realm of abortion and fetal protection, with the exception of free speech cases brought by abortion protesters and two major Supreme Court decisions that ultimately upheld a federal prohibition on late-term, so-called "partial birth" abortions.[17]

We might assume that a decline in the abortion rate coupled with a decline in litigation and Supreme Court decisions would mean that abortion and women's reproductive rights are less salient issues in contemporary politics than they have been in the past. But that assumption would be wrong. In the absence of Court challenges has come a proliferation of state-level laws meant to impinge upon access to abortion, protect fetal health, and regulate women of reproductive age, whether they are pregnant or not. Republican success in state midterm election races in 2010 bore significant fruit, and the passage of the Patient Protection and Affordable Care Act (called "Obamacare" by some), which mandates insurance coverage of a wide range of women's health needs including contraception, served as a lightning rod and motivator for conservative state legislatures.[18] Additionally, the rise of the Tea Party, with its extremely conservative views on issues related to women and reproduction, has moved even more moderate Republicans and their states to the right.

In the years 2011, 2012, and 2013, states passed 205 legislative restrictions on women's reproduction. In those three years, the states passed more restrictive laws than they had in the entire previous decade.[19] In 2013 alone, twenty-two states passed seventy laws—the second highest number of laws ever to be passed in this realm, limiting access to reproductive health services.[20] At the beginning of the new millennium, advocacy groups considered thirteen states "hostile" to abortion rights. By 2013, that number had more than doubled; twenty-seven states were considered hostile environments for the exercise of the rights articulated in *Roe v. Wade*.

Many of the bills that have passed in the several states since 2010 seem quite likely to withstand legal challenge: they extend mandatory waiting periods, record keeping, and informed consent provisions or provide further restrictions on access for minors. However, some constitutionally questionable "total bans" on the procedure have also been passed and will almost certainly fall to legal challenge. Nebraska has a ban on termination after twenty weeks, with no exceptions granted—not even to save the life of the mother. North Dakota has a total ban on the procedure after six weeks.[21] Texas Governor Rick Perry recently signed into law a bill similar to the one in Nebraska, banning all abortions after twenty weeks and, more significantly, requiring that "the procedure be performed at ambulatory surgical centers, [and] mandat[ing] that doctors who perform abortions obtain admitting privileges at a hospital within 30 miles and that even nonsurgical abortions take place in a surgical center." These provisions are significant because the majority of abortions in the United States are nonsurgical and early abortions; this law strictly limits access to the most commonly used procedure and the one safest for the mother. The Texas law was passed and signed after vocal opposition, procedural violations, and a marathon filibuster by State Senator Wendy Davis, who ran for Texas governor in 2014 and whose own early-in-life abortion procedure became a flash point in opposition to her candidacy for the governorship.[22]

Ten states have now passed laws mandating physically invasive, medically unnecessary transvaginal ultrasounds prior to termination of a pregnancy.

Such ultrasounds can detect fetal heartbeat long before fetal viability—sometimes as early as six weeks into a pregnancy—and these laws are coupled with legislation that prohibits abortion once a fetal heartbeat is detected. Arkansas lawmakers passed legislation that prohibited abortion after the detection of heartbeat by external fetal monitoring (usually around twelve weeks). South Dakota lawmakers have instituted a seventy-two-hour waiting period for abortion services, excluding weekends and holidays; South Dakota also requires faith-based counseling prior to any abortion, though this requirement is embroiled in litigation. Zoning regulations, transfer and hospital privilege arrangements, and spending bills that defund family planning clinics are also all being used to stop access to abortion services.

The state of Virginia passed a mandatory ultrasound bill in 2014 requiring that all women seeking to terminate a pregnancy submit to internal Doppler imaging prior to the procedure. Virginia's law is notable for the publicity surrounding it. One of the state senators responsible for the bill, a former chairman of the Virginia Senate's Health and Education Committees, Steve Martin (R) wrote this on his official Facebook page: "once a child does exist in your womb, I'm not going to assume a right to kill it just because *the child's host* (some refer to them as mothers) doesn't want it."[23] In this rhetoric, a woman is no longer even a "bad mother" if she desires abortion—she is a mere receptacle, a mere "host" for another life. A pregnant woman is no longer a rights-bearing citizen; she is a subject of the state. She is also ultimately responsible for the life and welfare of the fetus she "hosts."

The sad irony for those who care about both maternal health and fetal protection is that restrictive abortion laws and birth control policies simply do not result in lower rates of abortion. Restrictive abortion laws and anti–family planning policies do, however, make it more difficult for women to gain safe and affordable access to rights they have determined to exercise.[24]

Criminalizing Pregnant Women: Legislation and Prosecutorial Discretion

Previously, doctors who performed abortions were the targets of criminal sanctions advocated by pro-life organizations; women were not. In the years since 2005, though, mothers who obtain the means to abortion or attempt to abort are increasingly criminalized—as are the women who might help them. Reproductive rights attorneys point to the case of one Idaho mother who purchased RU-486 over the Internet. RU-486 is a pill that provides safe abortion in the first trimester, and it is legal in Idaho. She believed herself to be within the first twelve weeks of gestation, but she was wrong about the timing of her pregnancy. She unintentionally aborted a fetus close to twenty weeks along. She confided in her best friend, who alerted Idaho officials; she was arrested for feticide—a felony.[25]

A Pennsylvania mother purchased RU-486 for her sixteen-year-old daughter, who was pregnant and did not want to carry the pregnancy to term. The nearest abortion provider was more than an hour away, and the teen lacked health insurance. Her mother was sentenced to twelve to eighteen months in prison, fined $1,000, and mandated to do forty hours of community service. The conviction could have carried a seven-year prison term, so the sentence may seem lenient—but having a felony conviction will likely make it difficult for this nursing home aide and single mother to find work upon release.[26]

Certainly, there are women who will attempt illegal means to abort or miscarry a fetus or whose actions will intentionally result in harm or death to their unborn children. Society has long attempted to stop them from taking those actions and to punish them when it happens. The tragedies associated with women's lives when they are attempting to abort or do harm to themselves and their unborn children are often heartrending, though those circumstances often do not figure into decisions about prosecution and punishment. In 2011, Michelle Goldberg reported on several of these women in an article for *The Nation*. She tells the story of Bei Bei Shuai, a thirty-four-year-old woman living in Indianapolis. Goldberg writes that Shuai's pregnancy was near term when her relationship fell apart after she learned the child's father had been deceiving her and was already married. She ate rat poison in a suicide attempt, but friends rushed her to the hospital and she survived after receiving emergency care. At the hospital, according to Goldberg: "doctors performed a C-section, delivering her baby girl prematurely. ... [T]he baby had cerebral bleeding and died a few days later in her mother's arms. Shuai spent the next month in the psychiatric ward on suicide watch. Shortly after her release, she was charged with murder and attempted feticide, or fetal homicide, and has been locked up for more than a month, with little access to psychiatric care." Goldberg reports as well on a minor female known in court records as JMS, who was jailed for "criminal solicitation of murder" when in 2009 she paid a third party $150 to beat her severely enough to cause a miscarriage. At the time she made this agreement, JMS was living in a rural area of Utah with no electricity or running water; she did not have a driver's license, and the nearest abortion provider was three hours away. The father of the child she attempted to miscarry was serving federal time for producing child pornography—including the forcible coercion of JMS's performance in one of his pornographic films. Utah was unable to criminally prosecute her because her actions weren't illegal under the state's current abortion laws; lawmakers quickly moved to remedy that situation, should it arise in the future, and wrote legislation that would criminally penalize that desperate contract.[27]

Both Shuai and JMS took purposive action to end fetal life, and the states desire to hold them accountable. One might justifiably wonder if the state would better serve fetal life by attending to the structural and psychological impediments that led those women to their decisions.

Legislative and prosecutorial actions to restrict abortion and feticide are not by any means the only way that women are being impacted by the sudden, intense interest in the contents of their bumps. Indeed, pregnant women—and those who may be pregnant—are increasingly intruded upon, even when they desire to keep their pregnancies and birth their babies. As Terry Gross, the host of National Public Radio's *Fresh Air* reported in late 2013, "Pregnant women across the country are being subjected to arrest and incarceration, detentions in mental institutions and drug treatment programs, as well as forced medical interventions, including surgery, when medical professionals or law enforcement officials believe the pregnant woman may be endangering her fetus."[28]

NPR's reporting is cogent and correct. In the only existing comprehensive study of the issue, the National Advocates for Pregnant Women (NAPW) found that in the thirty years between 1973 and 2005, 413 women were prosecuted for fetal harm in 44 states.[29] In the decade since 2005, more than 250 cases have emerged. If this rate of prosecution continues unchecked, nearly one thousand women will be prosecuted in the next twenty years. This is more than double the rate of intrusion on women's reproductive lives in the years before 2005.[30] These cases impact women beyond those prosecuted; there is a ripple effect. Health care providers report that even one well-publicized case has a chilling effect on women in the community who might otherwise seek help.[31] And women of color and women living in poverty are disproportionately prosecuted and otherwise impacted by ramped-up prosecution.

Thirty-eight states have fetal homicide laws on the books. These laws were originally intended to add further criminal sanction to intimate partner violence when it results in the death of a fetus. But in spring 2014 the Tennessee legislature became the first political body to extend fetal protection law initially intended to protect pregnant women from intimate partner violence, in a way that criminalized women for "adverse outcomes" in pregnancy. Tennessee amended its criminal law with Senate Bill 1391; the bill made illegal drug use during pregnancy equal to "assault" and punishable by up to fifteen years in prison. The state's governor signed the bill over protests that noted that the law was "so badly written, it could affect all pregnant women in Tennessee, whether or not they use drugs, should something go wrong during their pregnancy."[32] Governor Haslam signed it even though penalties could accrue for women who tried and failed to access addiction-related services—in a state where only nineteen addiction treatment centers total offered treatment options for pregnant women.[33]

Even when addictions are under control, women's previous substance abuse problems may come back to haunt them. NAPW represents Alicia Beltran, a Latina who, during the course of receiving early prenatal care, at twelve weeks pregnant, disclosed that she had previously "struggled with her use of Percocet" and had previously used Suboxone, a medication meant to ease symptoms of withdrawal from opiates, before successfully kicking her habit. Alicia Beltran lives in Wisconsin, where a law on the books since 1998 defines and protects "unborn children" as existing "from the moment of fertilization" and which provides for civil and regulatory sanctions of drug use that impact those unborn children.

The law had previously languished within the code and had only been used selectively for those mothers who routinely or habitually resorted to drug use during pregnancy in a way that created "serious risk" to the fetus. Press descriptions of what happened to Beltran are chilling. Attorney Lynn Paltrow tells NPR listeners that Beltran, whose blood and urine analyses confirmed had stopped the use of all drugs, was visited at her home by five law enforcement officials who then detained her. Beltran was not arrested or charged under criminal law—which would have given her access to a state-appointed defense attorney. Rather, as Wisconsin's law is a civil code meant to protect children and unborn children, Beltran went through a civil commitment hearing, without benefit of counsel. The process went like this: "They put her in handcuffs, they took her to an emergency room where she was examined, and that examination said she looks fine, the baby looks fine. Nevertheless they took her to jail. They put her in leg shackles. They took her to a courtroom where there was already a lawyer appointed for her 12-week fetus, and she was not herself entitled to a lawyer."

Beltran, who had no medical insurance and lacked financial resources, refused to accept a prescription for Suboxone on the grounds that not only could she not afford it, she did not need it. The state's expert witness in these proceedings, who had not met Beltran or examined her, advocated her detention, writing, "She exhibits lack of self-control and refuses the treatment we have offered her."[34] The result: Beltran was forcibly sent to a ninety-day residential treatment program. She lost her job and when speaking with the *New York Times* upon her release, at six months pregnant, worried about retaining custody of her baby, once born.

The declaration in statutory law that a fertilized egg is a person with legal rights has significant ramifications for women who carry those fertilized eggs, even if they are not using or abusing drugs—and even if they have not done so in the past. In fact, Paltrow tells National Public Radio host Terry Gross that declaration renders women in jurisdictions with these types of "personhood" laws subject to numerous intrusions on their personal liberty and reproductive autonomy. State and medical officials in states with these laws have entitlement to pregnant women's medical records, they are "entitled to require her to undergo whatever medical procedures they think [are] best," and they are entitled to arrest her "if she doesn't obey."[35]

Jennifer Mason, who cofounded the organization Personhood USA in 2008 with her husband, Keith, explains the justification for such intrusion. "We believe," she says, "that every human being, regardless of their location, if they're in the womb or out of it, deserves those protections and those rights. . . . The baby is denied the [constitutional] right to life, the right to liberty and the right to pursue happiness at any point that they are [sic] killed in the womb."[36] Where in previous years and in more moderate forms fetal protection measures did take into account the potential need to abort in order to save the life of the mother, Personhood USA spokespeople deny that this could ever happen. Mason says, "We often get the question, well, what if there were a medical emergency," and you could save *either* the mother or the unborn child? "Well, doctors say that that doesn't happen, that there are not those cases" where you'd have to make that choice.[37]

Some of the legislation advocated by this organization would make tubal ligations for ectopic pregnancies illegal or at least more difficult to access. Ectopic pregnancies happen when a fertilized egg implants in one of the fallopian tubes; they are both nonviable pregnancies and life-threatening to women. Kansas, for instance, now has a law that redefines what "constitutes a medical emergency, so that pregnant women experiencing life-threatening complications—including hemorrhaging, infection and ruptured ectopic pregnancies—would be forced to wait at least 24 hours before obtaining an emergency abortion."[38]

Some of this legislation would also criminalize the inadvertent harm that comes to a fetus in the normal course of maternal life. Fifteen to twenty percent of all pregnancies will end in miscarriage or stillbirth, and these occur for a variety of reasons.[39] The potential that these could be criminalized via "fetal protection" and "personhood" laws is chilling. The national press recently broke the story of Christine Taylor, a pregnant Iowa woman whose blood pressure plummeted, causing her to fall down a flight of stairs. Paramedics said that she was fine, but she asked them to take her to the hospital to be sure her unborn child was not harmed in the fall. During the course of the examination, an emotional and concerned Taylor "admitted" to a sympathetic nurse that "very early in the pregnancy she had considered possibly having an abortion," though she was now committed to carrying the child to term. Her lawyer, Lynn Paltrow, reports:

> On the way home from the hospital . . . she is picked up by police and arrested on charges of attempted feticide. She's put in handcuffs. She's kept in jail for two days, until there is such a national outcry that they release her. But they release her saying, well, we released her because she was only in

her second trimester, but if this had happened when she was in her third trimester, we would have been entitled to keep her in jail on this charge of attempted feticide.[40]

Irony isn't the right word to use when describing the ways that laws meant to protect women and their children against intimate partner violence are used to prosecute women for their actions and inactions when pregnant. The right word for that is cruelty.

Medical Proxies for State Action

Jennifer Block's journalistic investigation of coercive practices relating to pregnancy and birth indicates that though states may not criminalize their actions, mothers who refuse the medical attention doctors and others think they, and their unborn baby, require do face governance via state proxies in the medical profession. One of the more contentious issues in reproductive justice is the ability of hospital staff, with and without a court order, to force a woman to undergo major surgery in the form of a cesarean section. The tragic case of Angela Carder in 1987 first brought national attention to this issue. Surgeons performed a C-section on Carder, though she had previously refused consent for the procedure and at the time was unable to provide consent, as she was rendered mostly unconscious due to treatments for inoperable cancer. Carder's baby died within hours of birth—too premature to be viable. Tina Cassidy writes that Carder "regained consciousness long enough to know her baby had been taken from her womb and was dead, [and] wept before she herself stopped living, two days later. They were buried together; the baby swaddled and placed in her mother's arms."[41]

Carder's parents sued the hospital; the resultant case was argued by attorney Lynn Paltrow and settled in her family's favor in 1990. The settlement established no precedent, but did alert hospitals to the need to create policies that "recognized a pregnant woman's right to control her own medical care."[42] Yet the threat to women's autonomy in decision making was clear. In 1987 alone, there were twenty-one court-ordered C-sections granted in eleven American cities. That number might not alarm us; more important is Cassidy's finding that hospitals were almost always victorious: nearly 90 percent of all hospital attempts to gain court orders were successful. And there are distinct and clear racial, ethnic, and class disparities: "Eighty-one percent of the women at the center of those court orders were black, Asian, or Hispanic; 44 percent were unmarried; and 24 percent did not speak English as their primary language." In addition, all of the women subject to court-ordered C-sections were poor; they were all treated at teaching hospital clinics or were receiving public assistance.[43]

The threats to women's autonomy—particularly the autonomy of poor women and women of color—are clear, and they persist.

A recent case highlights the fact that hospital staff are sometimes not even bothering with court orders when acting expressly against women's consent. In early 2014, thirty-five-year-old Rinat Dray was coerced and forced into having a C-section birth when an attorney for Staten Island University Hospital, without discussing the case with the hospital's bioethicists and without engaging a patient advocate, permitted doctors to override her explicit, conscious, and considered refusal to have a nonemergency C-section. The procedure was not only against her will, it was botched: the surgeons accidentally perforated her bladder during the procedure. In another case, where the woman's opposition to the surgery was so strong that she needed to be restrained: "hospital staff tie[d] her down with leather wrist and ankle cuffs while she scream[ed] for help."[44] The state no longer has to incarcerate uncooperative women or even provide judicial personnel for court orders; it has proxies in the form of hospital administrators willing to incapacitate women on their behalf.

Private Proxies: Employers

Cultural and legal vigilance also extends to those women who seek to responsibly avoid pregnancy by use of contraceptives. This vigilance is accomplished by proxies in the form of private employers who exercise their policing powers as proxies of the state. We live in an era where relatively safe, comfortable, and quite effective birth control is available for many women in the United States; yet still a (slim) majority of all pregnancies in the United States are unintended.[45] Unintended pregnancy rates have risen since 1981 among low-income and poor women; they have fallen for higher-income women. Without accounting for those pregnancies that end in miscarriage, 60 percent of unintended pregnancies result in birth; 40 percent are aborted. One way to avoid abortion, one might think, would be to decrease the number and rate of unintended pregnancies in this country. The provision of low-cost and effective birth control options for poor women would seem to be a good public policy option for those hoping to avoid abortion, as well as unplanned births.

However, state legislators are proposing to allow employers to erect significant barriers to accessing birth control. The National Women's Law Center reports that in 2014 there were forty-eight lawsuits pending in federal and state jurisdictions challenging the Patient Protection and Affordable Care Act's (PPACA's) mandate that employers' health plans cover contraception without co-pay, a benefit that impacts more than 27 million American women. Twenty states, as a matter of law, currently allow employers to refuse to comply with the PPACA, and more than seventy private for-profit employers take advantage of that permission.[46] The Supreme Court ruled in the *Hobby Lobby* and *Conestoga Wood* cases that both companies could refuse to comply with the mandate, citing religious objections to contraception. In *Hobby Lobby*,[47] the Court expanded on a jurisprudence of corporate citizenship that had previously reached a high-water mark in the hotly contested *Citizens United* and held that a corporate "person" with a closely held religious belief against contraception could refuse to cover birth control in an employee health plan.

In Arizona in 2014, legislators passed out of the statehouse a law that would have made it legal for an employer to *fire* a woman who uses birth control for "nonmedical" conditions (including avoiding pregnancy) if the use of birth control is against the employer's religious or moral beliefs.[48] The amended version of the bill struck that provision, but inserted language requiring employees to pay out of pocket for their birth control, then seek specific reimbursement for the prescription; it also allowed religiously affiliated employers to refuse to cover birth control in their employee insurance or health plan.[49] That same year, Ohio legislators considered a total ban on the use of intrauterine devices (IUDs), which in their copper form, provide the most effective long-term nonhormonal form of birth control available to women. The sponsor of the bill, Representative John Baker, has stated that he believes, contrary to medical evidence, that an IUD will prevent a fertilized egg (a person, under Ohio law) from implanting in the uterus, and thus cause an abortion. Baker told the *Columbus Dispatch*, "This is just a personal view. I'm not a medical doctor." Baker also advocates the death penalty for convicted rapists; however, his bill would make it illegal for insurance companies to provide coverage for abortion for women who become pregnant as a result of rape.[50] In this mindset, women are responsible for carrying their pregnancies to term—even if the only action they took on the way to becoming pregnant was to be the victim of a violent crime.

The responsibilization of women reached a laughable, and miserable, low in 2012, when Representative Todd Aiken told members of the press that "legitimate rape" could never result in pregnancy, as women's bodies had ways to "shut that whole thing down."[51] A responsible woman who is raped, Aiken theorizes, has a body that reacts in a way we know to be biologically impossible. In late 2014, Missouri state legislator Rick Brattin proposed a law that would require a woman seeking an abortion to have a notarized memo of permission from the father of the fetus—whether or not the woman had a current relationship with the man. When asked how this might impact women seeking to abort a pregnancy that was the result of rape or incest, Brattin returned to the language of "legitimate rape," telling reporters, "I'm just saying if there was a legitimate rape, you're going to make a police report, just as if you were robbed. . . . That's just common sense . . . you have to take steps to show that you were raped. . . . And I'd think you'd be able to prove that."[52]

There is a catch-22 to be found in all of this discourse. Women who seek to avoid pregnancy are doing something unethical or immoral—they are enjoying sex without the consequences. Women who become pregnant—even via rape—must have somehow enjoyed the experience. All women, then, are absolutely responsible for the outcome of any pregnancy and even the eventual life choices of the child, yet no woman, it would seem, can be fully trusted. Pregnant women, then, must be subject to surveillance and control.

The General Public as a Proxy for the State

Compared to the laws and prosecutions documented in this chapter, some of the modes of responsibilization undertaken by the public may seem light-hearted. Beginning in the 1980s, with the responsibilization of pregnancy, we see, for instance, a proliferation of parenting books pitched primarily toward a white, upwardly mobile and upper-middle-class readership.[53] In these books, women are encouraged to internalize the disciplinary norms of the various professional and medical fields attendant to pregnancy and its regulation and performance. These books actively teach women what pregnancy is like and how its symptoms are to be managed.

The more contemporary analogues are the three- to five-minute YouTube videos produced by *BabyCenter* and *HealthGuru,* which feature a multiracial cast of caring moms taking advice from a well-meaning doctor who starts nearly every video clip by telling her patient that the fetus is the size of a particular piece of fruit (a peach, perhaps, or a cantaloupe).[54] We learn through these books and videos that a "good" pregnant woman will submit to her doctor's care and will labor and deliver in a hospital. She cares more about the "outcome"—a healthy baby—than the "process"—a birth that went according to "plan." A well-disciplined pregnant woman can, with diligence, avoid the need for a forced, court-ordered, or emergency C-section. Docility and submission to the state and its multiple proxies will enable women to avoid criminalization and coercion. Good mothers perform their bumps appropriately: they live their pregnancies with hypervigilance; they choose healthy foods and avoid unhealthy ones; they exercise just enough and gain just enough weight; they avoid stress and rest when tired. This is self-discipline disguised as autonomy and self-care.

But still, there are the vigilantes, like the waitress in Arkansas who called the police to report a breastfeeding mother for child endangerment when that mother drank two beers over the course of ninety minutes while consuming food.[55] There are bartenders who refuse to sell pregnant women alcohol and strangers who comment with disapproval on their weight gain, their food choices, and their leisure activities. The popular culture makes clear that "pregnant women are doing it wrong," and their very wrongness, coupled with a "save the children" mentality, enables average people to feel completely justified in intervening in a pregnant woman's life. Dean Burnett, science editor for *The Guardian,* points out how extraordinarily stressful this can be for an expectant mom, then adds, "That's bad too; stress is very harmful to a baby, so if you're an expectant mother you'd better learn to find the whole process wonderfully relaxing ASAP, or you're risking harm to the baby and therefore a terrible human being."[56]

Sometimes control is accomplished by much more frightening vigilante proxies, like the man in rural Washington who drew a gun on a pregnant woman when she refused his demand, which he yelled out of his truck window at her while she walked down the street, that she put out her cigarette. "What kind of a pregnant woman," he asked indignantly, "smokes cigarettes?"[57] He continued to follow her and she called for help. When police pulled him over, they found two Glock semiautomatic weapons in his pickup truck. He pled guilty to felony harassment of the woman, who he did not know.[58]

Cupcakes, Fascism, and Baby Bumps

[Digital communication] is not nourishing. It's like snack food. You know how they engineer this food? They scientifically determine precisely how much salt and fat they need to include to keep you eating. You're not hungry, you don't need the food, it does nothing for you, but you keep eating these empty calories. That's what you're pushing. . . . Endless empty calories, but the digital-social equivalent. And you calibrate it so it's equally addictive. . . . You know how you finish a bag of chips and you hate yourself? You know you've done nothing good for yourself. That's the same feeling, and you know it is, after some digital binge. You feel wasted and hollow and diminished.

—Dave Eggers, *The Circle*[59]

Compared to the direct comments from strangers and threats of violence on city streets, advice columns and YouTube videos seem merely gentle. So do the magazines in the supermarket checkout lines, the commenters on *E!* online, and the writers at *TMZ*. We might understand that we're consuming junk food, but it's pleasurable and seemingly innocent.

Media coverage of the baby bump is a proxy extraordinaire, a technique of governance that works eerily well in contemporary society. Cultivating our obsessive attention to celebrity pregnancy helps to fulfill capital's need for expansion through perpetual commodification and patriarchy's need for a controlled and docile female population through normalizing and idealizing some female forms and performances of pregnancies. The celebrity baby bump has the power to channel moral panic and rebellion alike through techniques that laud self-surveillance via medicalization and self-discipline. The bump itself becomes a proxy for governmental interference in women's reproductive lives.

Images of celebrity baby bumps are so effective, and so convincingly postmodern, precisely because they aren't punishing—*they're fun*. We can understand them as, perhaps, some of the best "daydreams of communicative capital."[60] These daydreams are increasingly fluffy and sweet, and they serve to gently, almost invisibly, coerce us into self- and other- discipline and control. They are a perfect example of what Tom Whyman calls "cupcake fascism."[61]

Whyman's witty and prescient commentary for *The Guardian* notes that Brits and Americans alike would not be readily drawn into the fascist movements of the past. But, he writes, "you could get a huge mass of people to participate in a reactionary endeavour if you dressed it up in nice, twee, cupcakey imagery, and persuaded everyone that the brutality of your ideology was in fact a form of niceness."[62] The stranger who notes that "you're carrying low, so it must be a boy" is just trying to be nice—even as she engages you in coercive and judgmental dialogue about your plans for labor and delivery, circumcision, and breastfeeding. Looking at photos of pregnant Scarlett Johansson, Megan Fox, and Keira Knightley is just a nice way to spend a morning, as is shopping for a Jessica Simpson nursing bra or a Gwen Stefani design for the postpartum period. Cooing for Xtina's baby's photos or the glam lifestyle enjoyed by little North West seems like harmless fun indeed when compared to trying to avoid pregnancy, rape, and miscarriage—or being held responsible for any of them.

Consumption of popular culture media stories about pregnant celebrities likely helps us ameliorate our very real feelings of risk and anxiety, disconnection, and anomie. Yet very real material issues facing women during their reproductive lives are growing simultaneous to the growth of press coverage of celebrity pregnancies, though we don't often remark upon their simultaneity. The boom in views of Beyoncé's bump coincided with the introduction of more fetal protection bills than ever before. Our obsession with the Royal Baby, and Snooki's baby, and countless other celebrity babies coincided with an obsessive new desire to outlaw various forms of birth control. And while many of us were watching Kim Kardashian prepare to give birth, some of us were watching Wendy Davis filibuster in the Texas statehouse in an ultimately failed attempt to thwart that state's draconian anti–family planning laws.

At best, cultural obsession with pregnant celebrities and their burgeoning bumps is a mind-numbing and sometimes amusing distraction from very real issues facing women during their reproductive lives. At worst, though, these images and our consumption of them feeds into those very politics that would control us, as they enable us to feel comfortable being watched and judged, surveilled and regulated.

CHAPTER 6

REBEL RENDERINGS

FEMALE RAP ARTIST M.I.A. writes, produces, and performs rebellious and resistant, politically charged, and powerfully sexual lyrics.[1] Her hit single "Paper Planes" earned critical acclaim, a Grammy award, and top sales in 2007; she performed a sample of it at the 2009 Grammy Awards and brought the house down. Besides being musically innovative, her awards show performance was also a watershed moment in the history of public performances of pregnancy. When M.I.A. rapped "Swagga Like Us," she was the only female to share the stage with Lil Wayne, Kanye West, and Jay Z—and she did so at thirty-six weeks pregnant. She wore sensible white tennis shoes on her feet and sunglasses on her eyes, with a tight, mostly mesh, and otherwise tiny mini dress over her "bump."

About the dress, the United Kingdom's *Daily Mail* opined, "you won't find [it] in MotherCare." The reporter continued, "British rapper MIA redefined maternity wear. . . . [She] overlooked a traditional empire line dress in favour of a daring sheer confection that exposed most of her baby bump."[2]

Introduced that night by Queen Latifah as "mommy to be M.I.A.," M.I.A. perfected what bloggers began calling the "pregger swagga." The combination of her pregnancy, her politics, and the vehicle of hip hop on a mainstream stage was immediately interesting. Friends and colleagues emailed me, making sure I'd seen the performance and wondering if I found it as

FIGURE 6.1 M.I.A. performing at the Grammys. Photo credit: Getty Images

energizing, subversive, and rebellious as they—and millions of others—had. They asked whether I thought M.I.A. was doing something differently, performing her pregnancy differently, from the other women whose bumps I was watching.

That same semester, I was teaching a course on critical race and feminist theory for a group of engaged and interested undergraduate students. We were using, in part, a collection of essays from a volume titled *Embodied Resistance*;[3] its cover featured a gorgeous photo of a woman's tattooed back, and the text itself was filled with images and stories of attempted resistance to heteronormativity, gender normativity, and racialized and classed hierarchies. In the course, we were taking seriously the potential emancipation that can be found in living and performing with a resistant body. How, we routinely asked ourselves, can women resist the racially charged and gender-normative expectations placed on their bodies?

I began to wonder, Are there celebrity examples of resistance? Is M.I.A. one such example? Can rebellious performances of celebrity pregnancy provide strong enough counternarratives to displace, or at least radically trouble, the normative assumptions about pregnancy that we have seen replicated in most coverage of the celebrity baby bump? Even if they can do so, can they also resist the commodification of bumps, and all things pregnancy-related, and the governance of female bodies through surveillance and regulation?

As I watched celebrity pregnancies and the media that covered them, I became interested in the ways that some stars' pregnancies did seem to break the mold of feminine normativity that I have isolated as problematic in previous chapters. While most women were still easily categorized by the press as "good" or "bad" moms, or hot and sexy with a side of MILF, there was also a set of celebrity moms whose bumps seemed rebellious and disruptive of those categories. These nonnormative performances of pregnancy are emblematically evident in media representations of the bold bumps of Pink, M.I.A., and Christina Aguilera, all of whom performed their pregnancies in ways that appeared rebellious. I saw rebellion in purposeful and chosen absences, too—the absent bumps of Sarah Jessica Parker and Melissa Harris-Perry, both of whom had surrogates carry pregnancies on their behalf—and the absent fathers of female-headed households, whether they are celebrity women who parent alone (Sandra Bullock and Minnie Driver for example) or with their female partners (Jodie Foster and Melissa Etheridge come to mind). These women perform pregnancy and motherhood in ways that are reported in what comes close to a narrative of rebellion.

The Body Rebellious

Bodies may be a focus for control and management but this is a consequence of the unruly creativity of bodily desires. . . . There is always the possibility for resistance to forces, whether physical, biological or social, and efforts to manage bodies reflect the reality that bodies are not docile, that they are always in flux, always capable of becoming 'other.'

—Nick Fox, *The Body*[4]

Bodies can be lived in creatively, subversively, resistantly.[5] Sometimes, this resistance can be found in taking pleasure: pleasure in bodies that others find repulsive, pleasure in practices outside the norm, pleasure taking in the body itself, rather than in externalities and products.[6] Sometimes, the resistance can be found in bodily refusals to conform, in resistance to expectations, and in exuberant performances of self. Practices of daily resistance might form the groundwork for "subaltern counter-publics,"[7] and practitioners might engage in the telling of "counter-hegemonic tales" with their voices, their pens, their bodies.[8] I want to take seriously the possibility that such daily resistances might be effective "weapons of the weak,"[9] even when we are not in revolutionary settings—that daily lived and embodied practices of resistance are indeed tactics in the "art" of "not being governed."[10]

In their examination of "resistance" in practices of mothering undertaken by women who are often marginalized, Weingarten and colleagues point to the potential of such embodied resistance to craft new cultural narratives of motherhood. They pay particularly close attention to women of color, women parenting in poverty, and younger, unmarried, and lesbian mothers. Here, I pay close attention to the bold bumps of Pink, M.I.A., and Aguilera, as well as the determined absences of Foster, Bullock, Harris-Perry, and Parker. And I look toward the inscrutability of pregnant Mila Kunis and the press's seeming inability to write a narrative about her that fits with the ones already mobilized for other famous moms-to-be. In all of these women's perfor-mances of pregnancy and in the popular culture reaction to them, I do see rebellious bodies, helping to carve out spaces of resistance.

Bold Bumps

Disruption comes in many wondrous forms.

—James Scott, *Two Cheers for Anarchism*[11]

It is not coincidental that so many rebellious renderings of pregnancy seen in popular culture and media are those performed by musical artists rather than actresses. Recording as rock artists, indie artists, and rap artists, mu-sicians like Pink, Ani DiFranco, Madonna, Christina Aguilera, and M.I.A. are all claiming female space in musical genres that position themselves as antagonistic to cultural and political norms and dominant modes of rep-resentation.[12] The presence of female, let alone mothering, bodies in these genres is rebellious in itself. To a large extent, for most of its history and even when it is not aggressively misogynistic, "rock" as a genre has been gendered "masculine."[13] Key women artists across the past four decades have opened space for conversations in the popular culture around issues of sexuality, gen-der, and heteronormativity through their performances.[14]

Even more, perhaps, than rock 'n' roll, rap and hip hop are contemporary sites of resistance through music and culture jamming. Rap as a genre has been particularly marked as a space of cultural contestation over politics of race and representation,[15] where the voice of the contestation is a "black" one. Rap artists, Gwendolyn Pough argues, make "use of spectacle in ways that tell—in public—the stories that were once hidden from the larger public."[16]

Also long gendered "male," rap in a female voice can be powerfully sub-versive. Female rap artists often engage in "stage stealing" of the sort that Lau-rent Berlant examines in her treatment of "diva citizenship."[17] Berlant argues that moments of diva citizenship come when formerly disempowered women "steal the stage" and claim public space in episodic bursts that shake foun-dations. Of course, M.I.A. and Pink are not, individually, "disempowered" women—they are wealthy performers with major-label record deals. How-ever, they are female performers in genres that are often misogynistic and paternalistic, and they perform in ways that certainly attempt to trouble the sexual objectification of women and, in M.I.A.'s case, the racial and ethnic identity associated with musical stars. They are also performing at a particular moment of cultural history: a time of communicative capitalism in neoliberalism, where pessimism about the likelihood of structural change is paired with a carefree (and likely unwarranted) sense of optimism about the political power of clicking the "like" button or signing a virtual petition.[18] Berlant helps us to understand why Diva Citizens might emerge powerfully in the contemporary period. She argues that diva citizenship "tends to emerge in moments of such extraordinary political paralysis that acts of language can feel like explosives that shake the ground of collective existence."[19] While she also notes that moments of diva citizenship—of "stage stealing"—are impermanent enough to lack "world altering," structural significance, Berlant is quick to point out that such moments can indeed open and shift conversations.

Here is the importance, then, of M.I.A.'s Grammy performance. The pregga swagga claims power, and asserts her unwillingness to conform to norms associated with pregnancy and femininity. *Time* magazine named M.I.A. one of the top ten pregnant performers in all of history, and in a blog post titled "Preggers Like Us," put her on a list that included Lucille Ball's groundbreaking public pregnancy. The copy under M.I.A.'s photo read, in part, "Her belly wasn't a distraction." Rather, "it was a point of pride for women, men and hip-hop and rap fans everywhere: there was no way this star was going to miss her shot to represent as part of the group Queen Latifah introduced as the 'rap pack.' The only woman in the bunch, and boy (or girl?) did M.I.A. show it. Send her a congratulatory balloon at the hospital; she's probably there right now."[20] Indeed, she gave birth to son Ikhyd Edgar Arular Bronfman three days after the Grammy Awards performance. Ikhyd became the second most frequently searched celebrity baby of 2010—a clear indication of interest, if not revolution.

M.I.A. has continued to engage in the creation of controversial spectacle. Her diva-like feminist power was challenged by the National Football League in 2010, when the league sued her following a Super Bowl half-time performance with Nicki Minaj and Madonna (who denounced M.I.A.'s actions).[21] During the performance, M.I.A. "flipped off" the camera, aggressively offering a "fuck you" to the audience. In response to the NFL's $1.5 million suit against her, she countersued, making public statements that redounded with swagga. She took the league to task for its claim that its "wholesome" image was violated by her actions, arguing that such a claim is hypocritical in light of racist, misogynist, violent, and otherwise problematic behavior by owners, players, and coaches, and she early foreshadowed both the controversy surrounding concussions that *ESPN* and *Sports Illustrated* would break two years later and the scandal of league permissiveness regarding intimate partner violence committed by active players. In a 2013 statement, she said, "They're basically [saying] it's OK for me to promote being sexually exploited as a female, [rather] than to display empowerment, female empowerment, through being punk rock. That's what it boils down to, and I'm being sued for it."[22]

M.I.A. is not only a pregnant and mothering female rap artist; she is also a British Sri Lankan whose song "Paper Planes" does not only (or even primarily) address issues of drug dealing and gang banging in Bed-Stuy, but concerns itself with anti-immigrant sentiment in the United States and abroad. The controversies she courts are not only about gender and female empowerment. Her performances also raise issues of displacement, immigration, and belonging. According to public biographical accounts, M.I.A. was raised in northern Sri Lanka by parents committed to revolutionary and anticolonialist action. Her early life played out in a country disrupted by twelve years of civil war; her later childhood years were spent in refugee communities and derelict housing in London. Her songs contain references to the Tamil Tigers and the Palestinian Liberation Organization. She was initially denied a visa into the United States, after her vocal criticisms of the policies of the George W. Bush presidential administration caused her to be placed on a "risk list" by the Office of Homeland Security in 2006.[23] Via the "Homeland Security" remix of "Paper Planes," M.I.A. also comments on the use of extraordinary rendition, torture, and detention in the "war on terror."

M.I.A. represents an even more nonnormative performance of pregnancy in that the birthing mother is associated, traditionally and historically, with the creation, birth, and raising of citizens. Her body becomes an overt metaphor for the contested "body politic" of contemporary nation building: that body, as Rasmussen and Brown put it, that is "used in political theory to represent . . . both the ideal polity and to critique its actual manifestations . . . [which] is a powerful means of defining a political community, or the 'we' to which political appeals are made."[24] M.I.A.'s pregnant body in a context of her radical politics and the broader contexts of communicative capitalism and neoliberalism becomes a postmodern metaphor of the body politic that refuses, rather than constitutes, "a political geography that links citizenship to particular geographical and normative relationships."[25]

This metaphor and its refusal are powerfully transmitted through M.I.A.'s performance of pregnancy on the Grammys. As a way of understanding the radical nature of this refusal, it is useful to note the presence of a more conciliatory version of the body politic metaphor—one that is absent a refusal, yet still can be read as subversively powerful—visible in the performances of politically active mothering demonstrated by M.I.A.'s sometime collaborator: Christina Aguilera.

Aguilera's performances of pregnancy in 2006–2007, and more recently in 2014, are interesting for their similarities with M.I.A.'s.[26] I am also interested in the way that Aguilera's ethnic identity and party politics were constitutive parts of the discourses surrounding her pregnancies and the ways that they were shaped by the press and her actions to model a more acceptable, yet still potentially controversial, form of political engagement. During the run-up to the 2008 presidential election, Aguilera was quite active in the Rock the Vote efforts of MTV. She appeared at several events and spoke frequently of the importance of political participation for younger Americans and as an outspoken advocate for the rights of gay, lesbian, and transgender people.

Aguilera, an American-born pop star with Ecuadorian and Irish heritage, also interestingly embodies changing norms of citizenship and identity. With her ethnically marked name made even more interesting by the popular rendering of it: XTina, Aguilera's bleach blonde hair invokes racialized dichotomies that trouble our image of "Latinas" in interesting and important ways. Her politics regarding gay rights are considered progressive, and her message during Rock the Vote, though careful to be nonpartisan and avoid endorsing a candidate, was not well concealed enough that anyone was surprised when she later announced she had voted for President Obama. Yet her message was explicitly not partisan; rather, it was patriotic. In her public service announcement (PSA) for Rock the Vote, she crooned "America the Beautiful" to her infant son, Max, who she held in her arms, swaddled in an American flag.

Aguilera's PSA is powerful—the image of a mom holding a newborn wrapped in a flag is evocative of the sacrifices our sons and daughters might

one day make on behalf of democracy. The commercial is also, for rock afi-
cionados at least, an overt reference to Madonna's inaugural Rock the Vote
commercial. In that commercial twenty years prior, the pop superstar wore
a red bikini and an American flag cover-up, paired with the same bleach
blonde curls and candy apple red lip gloss that Aguilera wore in hers. Both
evoke a bygone era: they look like Marilyn Monroe and her ties to political
life via a suspected relationship with John F. Kennedy.[27] But the similarities stop there. There is no child in Madonna's commercial; the message is
grown-up and decidedly not maternal. Madonna's tag lines with the cam-
paign were resolutely aggressive and incredibly sexual. One print ad in the
series shows the pop star with the words "Vote or Else" captioning her pose;
in interviews she told reporters, "Voting is as important as having sex, because without either of them, there is no future," and "If you don't vote,
you're going to get a spanking."[28]

Aguilera's Rock the Vote efforts have a distinctly different tone. In print
work, the singer is shown with the words "The future is in our hands," and
a baby is in hers. In the extended video version of the PSA she directly addresses the camera, speaking of the importance of the suffrage movement,
the franchise for people of color, and the youth vote in the upcoming presidential election. The flag, her ethnic identity, the visual tribute to both Madonna and Monroe, and the image of the infant in her arms all write an
interesting and important story about sexuality, ethnicity, and nationhood.
Aguilera may be more babe than bold, but she troubles her evocative references to a more traditional era by inscribing a new politics of immigration,
race, and motherhood in the rock star portrayal.

Distinctly apolitical, Aguilera's contemporary performer Pink nevertheless embodies a form of motherhood that troubles and confounds the media
for being both absolutely maternal and fiercely independent. She confirmed
her pregnancy in November 2010 on the Ellen DeGeneres show, saying "I
didn't want to talk about it because I was just really nervous and I have had a
miscarriage before but if I was going to talk about it with anyone, it was going
to be with you."[29] She shows her vulnerability and concern in that moment,
but her performances while pregnant were high energy and invulnerable.

Much of the press coverage of Pink's pregnancy focused on how radical,
aggressive, and edgy she was. As a reporter for *Hollywood Life* put it, "Unlike

Mariah Carey who is singing Christmas tunes to her bump, it sounds to us like Pink's baby-to-be will be hearing a lot of edgy songs cooped up in Mama's belly!" Referring to Pink's husband, Carey Hart, who is a professional motorcycle racer, the writer goes on, "Hey, with Pink and Carey as your parents, you got to be a risk-taker!"[30] In interviews, Pink did little to dampen this image. "As soon as the baby can say 'mama,' I'm going on the road," she says. "We are going to be a traveling family gypsy band with garlands in our hair." My Baby Radio translates Pink's image this way: "She's got the spiky hair, the tattoos and she's got the attitude. There's no beating around the bush . . . Pink is one strong, independent woman."[31]

Further, Pink declined to discuss her pregnancy according to cultural expectations, wherein the woman tells a story of becoming incapacitated by morning sickness and more docile as a result. In one widely quoted interview, Pink compared herself to Kate Middleton, who famously suffered horrendous morning sickness, saying this of her experiences with pregnancy:

> I didn't have morning sickness at all; I just had genuine rage throughout my pregnancy. I'm talking *28 Days Later* rage. Demonic eyes. I wanted to kill everybody. I remember the first time my husband Carey p—d me off during my pregnancy and I bit his head off . . . his eyes glazed over, he was so scared. He realized this is how it was and he better not say another word. I wasn't pukey—I was just angry.[32]

Of this quote, the My Baby Radio blogger comments, "Fortunately, when Pink gave birth to Willow Sage last year, her hormones fell back into place."[33]

Pink refuses to perform her pregnancy according to norms, even though she is aware of them. Early in her pregnancy, she performed a rendition of her hit single "Raise Your Glass" at the American Music Awards, wearing a midriff-baring halter top and jacket combination, black harem pants, and a bandana in her hair. The *Daily News* gossip column reported that postshow the artist tweeted: "Thank you to everyone that rocked the stage with me 2nite." Referring to the swelling of her breasts accompanying pregnancy, she added, "My ta ta's were the stars of the show, let's be honest."[34] Though she objectifies her breasts in this post, Pink is an adamant breastfeeding mom; she engages in public breastfeeding in ways that desexualize that part of her body and remind viewers of their functional purpose. Postpartum, Pink tweeted and instagrammed gorgeous photos of herself breastfeeding—itself a nonnormative parenting practice in the United States.[35]

Given the taboos associated with breastfeeding, the photos of Pink nursing her daughter garnered the attention of the press. In one well-publicized shot, Pink is half-dressed in a floor-length white gown (she is getting ready to go onstage), her hair in an elegant but punk chignon. We see her tattooed back and a profile of her face. We also see her infant's head; she is clearly nursing. The photo was instagrammed in sepia tones that add a touch of instant nostalgia, a feeling of noir, a sense of glamour and high class. Another Instagram photo of Pink, dressed in a sleek black T-shirt nursing her eighteen-month-old in a Paris restaurant, was reproduced in poster form by probreastfeeding activists with the text, "Go Ahead. Ask Pink to Cover Up or Leave. I Dare You." Pink didn't perform her pregnancy quietly or meekly; even when taking a nurturing posture, she is portrayed as a ferocious and protective mama.

Other celebrity moms are also protective—but the focus of their protection comes from the intense privacy with which they guard their children, and their private lives, from the public eye. Sometimes the stars who are breaking norms associated with compulsory heterosexuality, embodied reproduction, and marital status are those who most crave and seek privacy. These celebrities raise the interesting and important question of rebellious parenting when it is typified not by presence, but by obvious absence: the absence of a man and, sometimes, the absence of a bump.[36] Lesbian celebrities and others who parent without the obvious presence of a father, as well as those celebrities who engage surrogates for their pregnancies or adopt their children are performing pregnancy and motherhood in rebellious ways by claiming maternal space absent men or absent the physical markers of pregnancy and birth.

Absent Men: Single Celebrity Moms

Though the image of the single mom has been a controversial one in American political and popular culture, *Parenting* magazine remains perky in a photo essay covering sixteen "single celebrity moms." The feature opens with this statement: "Whether they're single moms by choice, divorce or heartbreaking loss, meet famous single parent families and find out how celebs like Madonna, Sandra Bullock and Reese Witherspoon juggle the single life with kids. (Hint: they have help!) Plus, celebrity baby names we love!"[37] The photo essay goes on to profile Sandra Bullock and Sheryl Crow, both of whom adopted after breakups; Liv Tyler, Halle Berry, and Kate Hudson, who are custodial parents after divorce; and Michelle Williams, who parents solo after the death of her ex-husband Heath Ledger. Single celebrity women are mostly celebrated—they have the resources necessary to "do the job right" and parent well—while single moms in more average or conventional situations may find more disapproval or pity. Part of the celebration of these celebrity moms, then, is about their access to a lifestyle.

Part of media acceptance of these star moms comes too from their willingness to "play the game"—to acknowledge parentage or be public about their children's adoptions. This wasn't the case when Minnie Driver became a single mom in 2008. Driver was very emphatically, and very famously, tightlipped about the identity of her child's father. Though she announced the pregnancy on Jay Leno's *Tonight Show,* single-mom Driver decided not to expose her ex to public scrutiny, as they were no longer together and he was, in her words, "not famous."[38]

Driver's decision to be tight-lipped was vexing to the media. She recalled in 2012, "I was making a film at the time and the paparazzi would shout: 'Who's the sperm donor?' at me."[39] Even in 2014, a Google search of "Minnie Driver pregnant" returns more hits about the father's identity than any other aspect of the pregnancy—and until she announced his parentage and acknowledged the past relationship, much of the press focused rather salaciously on determining just who had "donated the sperm." This question is an undertone to much media coverage of lesbian moms' children.

Absent Men: "Celesbians" and Lesbian-Headed Households

Sexual politics have revolutionized in the past twenty-five years, almost simultaneous with our obsession with the baby bump. But heteronormativity remains hegemonic in the United States in our law, policy, and popular culture, and it remains extraordinary that we have celebrities that are "out" and working. In the past few years, magazines like *People* and *Us Weekly* have

begun featuring family photos of gay- and lesbian-headed households without being sensationalistic or prurient; this normalization represents progress
toward equality and acceptance. Shane Phelan has written brilliantly and persuasively on the power of "coming out," not as a moment of self-discovery,
but rather as a process of "becoming" lesbian.[40] As celebrities "become"
lesbian—as they claim their sexual identities and orientations—while we
watch, they are simultaneously working out their own sexuality and normalizing this process for a popular audience.[41]

Stars attempt to control the process of coming out, just as stars will attempt to control the release of pregnancy announcements and baby photos; and the process remains a high-stakes one for mainstream celebrities.
In fact, one of the most famous celebrities of the 1970s, 80s, and 90s, the
"intensively private" actress Jodie Foster, did not make a public statement
about her sexuality until 2012. In large measure because gay rights were not
yet salient, the mainstream press had long treated Foster's sexuality circum-
spectly, even though Foster has had a long relationship with her then-partner
Cydney Bernard, raising two sons.[42] Coverage of Foster's pregnancies in the
late 1990s offered tight-lipped answers from the star when pestered about the
fathers' identities. ABC News reported in 1998:

> Actress Jodie Foster is pregnant again, columnist Liz Smith reports, and
> as before, there's no word as to who the father might be. The 38-year-old
> actress, who has never married, is expecting her second bundle of joy in
> November. . . . However, the two-time Oscar winner won't dish on who the
> father is, or whether it's the same donor who fathered soon-to-be-3 Charlie.
> "I won't answer that," said the star. . . . Less than a year ago, Foster was the
> victim of false pregnancy rumors. Because one of her pals is actor Russell
> Crowe . . . speculation ran high that she and the gladiator were more than
> friends.[43]

A version of this report was reproduced in *People* magazine, *E! Online,* and
other mainstream sites, with heavy emphasis on the "missing" identity of the
father. Even after Foster made her sexuality public and married a female partner, celebrity gossip sites continue to obsessively wonder "who the father is,"
with many reports focusing on Foster's friend actor Mel Gibson as a likely
donor. Foster did not "become" a lesbian in terms of the public until her

acceptance speech for a Cecil B. DeMille lifetime achievement award at the Golden Globes in 2013. That evening, she acknowledged that there had long been speculation about her sexual orientation, but that those closest to her had always known the truth; she acknowledged her sons and thanked her former partner for coparenting with her.

Qparent, a webzine for parents who identify as queer, recently ran a feature of the twelve most influential lesbian and bisexual moms. While clearly offering a disruption of the heterosexual norm, features like that offered by Qparent also work hard to normalize same-sex couples and lesbian-headed households. Much like the photo editorials on People, Us Weekly, and other mainstream media sites, this article featured captioned photos of famous women and their children. Among them were singer Melissa Etheridge, comedian Wanda Sykes, television personalities Rosie O'Donnell and Sara Gilbert, and actresses Cynthia Nixon, Jane Lynch, and Jodie Foster. While the mainstream press evinces a deep desire to "out" the father in the press—to return some sense of patriarchy to the female-headed household—Qparent's coverage stressed the (female) partners of the (female) stars, and almost all of the pictures were "family" photos—the celebrity, her partner, and their children.[44]

While normalizing the families, the text also highlights the complexity of these families. Of Iron Chef star Cat Cora, Qparent reports:

[She] and wife Jennifer have four boys: Zoran, Caje, Thatcher and Nash. The children share the same anonymous sperm donor. From there, things get a little unusual. Both of the women had eggs harvested and fertilized by the donor sperm. Then Cat had Jennifer's embryo implanted and Jennifer had Cat's embryo implanted, so that each woman gave birth to her wife's biological child. That was for Zoran and Caje.

Then Jennifer had two eggs implanted, one of her own and one from Cat, which means the couple don't know for sure who Thatcher's biological mom is. At the same time Jennifer was pregnant with Thatcher, Cat was pregnant with Nash—the brothers were born just 4 months apart. Phew! Quite a family.[45]

These celebrity disruptions of heteronormative ideals of family life offer radical departures for popular culture and law. Even in legal rulings that have reinforced women's rights, the Supreme Court has been careful to offer the justices' views on the importance of heterosexual marriage and the presence of men to the lives of women and their children. In *Danforth*, for example, striking down spousal notification rules for married women seeking abortion, the court nevertheless reaffirmed the power of heteronormative marriage: "We are not unaware of the deep and proper concern and interest that a devoted and protective husband has in his wife's pregnancy and in the growth and development of the fetus she is carrying." Just as we saw with Dan Quayle's response to Murphy Brown's fictional pregnancy, the absent man has been a problem for politicians, the Court, and often for popular culture. With coverage of lesbian-headed celebrity families and attention to the bumps of "celesbian moms," contemporary popular culture is acknowledging what the state is starting to catch on to: families are not exclusively created, in Goodwin's words, "by heterosexual reproduction in the intimacy of a couple's house and the privacy of their bedroom,"[46] even in heterosexual celebrity marriages.

"Absent" Bumps

Recently, two high-profile women in heterosexual marriages made their surrogacy arrangements public. Made possible by technological innovation and covered avidly by the press, the pregnancies of Sarah Jessica Parker and Melissa Harris-Perry were not theirs to embody—or even to share publicly.

Parker and husband Matthew Broderick hired a surrogate mother to carry and birth their twin girls, born in 2009. Already parents to a son, James, the couple announced the surrogacy arrangement two months prior to the birth of the girls and stressed that infertility had led them to the process. They were successful in keeping the process, and the identity of the surrogate, a secret until close to the end of her pregnancy. The importance of keeping the arrangement private cannot be overstated. After her identity was revealed in the press, the surrogate was harassed and the subject of salacious exposés of her past. During the final weeks of her pregnancy, she had to be moved several times and kept in hiding. Eventually, a local police chief was convicted of felonies related to breach of privacy and theft of information from the surrogate: he was alleged to have been selling the information and items to paparazzi and disreputable members of the press.

Melissa Harris-Perry, an MSNBC news personality and political scientist—and therefore a rather unconventional celebrity already—announced the Valentine's Day 2014 birth of her daughter by posting Twitter photographs of herself, her husband James, and their baby in the hospital. Several celebrity news sources, including *People* magazine, picked up the story; some, like feminist publication *Jezebel*, speculated that the couple had adopted. Perry replied via Twitter, "Lovely to see so many stories welcoming our daughter. However @JamesHPerry and I did not adopt. Adoption is a loving choice but not our story." The next day, she posted the following statement on the MSNBC website: "Many people in our lives knew that we were expecting but most viewers of *MHP* were not aware of the impending arrival because I was not visibly pregnant."[47] The birth announcement goes on to tell readers that Perry gave birth to her first child, a daughter, at the age of twenty-eight. Years later, rendered unable to carry a pregnancy due to a hysterectomy to treat severe uterine fibroids, Perry used in vitro fertilization (IVF) and surrogacy. In her words, "we were blessed with a handful of potential Perrys." She continues, "It took two families, three states, four doctors, and five attorneys to get this little girl here."

In her statement, Perry cites an NBC news report that one in every hundred babies born in the United States in 2012 was conceived with the aid of advanced fertility treatment.[48] That number represents around 1.5 percent of all live births each year. Though Perry notes, and I agree, that this growth is exponential from mere years ago, it must be clear that 1.5 percent is still not anywhere near "normal," in the same way that 2 percent of births being planned out-of-hospital birth means that homebirth is still considered "fringe." Harris-Perry and her husband, like Parker and Broderick, undertook rebellious action in the construction of their family.[49] The "absent bump"—in other words, a bump not performed by the star who will raise the child—raises eyebrows and gets attention in ways that further denaturalize pregnancy and birth and again open realms of possibilities for ways of being pregnant and performing pregnancy and mothering.

There seems to be little room for debate: media portrayals of Sarah Jessica Parker and Melissa Harris-Perry show resistance to norms of embodiment surrounding pregnancy, as do stories about Jodie Foster, Cat Cora, Pink, and M.I.A. These rebellious renderings, though, coupled with the refusal of stars like Kristen Bell to lose all the baby weight in record time and the work of

Bell and Shepard, Garner and Affleck, and Halle Berry to stop profiteering from paparazzi photos all gave me some measure of hope for a resistant politics of mothering and resistant performances of the baby bump in the public eye. In their transgressive performances of nonnormative mothering, these celebrities are expanding the space available within which "legitimate" and "good" mothering takes place. Because attention to these pregnancies breaks to some extent from the tropes of "good girls, bad girls, and hot sexy mamas," media coverage of them seems to help to expand the available categories of performances of motherhood.

Simultaneously, though—and of course because they are celebrities—these women's images while pregnant and mothering are being used to sell and commodify, to brand them and associate them with particular practices that connect them to consumers. While they seem to be engaging in feminist acts of resistance against patriarchal norms associated with how we "should" be pregnant and parent, they are also rather wholeheartedly engaging in activities that serve to commodify the experience. Indeed, it is almost impossible for them not to.[50]

Additionally, the evidence of such resistance and rebellion manifested in these stars may serve to reinforce a dominant, regressive law and politics—one that seeks heightened surveillance and control. Postmodern disciplinary institutions—the dispersed state and its proxies in the market and the media—cannot trust, not completely, that we—female, pregnant, reproducing—are obedient, especially when the press gives us such compelling examples of refusal. Unable to guarantee our docility, those institutions have often used the excuse of the rebellious subject—the mother who doesn't enact her pregnancy as she "should"—to enact further surveillance and control on even the most docile, disciplined, and obedient bodies.

Clearly, if we are going to be disobedient, we should be wary. It is just as likely that nonnormative mothering practices will cause backlash as they will give rise to celebration. We still do have projects of governance that inspect, judge, watch, and penalize women for how they enact their pregnancies; the pages of this book are full of them. I am dismayed by and tired of such practices.

But the continued commercial and critical success of all of the women I've discussed in this chapter—simultaneous to their rebellious renderings of their pregnant and mothering bodies—gives me some reason to hope for expanded options for women in the performance of their more average, mundane pregnancies. This is welcome optimism because—I have to be honest—throughout the writing of this book, I felt increasingly hopeless about the implications of media coverage of and treatment of pregnant celebrities.

And then actress Mila Kunis announced her pregnancy, and the more attention I paid to coverage of her growing bump, the more hopeful I began to feel. The more I watched her and the press coverage of her pregnancy, the less certain I became of the narrative around and about her. That lack of a coherent narrative—Kunis's inscrutability to those who watch her closely—is a space for playful subversion. Kunis performs what I call a "micropolitics of inscrutability."

A Micropolitics of Inscrutability: Simply Living as Everyday Resistance

Mila Kunis is an American television and film star and the partner of Ashton Kutcher, who, coincidentally, was previously married to Demi Moore—a trailblazer in her own right, recall, when it comes to pregnancy. Kunis is a naturalized citizen who moved with her family to the United States from the former Soviet Union in 1991. Her heritage is Ukrainian, but she became famous for her role as the stereotypical spoiled rich American suburban girl Jackie Burkhardt on the extraordinarily popular series *That '70s Show,* which ran on Fox from 1998 to 2006. Jackie's naïveté and vanity bordered on parody, and Kunis's flat affect was brilliant. Her fictional character dated Ashton Kutcher's fictional character, Michael Kelso, though the two actors were not romantically linked until long after the series ended. Rather, she had a long and intensely private relationship with actor Macaulay Culkin; Kutcher was married to Moore for eight years.

Kunis had roles in feature films as early as 2001, but transitioned to film stardom in 2008 with her award-winning role in the Judd Apatow comedy *Forgetting Sarah Marshall.* Her breakthrough dramatic role was arguably that of Lily in the psychological thriller *Black Swan.* In that film, she played a psychotic ballerina against Natalie Portman's more innocent foil.

The press is often ill at ease with Kunis, who exudes self-confidence and has, as a writer for *Hollywood Reporter* puts it, "a smirk of self-assurance."[51]

The role of Lily seemed to exacerbate media discomfort while also gaining her critical acclaim. Critic Guy Lodge wrote this of her acting in *Black Swan:* "It's the cool, throaty-voiced Kunis who is the surprise package here, intelligently watching and reflecting her co-star in such a manner that we're as uncertain as Nina of her ingenuousness."[52] Yet she's slight and beautiful—or, as the press began to call her when her pregnancy began to show, "adorable." Her beauty seems to make her intelligence all the more surprising, and she refuses to consistently perform stardom as a bombshell. Kunis does have scantily clad magazine covers to her credit, and she is routinely named on lists of the "Sexiest Women Alive," or "Hottest Women" by men's magazines and in the celebrity-focused press. She acknowledged in 2013 that she was honored to be thought of as sexy. But, she told the *Los Angeles Times,* "You've got to base your career on something other than being FHM's top 100 number one girl. Your looks are going to die out, and then what's going to be left?"[53]

In her unscripted public appearances, Kunis often plays the tough or the heavy, though the press can't seem to believe it's really her. One widely circulated video of a press conference for the movie *Friends with Benefits* shows her speaking fluent Russian in a spirited defense of her costar Justin Timberlake.[54] In the ninety-second clip, we see Kunis chewing gum and repeatedly saying "Huh?" while also giving hard stares and an almost existential critique of a reporter's question. At one point the reporter asks Timberlake, already a successful musician, why he has become an actor. Kunis fixes her with a stare and asks, "Well, why are *you* here?" At the end of the exchange, Timberlake— who has been listening to a time-delayed translation on an earpiece, laughs and says of Kunis, "She's my bodyguard." Kunis, according to coverage of the event, "smacks down" the Russian reporter and is "definitely someone you'd want to have in your corner" in a fight. Yet the media still finds her too cute and adorable to be fully threatening.

E! Online posted a photo of Kunis and Kutcher visiting her family in Los Angeles in June 2014.[55] As with much of the coverage of her pregnancy, the author cannot seem to write a coherent story about Kunis. She writes that Kunis "flaunts" her bump in a "tight top" (actually, a Nike workout top and matching pants); her belly is a bit too big (but she has an "adorably protruding belly button"); her hair is in a "messy (but cute!) bun," and she's not wearing any makeup. The main text of the first two sentences of the paragraph set up a Britney Spears comparison—a bad girl performing her pregnancy poorly. But the author finds Kunis too "adorable" to censure, and parenthetical asides construct her as harmlessly cute and healthily diligent. Writing about the same photo, an author for *US Weekly* notes that Kunis is "one low-maintenance mom-to-be" in a "sweet romance" with Kutcher; she is "cutely casual" and "no fuss."[56]

But what happens when the object of Kunis's takedown isn't a Russian reporter, but an American man and when she seems decidedly "high maintenance?" In early summer 2014, Kunis appeared on *Jimmy Kimmel Live,* and a scripted portion of that interview soon went viral: within five days of the show airing, the authorized YouTube video had been seen 1.5 million times. At the beginning of the skit, Kimmel tells Kunis, "My wife and I are pregnant; we are having a baby soon." In response, Kunis unclips her microphone and stalks to center stage in a fake huff, announcing, "I have a very special message for all soon-to-be-fathers: stop saying you're pregnant!" She asks rhetorically, "Do you get to squeeze a watermelon-sized person out your lady hole? . . . When you wake up and throw up, is it because you're nurturing a human life?" No, Kunis answers, "It's because you had too many shots of tequila," which is off limits for women, who, she announces, "*can't have anything,*" because "we've got your little love goblin growing inside of us." Kunis knows that pregnant women are surveilled, that their actions are regulated. Certainly she is surveilled; but in the skit she acknowledges that it is *all* of us—all women pregnant or at risk of becoming so. Her solution, in this skit at least, is to form a coalition of resistant pregnant women. At the close of her monologue, Kunis is joined on stage by a multicultural group of pregnant women, holding pints of ice cream and plastic spoons, who announce, "You're not pregnant, we are!"[57]

The commentator for Yahoo TV who introduces this clip has a complex reaction to Kunis's words. She introduces the segment with sympathy for Kimmel, who was "bumped" from the conversation by Kunis and her "rather large baby bump" and notes with disdain that Kunis has already perfected her "classic mom shush." And though she says Kunis is her "hero," she does it in language and tone that parodies the idea and can only find common ground in gentle man hating: she closes her commentary with a sigh, saying, "Men, ugh." Yet another treatment of the skit announced "Kunis Against

FIGURE 6.2 Mila Kunis on *Jimmy Kimmel Live*. Photo credit: ABC News. Sourced at: desmoinesregister.com

Men" for its headline before clarifying that she is against men "saying they are pregnant."

But we know that Kunis isn't "antimen"—we've seen her defend Justin Timberlake and gush over the moment of her engagement to Kutcher. We also know that she isn't really disgruntled with being pregnant. Kunis articulates pregnancy as a choice—as something she "wanted" and "loves." She has internalized norms associated with a biopolitics of responsibilization and has been frequently quoted, from an earlier appearance on the *Ellen DeGeneres Show,* saying, "I did this to myself—I might as well do it right. . . . I wanted this. It's like, no one made me do this." But she also disrupts this responsibilization by planning an out-of-the-mainstream unmedicated labor and delivery and talking about it graphically and raunchily. Kunis also says she looks forward to being a parent, telling *US* Weekly that she hopes her children will not be "assholes." Speaking of her plans for parenting with Kutcher, she says, "Both of us just want to have well-behaved, honest, nice children who people meet and say, 'That's a good kid.'"[58]

In the same article, though, she says that she expects her "vag" will be "shredded" by birth and that she's thrilled her breasts have swelled during pregnancy. Kunis seems unwilling or unable to perform her pregnancy in a way that fits "good girl" stereotypes, yet she is not tabloid fodder and clearly hasn't been typed a "bad girl." Kunis reads in the mainstream press as almost too raunchy to be intelligent, but simultaneously too intelligent and independent to be "hot and sexy" and too young to play the MILF. She actually seems to not be *performing* the pregnancy at all; rather, she's simply *being* pregnant. Pop culture commentators don't seem to know what to do with Kunis, and she gives them very little to work with.

During her pregnancy, Kunis didn't have a Facebook page, a Twitter account, or an Instagram, and though she's sacrificed some of her famously "intense" attachment to her own privacy by being public about her pregnancy, she planned to maintain her privacy with Kutcher, who she said would stay "head-to-head" rather than "head-to-vag" during the birth.[59] After their daughter was born, the couple gave her the gender-inscrutable name "Wyatt Isabel," and Kutcher, famous for his practical jokes on the MTV series *Punk'd*, released a photo of the baby—embedded in a gallery of photos of babies (some human, some not), promising that one of them was his daughter, but refusing to indicate which one. It is precisely here, in a micropolitics that relies on jokes and joy, and in a refusal to give mainstream and tabloid press a coherent script, that I see a place of hope, a possibility for Kunis's own self-definition that the rest of us could model.

The tradition of law and society scholarship has long been diagnostic and critical of the status quo. It has also been emancipatory and hopeful. In his five-volume compilation of "possibilities," Boaventura de Sousa Santos argues that there are viable alternatives to neoliberalism and that it is the job of scholars to point them out and make them known.[60] He argues that we must attend to silences—spaces that aren't making the news, people that aren't grabbing headlines—in order to find some of the most radical actions toward liberation.[61] His work highlights the local, discrete, contextualized resistances to neoliberal attempts at hegemony and shows them to be vibrant and important.

Inscrutable and rebellious performances of celebrity pregnancies may feel very different from a worker's collective in the global south or the Occupy Movement or the loosely coordinated, widespread, and quite effective protests in the wake of events in Ferguson, Missouri. *But the stakes are just as high, and the potential for emancipation just as present.* In an earlier article, Santos argues that we can employ new metaphors for conceiving of, and living with, law. These metaphors include "the baroque," which relies on carnival, celebration, and radical joyful action—and "the frontier," which is where we make new rituals and traditions out of the simple practices of our daily lives.[62] Santos's later work makes clear that "different forms of oppression or domination generate equally distinct forms of . . . resistance, mobilization, subjectivity, and identity."[63] Surveillance and regulatory control of women's bodies through the proxies generated by the presence of a "bump" are uniquely neoliberal in their current manifestations. It makes sense, then, that the uniquely neoliberal manifestation of contemporary celebrity would be the place we should look to find counterhegemonic strategies of resistance.

Similarly, at the close of his emancipatory musings in *Two Cheers for Anarchism*, political theorist and activist James Scott writes that "our desire for clean narratives and the need for elites and organizations to project an image of control and purpose all conspire to convey a false image of historical causation."[64] Kunis denies the press the ability to write a clean narrative of her pregnancy. By remaining inscrutable, Kunis highlights the fact that the project of governing pregnant women through attention to their bodies and behaviors is an incomplete project, and necessarily so. As James Scott reminds us, "Most revolutions are not the work of revolutionary parties but the precipitate of spontaneous and improvised actions . . . disorderly, unpredictable, spontaneous action."[65] If Kunis and Kutcher can seem spontaneous and improvised, perhaps so can we.

No, we cannot hang our liberation on the baby bump of Mila Kunis, even when we read her inscrutability next to the outright rebellions of artists like M.I.A. and the subversions of Minnie Driver, Jodie Foster, and Sarah Jessica Parker. And we might pause before getting too caught up celebrating any part of the cultural force at work in the coverage of stars' pregnancies. There are structural and political forces to be reckoned with, and we should not be overly distracted by cupcakes and glossy photos. But the fact that resistance and rebellion exist and are celebrated in popular culture is important. Such resistance, intentional or not, can be difficult. Resistance to domination need not always be purposive and intentional in order to exist; nor need it always be directly revolutionary.

Writing about resisting the ageism of contemporary culture, Margaret Morganroth Gullette put it this way: in conditions of hegemony, sometimes "any lame thing will do to break the automaticity."[66] Certainly, the accumulation of daily resistant practices of inscrutability do just that—they make us think, and in so doing, open space for possibilities beyond the automatic, beyond the habitual.

Perhaps one day we *will* inhabit entirely a society of complete control. Dave Eggers's dystopic novel *The Circle* chillingly envisions a world—not too far off—when we rate every interaction, map every location, photograph every beautiful thing, share every story. He sees the role of capital in creating markets for these previously private data points and imagines the structural and normative forces that will work to force us to share parts of ourselves that we might prefer to keep sacred. Perhaps some day, indeed, that will be our world.

I hope not.

As of now, we live in a society of incomplete control. Surveillance is necessary precisely because the project of crafting the perfectly docile neoliberal consumer-subject-citizen is necessarily incomplete. Consumerism only goes so far in controlling and channeling our impulses, especially when most people can't afford (or don't want to buy) $80 yoga pants. Even dominant culture representations of yummy mummies must acknowledge the Halle Berrys and Salma Hayeks in our midst; we need only look at media coverage of Britney Spears to recall that even white, wealthy, thin females sometimes seem to be inadequately disciplined. And we must be honest—the majority of women are not celebrities, not even pale versions of yummy mummies: we are not white or wealthy or thin. Most of us are simply living our lives—with the luxury of flying under the radar. Our bodies are not completely docile, not wholly tamed. To the extent that we can remain inscrutable to those who might watch us, perhaps we can remain a bit more free.

Self-surveillance has not (yet) become completely hegemonic; we are not completely and totally disciplined and docile—nor are those we watch and want. We witness a state, political actors, and their proxies that still seek to surveil and regulate women, in large part because they worry about their lack of capacity to enact control. We witness state formations that offshore, as it were, their reach to other domains and proxies.

In the coming years, some of us will choose to enact our pregnancies boldly and radically. Some of us will be pregnant absent what convention tells us we need: a bump, a husband, modesty, a convincing narrative. Some of us will refuse to be, or to remain, pregnant.[67] In these ways, we will enact a micropolitics of resistance and inscrutability. Emancipation and liberation are achieved through small, inscrutable daily practices of living under the radar of the watching state and its proxies; all women can attempt those small resistances. Individual action will not be sufficient, of course, but coordination is not always necessary when we participate in a politics that engages structural inequalities perpetuated by the global spread of neoliberal capital formations. Doing so, we will engage in imagining and enacting counterpublics and writing counternarratives that may one day have the power to successfully resist neoliberal formations that have power over us. In that way, we can begin to inhabit those domains reserved for the state and its proxies, reserved for commodification and surveillance. We can together endeavor to become counterproxies: the resistant, refusing, rebellious, and inscrutable (often, maternal) bodies upon which freedom may be written.

NOTES

Notes to Introduction

1. Website visitor data gathered from www.SEMRush.com. SEMRush data tracks web visitors worldwide, with searchability for specific terms, locales, and dates on each site searched.

2. Throughout the book, I will use "star" and "celebrity" interchangeably, though there are interesting differences in their construction and meaning, from the perspective of celebrity studies and cultural theory.

3. Mann 2012; Harvey 2005.

4. Foucault 2010 (1978–1979).

5. Buttenwieser 2007, 23.

6. Buttenwieser also notes that attention to celebrity pregnancy as an individualized and personal issue means that structural problems—lack of access to "affordable child care, paid parental leave, and universal healthcare among them," go unremarked upon in the press (26).

7. Yanow and Schwartz-Shea 2006; Yanow 2003.

8. As Wendy Brown puts it, for interpretivists "causation is a poor analytical modality for appreciating the genealogical relationship . . . *a relationship that is complexly interconstitutive*" (Brown 1995, 183; emphasis added).

9. Cramer 2012; Cramer 2009.

10. DeVault 1990; Smith 1987.

11. Alexander-Floyd 2012; Bedolla 2007; Hancock 2007; Strolovitch 2007; Crenshaw 2001; Collins 2000; Collins 1998; Crenshaw 1989.

12. Banks 1999; Austin 1999; Montoya 1994; Roberts 1992; Caldwell 1991; Ikemoto 1991; Wildman 1984.

13. West 1987.

14. Ruddick 1995.

15. Anzaldua and Moraga 1995 (1981); Walker 2004, 2001; Lorde 1995, 1984, 1978.

16. Jordan-Zachary, forthcoming.

17. Firestone and Koedt, 1970.

18. Cruikshank 1999; Stone 1997.

19. Gullette 2002; Roberts 1998; Solinger 2007; Fineman 1995; Bassin, Honey, and Kaplan 1994; Collins 1992; Rothman 1988–1989.

20. Sarat 2000.

21. By taking a constitutive understanding, scholars in the field necessarily grapple with the indeterminacy of law, the relationships between the "semi-autonomous social fields" of law and society (Moore 1973), law's potential to be responsive, its role in social control, and its lack of complete hegemony (Lazarus-Black and Hirsch 1994; Scott 1985). Sociolegal scholars are very interested in law and its potential for disruption, via its deep relationship with culture and society (Darian-Smith and Fitzpatrick 1999; Mertz 1994).

22. Nonet and Selznick 2001 (1978); Erlanger, Chambliss, and Melli 1987; Ewing 1987; Teubner 1983; Moore 1973.

23. Passavant 2001; Norrie 1999.

24. Sarat and Kearns 1998.

25. As Kitty Calavita puts it in her "invitation" to the field, law and society scholars are interested in "law *as it is lived* in society" (Calavita 2010, 3; emphasis added). They thus realize that "law [is] far from an autonomous entity residing somewhere above the fray of society—[law] coincides with the shape of society and is part and parcel of its fray. . . . [L]aw is not just shaped to the everyday life of a society, but permeates it, even at times and in places where it may not at first glance appear to be" (Calavita 2010, 8).

26. Denvir 1996.

27. Denvir, xii.

28. Clover 1998; Garber 1998.

29. Sarat 2011; Manderson 2011. Richard Sherwin makes a further important point related to the project I undertake in this book. Sherwin stresses the importance of understanding the visual rhetorics of popular culture, not just the narratives of them (Sherwin 2011, 110–111). He writes, "It is important to realize that the way we respond to visual images is different, as a perceptual and cognitive matter, from the way we respond to words alone" (Sherwin 2011, 110).

30. More recently, though, Lorenz has theorized music as a form of jurisprudence; and Susan Burgess's work on YouTube representations of the discourses of the Founding Fathers uses popular culture to elaborate an understanding of foundational political theories of liberty and democracy. Burgess 2009; Lorenz 2005.

31. Rapping 2003.

32. Sarat and Kearns 1998, 2.

33. Coombe 1998, 37.

34. Ibid.

35. Coombe, 51.

36. Sarat and Kearns, 47.

37. Though it is not the focus of her essay, Coombe does not disagree. By the end

of it, she writes, "The heuristic value of exploring law *culturally*, I suggest, is a more focused and politicized emphasis upon meaning in domains traditionally preoccupied with questions of power. Similarly, the dividends realized from studying culture *legally* is the greater specificity and materiality afforded to understandings of power in fields largely focused upon meaning. The social force of signification and the material weight of meaning are simultaneously brought to the fore in such endeavors" (Coombe, 60).

38. Haltom and McCann 1994.

39. Van Krieken 2012; Sternheimer 2011; Dyer and McDonald 2004; Dyer 2003; Wojcik 2003; Schickel 2000; Marshall 1997; Inglis 1988. These more contemporary renderings—and this book, as well—owe much to Marcuse (1964); Althusser 1997 (1971); Adorno and Horkheimer (1944); and Bourdieu's work on charisma (1980).

40. Marshall 1997, ix.

41. In chapter two, I unpack the now commonplace that "celebrity" is a space within which we "idealize" and "identify" stars as individuals. We idealize particular types of pregnancies and pregnant bodies and allow them to tutor women on the proper expression of their reproductive capacities. Chapter three takes up Dryer's thesis that celebrity becomes a commodity. Though my work here is informed by the work of Marshall and Dyer, neither of them elaborate a theory of surveillance as attached to celebrity; I contribute that piece in chapter four.

42. Marshall, x; emphasis added.

43. Marshall 72.

44. Dyer 2007a, 80–81.

45. Marshall, x and 43.

46. Dallek 2000; Rogin 1987; Dallek 1984.

47. Dyer 2007a, 79.

48. Wojcik, 224.

49. Marshall, 72.

50. Van Krieken, 10.

51. Marshall 17; see also Dyer.

52. Marshall, 85.

53. Marshall, 9.

54. Dixon 2003, 99.

55. Marshall, 58.

56. Marshall 4; see also Dyer 2007a.

57. Marshall, 92.

58. Dixon, 96.

59. Marshall, 93.

60. Marshall, 92.

61. Marshall, 62.

62. Dyer 2007a, 83–84.

63. Liesen and Walsh 2012, 6.

64. Liesen and Walsh, 6.

65. Dean 2009; Hardt and Negri 2001 and 1994; Simon 2001; Rose 1999. Passavant

grants that "the present state formation functions to achieve its ends in a significantly distinct manner from the Cold War state," yet he asserts, "nonetheless, just because the post-Fordist state of today governs through a neo-liberal rationality, we should not mis-characterize this state formation as either small, weak, or as heralding the end of 'big government'" (Passavant 2005, 2 and 4).

66. Dean writes, "to succeed . . . neoliberalism depends on the organized political occupation and direction of governments, on the use of the bureaucratic, legal, and security apparatuses of the state in ways that benefit corporate and financial interests" (Dean, 49.)

67. Dean, 11.

68. Dean, 132–133. Dean terms our present state formation "communicative capital-ism," which she defines as "the materialization of ideals of inclusion and participation in information, entertainment, and communication technologies in ways that capture resistance and intensify global capitalism" (2).

69. Inglis 1988.

70. Dean 2009, 4 and 16.

71. As Foucault predicted, a "veritable discursive explosion" has developed "around the mother/child relationships" through several techniques, including the deployment of a "normalizing, discursive power" (Liesen and Walsh, 6.)

72. Ouellette 2011, 159.

73. Ouellette, 164.

74. Dean 2009, 132.

Notes to Chapter 1

1. Longhurst 2002, 464.

2. Longhurst, 455.

3. Importantly, one of the downsides to this protective attitude was that women were also considered unfit to "participate in civic life, branded as inferior to men, de-nied economic rights, and subjected to their husbands' rule in the family" (Cushman 2001, 1). Men, conversely, while given power and authority in the home as the "head of household"—performed most of their life in the public sphere: at work, in church, in government. Of course, the purported split between "public and private" spaces is most certainly socially and legally constructed, rather than naturally occurring. Such a split is enormously problematic, as it denies that significant numbers of women were already in paid and unpaid employment far prior to the 1950s and 60s. A reification of the public-private split can also work to deny the infiltration of patriarchy into the home—the private sphere—which is constructed as the "female" realm in this narrative. And it fails to recognize that many women still have not entered "public life" in a way that renders them powerful advocates on their own behalf. In fact, the "public" and the "private"—the state and the social—are mutually constitutive realms. The language and reality of the ideology of separate spheres, though referring to a construction, has had profound implications for women's lives. When looked at from the frame of a public-private split, women have viewed feminism as the emancipatory process of becoming

accepted and powerful in public spaces. Feminism, then, is the vehicle by which women enter public life by holding paid employment, for example, and run for office. It also becomes a vehicle through which issues of pregnancy, birth, abortion, and parenting become visible—and enter the realm of public policy, jurisprudence, and legislation. See Bottomley, Gibson, and Meteyard, 1987; Harstock 1983; Solinger 2007; and Fraser 1997.

4. Earle 2003, 248.

5. When actress Lucille Ball and her in-life and on-screen husband, Desi Arnaz, were expecting their first child in 1952, the network took the revolutionary step of writing it into the story line of their television show. However, the television network and Federal Communications Commission agreed that the word "pregnant" could not be used to describe her condition and the Ball-Arnaz couple stayed in separate beds for the duration of the sitcom. See Davis-Floyd 1992; and Solinger.

6. See, for example, Luker 1985; Fineman and Karpin 1995; Cushman 2001; Baer 1999; Solinger 2007.

7. Vogel 1990; Rubin 1984; Fineman 1995; Edwards 1996; Solinger and May 2000; Lens 2003; Schneider and Wildman 2011.

8. Solinger 2007, 13.

9. The institution of slavery relied upon white control of the reproductive capacity of black men and women, and slave masters instituted brutal means to ensure the forced reproduction of those they held in captivity. Using rape to force enslaved women to reproduce, the state and plantation owners denied them of the ability to make human choices about their reproductive capacity—and that denial occurred in the service of economic self-interest and state building (Roberts 1987). At the same time, colonial overseers brutally sterilized hundreds of thousands of indigenous women as a part of state-building policies (see Carpio 2004; Lawrence 2000; Torpy 2000; Smith 1999; Lujan 1996; Rodriguez-Trias 1978; Dillingham 1977). Whiteness as we understand it today was not the only metric by which worthiness to parent was measured. Eugenicists also tied moral worth to intellectual development and valued some people over others (Roberts 61–65). In the early 1900s, twenty-three states had general prosterilization laws in place; by 1940, at least forty thousand women had been sterilized. One of the most famous of these is Carrie Buck. The Supreme Court affirmed the state's mandate of her sterilization in 1927, in a decision that is appalling for its brutal language and impact. Of the state of Virginia's decision to sterilize seventeen-year-old Buck, Justice Oliver Wendell Holmes wrote, "It is better for all the world if, instead of waiting to execute degenerate off-spring for crime, or to let them starve for their imbecility, society can prevent those who are manifestly unfit from continuing their kind." Buck was sterilized after giving birth to a daughter, Vivian, while held at the Virginia State Colony for Epileptics and Feebleminded, to whose care her foster parents had committed Buck, after she became pregnant as a result of rape. Speaking of the fact that Carrie Buck was the daughter of a woman also deemed "unfit" to parent, and also committed to the Colony, because of a history of prostitution, "immorality" and sexually transmitted diseases, Holmes concluded, "Three generations of imbeciles is enough." *Buck v. Bell* 24 U.S. 200 (1927).

10. Bassin, Honey, and Kaplan 1994, 2.

11. Solinger 2007.

12. Cushman, 165.

13. Wildman 1984, 271.

14. Solinger, 92.

15. *Muller v. Oregon* 208 U.S. 412 (1908).

16. *Bradwell v. Illinois* 83 U.S. (16 Wall) 130 (1873).

17. Solinger, 13.

18. Cushman, 165.

19. Cushman, 165.

20. Quoted in Cushman, at 165–166.

21. *Cleveland Board of Education v. LaFleur* 414 U.S. 632 (1974).

22. Shortly after the LaFleur case was decided, the Court heard *Turner v. Department of Employment Security of Utah* 434 U.S. 44 (1975). In its *per curiam* decision, the Court ruled that Utah's denial of unemployment insurance to pregnant women, from three months prior to their due date until six weeks after, was an unconstitutional violation of the due process clause, as well as the doctrine newly announced in *LaFleur*.

23. 381 U.S. 479 (1965).

24. 405 U.S. 438 (1972).

25. 410 U.S. 113 (1973).

26. Luker, 22–23.

27. 428 U.S. 52 (1976).

28. Munford and Waters 2014, 45.

29. Munford and Waters, 148; also the Archive of American Television at http://www
.emmytvlegends.org/interviews/shows/maude; last accessed June 9, 2014.

30. http://www.tv.com/shows/category/comedy/decade/1970s and http://www.tv
.com/shows/category/drama/decade/1980s; both accessed last June 8, 2014.

31. Lehman, 1–2. In her genealogy of the designation, Lehman writes: "The term 'single girl' emerged in the 1960s as an appealing alternative to 'spinster,' and it characterized the unmarried woman as youthful and playful well into her thirties. By calling themselves 'girls,' single women treated the period between schooling and marriage as an extended adolescence and resisted the adult pressures to marry and have children" (Lehman, 3). But it was always clear, to the audience and to the "girls," that eventually they would "grow up"—marry, have sex, have children—and move to separate beds and flannel nightgowns. Thus, professional (and even sexual) aspirations could be played with, toyed with, and then put aside when "real life" began. Being a "single girl," Lehman writes, provided young women "the opportunity to live a little before getting married"; it did not constitute "opposition to marriage itself" (Lehman, 70).

32. And, a decade or so earlier, *Peyton Place* (1956) and *Sex and the Single Girl* (1962).

33. The single woman of the 1970s was portrayed in the media as a "living liberated" (Lehman, 116). This portrayal of a particular kind of "liberation" had mixed effects. "On the one hand, media identified a woman's decision to live alone and pursue a career as a political act, and sitcoms gently broached singles' struggles for equality in the workplace. On the other hand, mainstream media's overreliance on the successful

white middle-class single woman as a symbol of feminism minimized the movement's relevance across lines of class, race, and marital status, and it suggested that women had 'made it' in a male-dominated world" (Lehman, 117).

34. Lehman, 96.

35. Friedman 2007.

36. The demographic of single, urban, professional young women, and their purchasing power, *was* expanding in this era. Lehman notes, "In the early 1960s, unmarried women were a smaller, marginalized demographic group. . . . [B]y the mid-1960s, single working women had become an economic force in their own right—according to *Time*, urban singles [men and women] were a $70 billion market by 1967" (Lehman, 3).

37. Cushman, 173.

38. Strebeigh 2009, 118.

39. Strebeigh, 80–85.

40. Feminist legal theory at the time was rather silent, but within two decades, many feminist scholars expressed anger and shock at this reasoning. As Christine Littleton wrote in 1991, "The phallocentricity of equality is most apparent in the extraordinary difficulty the legal system has had dealing with the fact that women (and *not* men) conceive and bear children" (Littleton 1991, 42).

41. 417 U.S. 484 (1974).

42. 429 U.S. 125 (1976).

43. Strebeigh, 417, emphasis added.

44. In 1977, and in line with developing jurisprudence in the realm of abortion, the Court moderated its tone a bit, stating in *Nashville Gas Co. v. Satty* (434 U.S. 136 [1977]) that employers could withhold benefits to pregnant women, but those women could not be *unduly burdened* by employment policies, if and when they returned to work; that is, once they were no longer pregnant, women could not face workplace discrimination. The Court would continue to develop the "undue burden" standard—most predominantly in its jurisprudence surrounding abortion rights.The Court began to articulate this standard in *Bellotti v. Baird* 443 U.S. 622 (1979), ruling that state regulations that "unduly burdened" a woman's access to abortion would be struck. In this case, the Court once again struck a law requiring parental permission for a minor's abortion, absent a judicial bypass option. And the Court once again reified a normative American family where rational decision making in a context of love and access to resources was present. Powell wrote, "Parents naturally take an interest in the welfare of their children—an interest that is particularly strong where a normal family relationship exits and where the child is living with one or both parents," though he and the justices joining his decision recognized that not all minor females would have access to a "normal" and functioning family. It was not until 1992, and Justice O'Connor's decision in *Planned Parenthood v. Casey* (503 U.S. 833 [1992]), that we would see a full articulation of the undue burden standard, and in the intervening years the Court permitted states and the federal government wide latitude to burden access to the right.

45. See Cruikshank 1996.

46. Lichtenstein 1994, 199.

47. Zeisler 2008, 74.

48. *Cagney and Lacey* aired from 1982–1988. As would continue to be true in other popular culture renderings from 1980 on, the primary controversy surrounding the series concerned Cagney's sexual orientation. Sharon Gless replaced the original actress portraying Cagney in the show's second season, in large part because she cut a more traditionally feminine form and was not associated with gay rights or lesbian identity. See Zeisler, as well as http://www.emmytvlegends.org/interviews/shows/cagney-lacey; last accessed June 12, 2014.

49. See Faludi, 1991, for an account of the backlash against women raging in the late 1980s.

50. Lehman, 164. Fred Strebeigh argues that congressional passage of the ERA, more than forty years after its first introduction as a bill, actually led the U.S. Supreme Court to do *less* to remedy discrimination against women in the workplace in the 1970s and 80s. He convincingly demonstrates that the justices preferred legislative options for rights claiming and, believing a legislative and constitutional remedy was soon at hand, the Court ruled more narrowly for the next decade than it might have, absent provisional passage of the ERA (Strebeigh, 61). However, the amendment faced resistance from cultural conservatives in the Church of Latter Day Saints, as well as fundamentalist evangelical Christians, embodied most emphatically in Phyllis Schlafly. The amendment had also faced resistance from progressives like members of the executive committee of the American Civil Liberties Union, and even the League of Women Voters, which, until the early 1970s, feared that the amendment's provisions might overturn restrictive labor legislation that "protected" women (Strebeigh, 117), the residue of *Muller v. Oregon*. Ultimately, the states failed to ratify the ERA, and the Court had the opportunity to rule on cases that impacted women's work lives, as well as their reproduction—but it did so absent a constitutional mandate to gender equality, and via a stingy reading of the 14th Amendment's Equal Protection Clause.

51. Olsen 1993, 91.

52. Part of this managerial move was necessitated by the growing divorce rate; Rubin notes that by 1984, nearly one in every two marriages would end in divorce. See Rubin throughout, but especially pages 36–37 and 106–107.

53. Abortion "all but disappeared from the horizons of popular culture" by the late 1980s (Zeisler, 149).

54. Solinger, 150.

55. Fineman 1993.

56. Karpin 1997, 131.

57. The 1980s was a time of increasing restrictions on abortion access. The Court's decisions after *Harris v. McRae*, in *City of Akron v. Akron Center for Reproductive Health* (462 U.S. 416 [1983]) and *Thornburgh v. American College of Obstetricians and Gynecologists* (476 U.S. 747 [1986]) both revisited some of the issues at stake in previous restrictive laws—reaffirming the Court's previous holdings—as well as covered new ground, with the Court rejecting limits on the types of procedures by which abortion could be performed and rejecting limits on the locations allowable for legal abortion. In 1986,

Missouri enacted sweeping legislation meant to limit access to abortion, including a preamble that defined "life" as beginning at conception, a prohibition of the use of public facilities to perform abortion, a prohibition against state or public employees from performing abortion, a prohibition on the use of any public funding for counseling that offered abortion as an option, and a requirement that physicians perform fetal viability testing prior to termination. Reproductive Health Services challenged the laws, and by 1989 *Webster v. Reproductive Health Services* (492 U.S. 490) had made its way to the Supreme Court. Writing for a fractured Court, Chief Justice Rehnquist mustered a slim majority in favor of most of the law's provisions; most significantly, the Court retained Missouri's ban on public funding for all aspects of abortion-related services. The decision had tremendous impact, and not only in Missouri. Emboldened, federal antichoice legislators mobilized to pass the so-called "gag rule," which was upheld by the Court in 1991's *Rust v Sullivan* (501 U.S. 173) and remained in place until 1993, when President Clinton removed it by executive order.

58. Zeisler, 92.

59. http://www.washingtonpost.com/entertainment/tv/murphy-brown-a-television-trailblazer/2014/01/09/8b0deaae-7401-11e3-8b3f-b1666705ca3b_story.html; last accessed June 3, 2014.

60. Even more Americans tuned in for the next season's opening show, when Murphy dumped a truckload of potatoes on Dan Quayle's lawn, taunting him for his nationally televised spelling error, and in response to his vocal critique of her character. For that episode, viewership was seventy million (41 percent of households with television). http://www.washingtonpost.com/entertainment/tv/murphy-brown-a-television-trailblazer/2014/01/09/8b0deaae-7401-11e3-8b3f-b1666705ca3b_story.html; last accessed June 3, 2014.

61. Curiously, as the culture wars instigated in the 80s became a prominent subject of study in the 1990s (Whitehead 1994; Hunter 1992), simultaneously, legal studies scholars became interested in the "cultural lives of law" (Sarat and Kearns 1998). The culture wars themselves seem to have instigated a "cultural turn" in critical scholarship.

62. Zeisler, 92.

63. Quayle 1992.

64. Political scientist Iris Marion Young provided a corrective to claims like those made by Quayle. She wrote, "[L]et us dwell for a moment on the facts about births to unmarried women. In 1990, 26 percent of all births in the United States were to unmarried women. Contrary to the image that 'illegitimacy' is a Black phenomenon, 56 percent of these women were white, and 41 percent were African American. Again contrary to popular image, the rate of births to unmarried Black mothers has been falling in the last twenty years and rising very significantly among white mothers" (Young 1995, 539). Young continued, "The primary cause of the poverty of children in single-parent households is women's lack of earning power. In 1990, the median weekly earnings for women twenty-five years and over was $400, compared with $539 for men. About 40 percent of women maintaining households alone are full-time year-round workers, and another 27 percent work seasonally or part-time. But more than 21 percent of families headed

by employed women have incomes below poverty, compared with 4 percent of families headed by an employed man" (Young, 541).

65. Roberts 1998, 112.

66. Roberts 1998, 193.

67. Roberts 1998, 153. We have a cultural aversion to women using drugs while pregnant and generally see it as a bad thing. Certainly, babies born to actively addicted and using mothers have difficulties, especially immediately after birth, when they may feel the symptoms of withdrawal; addicted mothers also often lack proper nutrition and self-care, and their babies may have lower birth weight as a result. However, there are very few longitudinal studies of children born to addicted mothers which show that brain function is significantly different from infancy to five years old in children who were exposed to opiates, versus those who were not. Barbara Levy, vice president for health policy for the American College of Obstetrics and Gynecology (ACOG), explains that ACOG takes the position that women's drug use while pregnant should be treated, not criminalized, and that treatment should focus on prenatal care and holistic health. In fact, mandated treatment that involves "cold turkey" withdrawal from drugs may be more harmful to the fetus; Levy reports, "From a medical standpoint abruptly discontinuing some of these . . . can result in very negative outcomes for the baby. They can result in premature labor. They can result in fetal distress . . . they can even result in fetal death" (Gross 2013). The American Medical Association, the American Academy of Pediatrics, the American Nurses Association, and a host of other professional associations and children's rights advocates oppose laws that would further criminalize maternal addiction, for precisely the reasons stated by Levy. http://advocatesforpregnantwomen.org/medical_group_opinions_2011/Medical%20Group%20Positions%202011.pdf; last accessed June 10, 2014.

68. Roberts, 153; emphasis added. Women of color were not silent in the wake of these moments of backlash and danger for mothers, and they helped to push feminist discourse away from focusing solely on termination as the only area of reproductive politics worth engaging in—feminists of color consistently and necessarily challenged white allies to broaden their definition of reproductive justice (Silliman et al. 2004; Nelson 2002)—and began a renewed critique of the nation-building and empire-serving aspects of U.S. reproductive policy.

69. 499 U.S. 187 (1991).

70. Cushman, 179.

71. *Friends* was the most popular sitcom of the 1990s; it ran from 1994–2004, was rated by *Time* magazine as one of the most popular television shows "of all time." When its finale aired on May 6, 2004, 52.5 million Americans tuned in, making it the fourth most watched season finale in history and the most watched single television show of the decade.

72. Davis-Floyd at 26, citing Oakley (1984) and Rothman (1982). Davis-Floyd further notes that "concurrent to this rise of respectability has been pregnancy's redefinition from a private and feminine to a public and medical event." I return to this insight in chapters four and five.

Notes to Chapter 2

1. Earle 2003, 251.
2. Longhurst 2002, 458.
3. Bordo 1997, 94.
4. McRobbie 1993, 416.
5. Bartky 1999, 142–143; emphasis in original.
6. Fox defines embodiment as "the process by which social worlds and biological bodies constitute each other" (Fox 2012, 54).
7. Gullette, 189.
8. See Butler, 1993, for an examination of embodiment as materialization and performativity.
9. Gullette 2004, 162. Drawing heavily on Bourdieu's conceptualization of *habitus*, Gullette argues that aging is itself natural, but that our understandings and performances of aging are constituted by a culturally contextualized and produced "age ideology." In the contemporary United States this ideology is constituted by a pattern of "gendered and racialized constructs, relations of difference depend[ing] on the din of representations, unseen internalizations, unthinking practices, [and] economic structures of dominance and subordination" (Gullette 2004, 27).
10. Gullette 2004, 101.
11. Fox, 42.
12. Stacey 2007, 323.
13. Young 2006, 95.
14. Gullette 2004.
15. Bourdieu 1990.
16. Young 2006, 96.
17. Ibid.
18. Francus 2012, 120 and 194.
19. Foucault 2010 [1978–1979]; Bordo 2004; Bartky 1999.
20. Fox, 48. See also Featherstone 1991.
21. Ussher 2006, 91.
22. Charles and Kerr 1986.
23. Brewis and Sinclair 2000.
24. Earle, 247.
25. Bailey 2001, 120.
26. Earle, 249.
27. Bailey, 116.
28. Bailey, 121–122.
29. Bordo 1997, 105.
30. While many women want visual proof of their pregnancy via the baby bump and are excited by the physical changes they undergo, pregnant women are also at significant risk of body size distortion and body image problems. As psychologists Sumner et al. report, "[W]omen develop a particularly distorted body image during pregnancy, overestimating [their actual size] by more than non-pregnant women" (Sumner et al.

1993, 203). And, their pilot study finds, media images exacerbate this tendency toward distortion. "At 16 weeks gestational age, viewing pictures [of skinny models] from these [fashion] magazines led women to overestimate the depth of their abdomens by more than usual. At 32 weeks, in addition to that sensitivity, they responded to the pictures by an increase in their perceived general body width" (206–207). As can be expected, they conclude: "It should be remembered that body image distortion has a very real emotional impact on women, and that it cannot simply be dismissed as a perceptual distortion, particularly during pregnancy" (207).

31. http://www.lifeandstylemag.com/posts/jessica-simpson-opens-up-about-preg nancy-weight-battle-shows-off-slim-body-35203; last accessed May 6, 2014.

32. Krupnick, Ellie. March 13, 2012. "Jessica Simpson on the Tonight Show: Pregnant in Six Inch Heels!" The Huffington Post; http://www.huffingtonpost.com/2012/03/13/ jessica-simpson-tonight-show_n_1341337.html last accessed 4/20/15.

33. http://www.tmz.com/category/jessica-simpson-pregnant; last accessed May 6, 2014.

34. Wetherbe, Jamie. 2013. "Nude Sculpture of Pregnant Kim Kardashian Unveiled in L.A." *Los Angeles Times,* June 6. http://articles.latimes.com/2013/jun/06/entertain ment/la-et-cm-kim-kardashian-pregnant-nude-sculpture-20130605; last accessed May 6, 2014.

35. http://www.tmz.com/category/kim-kardashian-pregnant; last accessed May 6, 2014.

36. Ibid.

37. Ibid.

38. http://www.thesuperficial.com/hilary-duff-huge-fat-post-pregnant-haylie-duff -06-2012; last accessed May 6, 2014.

39. Thomas, Liz. "Look Everybody! Nicole Kidman Tries to Make Her Baby Bump as Big as Possible." http://www.dailymail.co.uk/tvshowbiz/article-567217/Look-every body -Nicole-Kidman-tries-make-baby-bump-big-possible.html; last accessed May 6, 2014.

40. http://www.justjared.com/2008/06/09/nicole-kidman-baby-bump-4; last ac cessed May 6, 2014.

41. It is interesting to note that both women have had long relationships with the actor Tom Cruise. Kidman, now married to Keith Urban, was Cruise's wife for eleven years and adopted two children with him. Urban and Kidman have two children, one born to Kidman, the other born to a surrogate. Katie Holmes and Tom Cruise were married in 2006, seven months after Holmes gave birth to daughter Suri. The pair di vorced in 2012.

42. http://www.ivillage.com/ins-outs-katie-holmes-baby-bump-0/1-a-22616; last ac cessed May 6, 2014.

43. http://www.tomcruisewatch.net/is-katie-holmes-pregnant; last accessed Oct. 16, 2008. Holmes was not, we now know, about to become a mother for a second time.

44. Conby, Medina, and Stanbury, 3.

45. McDonald 2012, 26, citing the Quigley Poll 2010.

46. McDonald, 254.

47. Brantley 2006, E6; cited in McDonald, 254.

48. Brantley 2006, E6; cited in McDonald, 254.

49. McDonald, 266.

50. http://www.moono.com/news/news00224.html; last accessed Oct. 25, 2008.

51. *Us Weekly,* Aug. 18, 2008, page 86.

52. http://www.usmagazine.com/julia_roberts_0; story from December 29, 2006; last accessed Oct. 16, 2008.

53. http://www.celebitchy.com/category/jennifer_garner; last accessed Oct. 16, 2008. Their children are named Violet Anne, Seraphina Rose Elizabeth, and Samuel.

54. http://www.okmagazine.com/pixandvids/gallery/9830/5; last accessed Oct. 25, 2008.

55. http://www.celebwarship.com/wp/?p=2851; last accessed Aug. 1, 2009.

56. http://popsugar.com/11020; last accessed Oct. 16, 2008.

57. Ussher, 161.

58. http://bumpshack.com/2006/07/13/pregnancy-not-always-pretty-for-britney-spears; last accessed Sept. 30, 2008.

59. http://thesuperficia.com/2008/05/britney_spears_stops_at_a_clinic.php; last accessed Oct. 16, 2008.

60. http://www.okmagazine.com/pixandvids/gallery/9830/5; last accessed Oct. 25, 2008.

61. Cooper 2008.

62. Harris, Mark. 2008. "The Mommy Track." *New York Times,* Oct. 19, AR 1.

63. Pitt and Jolie reportedly met on the set of their film Mr. and Mrs. Smith—ironically, a film about an average American couple in the next door of suburbia who are secret agents sent on a mission to kill each other.

64. As a reporter for the *New York Times* wrote in mid-October 2008, in an article about Jolie titled "Mommy Track," "Angelina Jolie Is Many Things: Parent, Daughter, Advocate, Action Star, Actress—but Not America's Sweetheart." Harris, Mark. 2008. "The Mommy Track." *New York Times,* Oct. 19, AR 1.

65. Cooper, 34.

66. Jolie 2013.

67. In her editorial, Jolie writes this about her double mastectomy, "I do not feel any less of a woman. I feel empowered that I made a strong choice that in no way diminishes my femininity" (Jolie 2013).

68. Chodorow 1999, 217.

69. Aug. 18, 2008.

70. Longhurst 2002, 470.

71. Wojcik 2003, 244, emphasis added.

72. Ussher, 161.

73. http://www.okmagazine.com/halle-berry-slideshow; accessed Oct. 25, 2008.

74. http://www.tmz.com/2014/01/30/halle-berry-post-pregnancy-photo-hot-body/ last accessed 4/20/2015.

75. http://bumpshack.com/2007/09/22/salma-hayek-gives-birth-to-baby-girl/salma
-hayek-with-milk-jugs; accessed Aug. 1, 2009.

76. Shildrick and Price 1999, 3.

77. Media attention to Kate Winslet's pregnancy is a case in point. In his article on white British actress Kate Winslet's stardom, Redmond notes that Winslet's success is made possible by her tapping into two important myths of modern life: the myths of individualism and success. He also notes that her seeming self-control, central to her success, is "racially coded" (Redmond 2007, 264). Coverage of Winslet's pregnancy reinforces these codes. On September 5, she "hid her baby bump and held [her] husband's hand," while "wearing sensible flats" and holding "her hand over her tummy for even more coverage." On September 18, the British press noted that she "glowed" on a "dinner date with [her] husband" even as he "protected" her from the rain. Even her male costar, Josh Brolin, gushed about her "pregnancy glow." Indeed, the only one threatening to explode, in this coverage, is her "gushing" costar—a safe, to be sure, white man. See http://www.usmagazine.com/celebrity-moms/news/kate-winslet-hides-baby-bump -in-black-dress-holds-husband-ned-rocknrolls-hand-201359; http://www.express.co.uk/ news/showbiz/430352/Pregnant-Kate-Winslet-glows-on-dinner-date-with-husband -Ned-Rocknroll; and http://www.eonline.com/news/457932/kate-winslet-costar-josh -brolin-talks-about-her-pregnancy-glow-moving-baby-bump-moment; last accessed Apr. 20, 2015.

78. Dean 2009, 69.

79. Longhurst 2002, 467.

80. Beltran 2007, 282.

81. Beltran, 282.

82. Bordo, 2004.

83. Collins 1998; Roberts 1998; Jordan-Zachery, on file with author.

84. http://www.usmagazine.com/celebrity-moms/news/beyonce-it-was-harder-to- breathe-performing-while-pregnant-20112111; last accessed Jan. 8, 2014.

85. Redmond, 263; emphasis in original.

86. Redmond, 267.

87. Bloggers SherpaWoman and Erica Ehm (who writes the Official Yummy Mummy Club's Guilt-Free Dictionary) have attempted to "reclaim" MILF and offer a different definition. MILFs, they write, are Modern Inspired Lifemaker Freakin' multitasking babes.

88. www.goop.com.

89. http://www.huffingtonpost.com/2014/02/18/gwyneth-paltrow-affair_n_4810117. html; last accessed May 1, 2014.

90. http://www.urbandictionary.com/define.php?term=yummy%20mummy; last accessed Jan. 4, 2014.

91. Ussher, 4.

92. Stacey, 323.

93. Dworkin 1974; emphasis added.

Notes to Chapter 3

1. http://www.eonline.com/uberblog/families/index.2.html?categories=families; last accessed Oct. 4, 2008.

2. http://www.tmz.com/2014/03/03/scarlett-johansson-dauriac-pregnant; last accessed Mar. 4, 2014.

3. Google Analytics (www.google.com/trends) allows users to search for trending topics in Google searches, controlled for month, region of the world, and category. It is clear that celebrity pregnancies are often searched and generate hits to hundreds of websites; Google even has "celebrity pregnancy" as a top-ten trending topic for 2014. For any given pregnancy, and any given month and year, we can track the ratio of searches for those celebrities against all searches and against specified searches (such as celebrity marriages or the Oakland A's).

4. Sheryl Sandberg's book *Lean In: Women, Work, and the Will to Lead*, advocating that women step up their career game, has been a *New York Times* bestseller since it was published by Knopf in early 2013.

5. Grossberg 1988, 178–179.

6. McDonald 2012, 4 and 46; Dyer 2007b, 86.

7. Marshall 1997, 63.

8. Sternheimer 2011, 11.

9. Sternheimer, 187.

10. Sternheimer, 11.

11. Stacey 2007, 318.

12. Stacey, 324.

13. Swigat 1998, 26.

14. Lavrence and Lozanski 2014, 86.

15. http://www.ibisworld.com/industry/maternity-wear-stores.html; last accessed May 17, 2014.

16. Richard Joslin, Peter Leuck, Chad Martino, Melissa Rhoads, Brian Wachter, Robin Chapman, and Gail Christian. "Gap Inc.: Has the Retailer Lost Its Style?" www.cengage.com/management/webtutor/ireland3e/cases/gap.pdf.

17. http://www.destinationmaternitycorp.com/WhoAreWe.asp.

18. The website Stylelist has "pregnancy galleries" for both Diana and Kate at http://www.stylelist.com/view/princess-diana-the-pregnancy-years. After looking at the galleries, readers are urged to see Hilary Mantel's stunningly good essay on Kate's pregnancy (and royalty in general) for the *London Review of Books* in 2013: http://www.lrb.co.uk/v35/n04/hilary-mantel/royal-bodies.

19. http://www.seraphine.com/maternity-clothes/celebrity-style-1.html.

20. http://www.glamourmagazine.co.uk/celebrity/celebrity-galleries/2009/01/15/celebrity-pregnancies#!image-number=30; last accessed May 9, 2014.

21. http://fashion.telegraph.co.uk/news-features/TMG10792653/Gwen-Stefanis-post-pregnancy-snap-back.html; last accessed May 12, 2014.

22. As she tells it, Stefani's experiences with pregnancy mitigated against a heavy touring schedule while carrying her children. She told *Elle* magazine in 2011 that she felt

this way while performing during her pregnancy: "Certain songs would make me want to puke. You feel pretty gross when you are first pregnant. You don't feel cute, you feel disgusting. You're getting fat. It was hard. . . . I mean, I'm very vain," she added. "That would be my middle name. Of course I am, you know what I mean? I love the visual" (Candace Rainey, "The All-Star: Gwen Stefani," *Elle,* May 4, 2011. http://www.elle.com/culture/celebrities/a11609/gwen-stefani-interview; last accessed Apr. 29, 2015). The *Independent U.K.* reported in 2011 that Stefani said she felt "so gross" after giving birth that she could not even write music. The paper quoted her in this way, "I hadn't planned on doing a tour; I'd had Zuma, I felt so gross—I got so big and felt so out of touch and not cool. I was trying to write this cool record and nothing came out" ("Gwen Stefani Couldn't Write Songs after Giving Birth," *The Independent,* Mar. 14, 2011. http://www.independent.co.uk/news/people/news/gwen-stefani-couldnt-write-songs-after-giving-birth-2241658.html; last accessed Apr. 29, 2015).

23. http://www.shoplamb.com/about-gwen; last accessed Jan. 12, 2014. L.A.M.B. is an acronym for Love Angel Music Baby.

24. http://www.lilsugar.com/Pregnant-Celebrities-Spring-Maternity-Dresses-Less-22588480#photo-22588489.

25. Stout 2014, B3.

26. See Vertesi present at the fourth annual Theorizing the Web conference (TtW4), April 2014; http//mashable.com/2014/04/26/big-data-pregnancy (last accessed May 1, 2014) for details and links; you can watch all of the TtW4 panels on YouTube.

27. Stout.

28. http://www.dailymail.co.uk/tvshowbiz/article-2768973/Father-Ashton-Kutcher-tweets-snap-kid-friendly-10-2-million-Beverly-Hills-love-nest-fianc-e-Mila-Kunis.

29. http://celebritybabies.people.com/2014/05/21/ashton-kutcher-mila-kunis-baby-shopping-juvenile-shop-sherman-oaks.

30. *PopSugar,* Jan. 28, 2014.

31. BuyBuy Baby is a baby and infant-needs retailer. It was started in 1985 and was purchased for $67 million in 2007 by the Bed Bath & Beyond global brand that also includes World Market, Harmon Face Value stores, and Christmas Tree Stores. http://www.fool.com/investing/general/2007/03/26/buybuy-baby-gets-bought.aspx; last accessed Jan. 13, 2014. BuyBuy Baby's commercial website notes, "Our stores are approximately 28,000–60,000 square feet and offer over 20,000 products to choose from." http://www.buybuybaby.com/store/static/BabyAboutUs; last accessed Jan. 10, 2014.

32. Nadesan 2002.

33. Gullette 2002, 35. See also Schor 1998.

34. Lacey Rose. 2002. "In Pictures: Most Expensive Celebrity Photos." *Forbes,* May 22. http://www.forbes.com/2009/07/01/michael-jackson-magazine-business-media-jackson_slide_2.html; last accessed June 3, 2014.

35. Rose 2002.

36. http://www.huffingtonpost.com/2013/12/10/beyonce-shares-blue-ivy-photo_n_4420801.html; last accessed Apr. 20, 2015.

37. See chapter four for a discussion of a California law championed by Garner, Af-

fleck, and Berry, which provides misdemeanor penalties for photographers who harass celebrity children.

38. *The Business Standard,* Aug. 12, 2014; http://www.business-standard.com/article/ pti-stories/kim-kardashian-kanye-west-won-t-sell-baby-pictures-113081200305_1.html; last accessed Mar. 6, 2014.

39. http://www.redbookmag.com/fun-contests/celebrity/kristen-bell-interview #slide-1; last accessed June 2, 2014.

40. http://miamiherald.typepad.com/worklifebalancingact/2014/03/gwyneth-pal-trow-ignites-outrage-from-working-mothers.html; last accessed June 8, 2014. "Regular mom" Mackenzie Dawson penned an open letter to Paltrow, published in the *New York Post.* It read, in part, "Thank God I don't make millions filming one movie per year' is what I say to myself pretty much every morning as I wait on a windy Metro-North platform, about to begin my 45-minute commute into the city. Whenever things get rough, all I have to do is keep reminding myself of that fact. It is my mantra. And I know all my fellow working-mom friends feel the same. Am I right, ladies?" http://ny post.com/2014/03/27/a-working-moms-open-letter-to-gwyneth-paltrow; last accessed June 8, 2014. The *Post* reports that Dawson's letter had 3.6 million readers by early summer 2014.

41. Jane Ussher's work notes the tendency toward "hysterization of women's bodies" postmotherhood (Ussher 2006, 96). While she is much more concerned with postnatal depression as a construct and the role of idealized mothering than with the idealization of the pregnant and postbaby body itself, her work shows clearly how important the image of the "good mother" is to women and how willing they become to self-police, self-silence, self-castigate, and self-deny in order to appear "good"—in control, nurturing, calm. There is no shortage of "role models" in the popular press.

42. Paxman 2014.

43. Min 2012, 162–163.

44. Lavrence and Lozanski 2014, 83.

45. Longhurst 2001, 20.

46. Amanda McMillan. 2014. "Pre-Baby Body or Bust!" *Health.* http://www.health.com /health/gallery/0,,20603375,00.html; last accessed June 5, 2014.

47. McMillan.

48. McMillan.

49. Min, 3.

50. Min, 7.

51. Rothman 1989.

52. Min, 134.

53. Min, 8.

54. Radin and Sunder theorize that "the unstable meanings of commodities make them potentially or actually liberating, and not just potentially or actually subjugating" (Radin and Sunder, 14), and they hypothesize that commoditized movements associated with pop singer Madonna, the holiday Kwanzaa, and role of the Nature Conservancy in buying up and "saving" land at risk of development might bring us into a "new age

of freedom through commodification," what Appadurai called "commodity resistance" (Radin and Sunder, 14 and 23). There is "optimism" in these actions, Radin and Sunder argue, and that optimism might be what makes such moments "progressive" (23). They write, "We cannot be progressive if we do not have some optimism—that we can get from here (not so good) to there (better)" (23). For a treatment of the commodification of gay subversive spaces, see Bell and Valentine 1995. For an examination of postfeminism and commodification, see Showden 2009.

55. Eisenstein 1997, 32, emphasis added. Eisenstein notes the same processes at work in the capitalist cooptation and capture of previously radical calls for "multiculturalism."

56. Lululemon yoga wear is exceptionally expensive; the average price of a pair of pants on the website is $82, a "daily practice" long-sleeve T-shirt retails for $68, and a pair of "light as air" underwear will run you $16. If you were outfitted head to toe—socks to headband—in lululemon, you'd be wearing at least $175 worth of workout gear. I last browsed the lululemon retail site, lululemon.com, on May 15, 2014.

57. Lavrence and Lozanski, 77, citing Bishop 2012.

58. Lavrence and Lozanski, 76–78.

59. N. Rose 1999.

60. Lavrence and Lozanski, 85.

61. Lavrence and Lozanski, 80.

62. Sloane and Sloane 2002, 141.

63. Sloane and Sloane, 160.

64. Sloane and Sloane, 98.

65. Sloane and Sloane, 98.

66. "Every hospital that attains the Baby-Friendly designation moves us closer to reaching the Healthy People 2020 goal of increasing the proportion of live births that occur in facilities that provide recommended care for lactating mothers and their babies. . . . Currently, 6.9% of births occur in Baby-Friendly designated facilities. The Healthy People 2020 goal is 8.1%." https://www.babyfriendlyusa.org/find-facilities; last accessed May 18, 2014.

67. Solinger 2007, 202.

Notes to Chapter 4

1. http://www.celebitchy.com/12351/jennifer_garner_gets_locked_out_of_car_by_her_two_year_old; last accessed June 2, 2014.

2. Dean 2009, 128.

3. Dean 2009, 145.

4. For an interesting fictional treatment of this, see Jonathan Kellerman's 2013 mystery novel *Guilt*.

5. http://www.eonline.com/news/459304/jennifer-garner-confronts-paparazzo-while-out-with-her-children-see-the-pic; last accessed Dec. 27, 2014. Readers will have noticed that I reproduce images in portions of this text; I decided only to use photos that were taken as part of publicity appearances or as cover photos for magazines. I decided not to use any photos that included children of the stars and to avoid all paparazzi

photos. Because Garner and Affleck entered this photo into the legislative record, I reproduce it here—breaking my "no paparazzi photos" rule.

6. http://www.momtastic.com/entertainment/174481-photos-celebrity-families-out-and-about-ali-larter-sarah-jessica-parker-and-more; last accessed Dec. 8, 2014.

7. http://www.babyrazzi.com/2014/01/06/page/2; last accessed June 2, 2014.

8. http://www.popsugar.com/Jennifer-Lopez-Bikini-Photos-Babies-Marc-Spain-1736125; last accessed Dec. 14, 2013. The headline of this article reads "For LOTS more photos of Jennifer in a bikini and with her babies, just click here."

9. http://www.usmagazine.com/celebrity-moms/news/mila-kunis-ashton-kutcher-visit-iowa-pregnancy-reveal-picture-2014313; last accessed June 12, 2014.

10. Senate Bill 606; amending Section 11414 of the California Penal Code. Introduced in late February 2013, the bill was signed by Governor Brown in late September; it passed through committee and on the assembly floor with no votes in opposition.

11. History of the bill provided by the Senate Rules Committee.

12. August 13, 2013, hearing of the Assembly Committee on Judiciary.

13. http://www.nydailynews.com/entertainment/gossip/jennifer-garner-joins-halle-berry-fight-tougher-paparazzi-laws-article-1.1426589; last accessed June 10, 2014.

14. The bill opens the possibility of civil suit against photographers and harassers, but does not make the publication of any stolen images a crime. The Motion Picture Association of America, California Broadcasters Association, California Newspapers Publishers Association, and National Press Photographers Association opposed it. Testimony in support of the bill was offered not only by celebrity families, but by the Screen Actors Guild—American Federation of Television and Radio Artists, several branches of California law enforcement, the National Organization for Women in California, and legal scholars Gary Williams (Loyola of Los Angeles) and Erwin Chemerinsky (University of California at Irvine).

15. Kirthana Ramisetti. 2014. "Kristen Bell, Dax Shepard Boycotting Magazines That Publish Paparazzi Photos of Celebrity Kids." *New York Daily News,* Jan. 28.

16. N. Rose 1999, 85.

17. Dean 2009, 38–44.

18. Dean 2009, 49.

19. Von Drehle with Calabresi 2013; Passavant 2005.

20. In addition to Passavant, see the work of Benjamin Fleury-Steiner and various coauthors for different ways that this construction is accomplished (Longazel and Fleury-Steiner 2013; Fleury-Steiner, Dunn, and Fleury-Steiner 2009).

21. A couple of weeks after I wrote this last sentence, researcher and surveillance avoider Janet Verseti told an interviewer that people "don't like being stalked by a pair of shoes they looked at once on the Internet two years ago" (Goldstein 2014, 6). Indeed!

22. Passavant 2005, 5.

23. Kashmir Hill at *Forbes* magazine broke this story; http://www.forbes.com/sites/kashmirhill/2012/02/16/how-target-figured-out-a-teen-girl-was-pregnant-before-her-father-did; last accessed June 10, 2014.

24. Goldstein, 2.

25. Goldstein, 5.

26. Ussher 2006, 87–88.

27. A recent study suggests that "maternal diet around the time of conception can influence certain properties of the child's DNA [which] could have lifelong implications" (Alford 2014).

28. Davis-Floyd 1992, 7.

29. Mitchell 2001, 49.

30. Robbie Davis-Floyd, the scholar in the United States most knowledgeable about rituals of birth, the role of the doctor, and the criminalization of midwifery, argues that the impact of many of the technological changes surrounding birth from the 1950s to today stems from the play of a binary between science and nature, constructed in technocratic societies as a way to give primacy to science and technology. In identifying this binary, Davis-Floyd argues in a vein similar to ecofeminists like Carolyn Merchant that the technocratic and scientific models seek to control nature—which here means to control pregnancy—which means to control women. Davis-Floyd argues that technocratic rituals of birth are meant to "fence in" the power of the process in order to continue to disempower women (Davis-Floyd, 61).

31. Mitchell, 90.

32. See Davis-Floyd, 109–111, and Block 2007, 13–35. Block reports that 83 percent of laboring women had IVs, 56 percent had urine catheters, and 76 percent had epidurals or spinal anesthesia.

33. Block puts it this way, "Once a woman's water is broken—spontaneously or deliberately—she is on a deadline" (Block, 13).

34. Cassidy 2006, 21.

35. Mitchell, 67.

36. Mitchell, 106–107.

37. Mitchell, 5–6.

38. Mitchell, 174.

39. Mitchell, 66.

40. Block, 63.

41. http://www.ohbabymagazine.com/blog/%EF%BB%BF%EF%BB%BFsarah-drews-blog-the-incredible-first-ultrasound; last accessed June 3, 2014.

42. http://abcnews.go.com/blogs/entertainment/2013/01/beyonce-shares-blue-ivy-ultrasound-in-new-trailer; last accessed June 3, 2014.

43. http://www.hollywood.com/news/celebrities/3499011/tom-cruise-causes-ultrasound-crackdown; last accessed Nov. 11, 2014.

44. http://www.mommyish.com/2013/02/13/evan-rachel-wood; last accessed Nov. 9, 2013.

45. Young 2003; Fraser 1989.

46. Francus, 28.

47. Ussher, 6.

48. Kipnis 1988, 156.

49. Bumiller 1997, 156.

50. Bumiller, 156.

51. Mitchell, 148.

52. Bumiller 157; see also Petchesky 1987. Interestingly, the role of amniocentesis technology in abortion politics, and in the cultural imagining of celebrity pregnancy, is a bit more contested. For instance, a devastating amnio result can serve to medically justify a late-term abortion. Rayna Rapp's prescient sociology of the procedure indicates that though it was "initially recommended for relatively small numbers of older pregnant women, the test is rapidly becoming a pregnancy ritual for certain sectors of the highly educated urban middle class" (Rapp 1994, 206). However, perhaps because it involves the insertion of a long needle into the belly of a pregnant woman rather than the photo-capture of a fetal image, or perhaps because it often occurs after an ultrasound detects potential fetal anomaly, the amnio procedure has not become "popular" in the media coverage of celebrity pregnancy.

53. http://www.jillstanek.com/ultrasound/halle-berry-pro.html.

54. Paul 2010, 50.

55. Paul, 53.

56. Paul, 50.

57. Cassidy 2006, 50–54.

58. Walter Winchell famously thought that gossip would play a democratizing role, by allowing average people a window onto the failures and foibles of the rich and famous. See Gabler 1995.

59. Geraghty 2007, 100.

60. Mitchell, 42.

61. Besnier 2009.

62. Dean 2009, 31.

63. See Besnier; Minh-ha 1989.

64. Besnier, 40.

65. Davis-Floyd, 22–25.

66. Miller and Rose 1995, 434.

67. Davis-Floyd, 27.

68. Mitchell, 86.

69. See Beck 1994; Beck 1992.

70. Fox, 148.

71. Rose, 1999.

72. Fox, 148–149; emphasis added.

73. Ussher, 40–44.

74. Fox, 147.

75. Fox, 129.

76. Fox, 154–155.

77. "There is no need for arms, physical violence, material constraints, just a gaze. An inspecting gaze, a gaze which each individual under its weight will end up interiorizing to the point that he is his own overseer, each individual exercising this surveillance over, and against himself" (Foucault 1977, 155).

78. Min, 134.

79. Min, 188.

80. Min, 134.

81. See Nancy Fraser's brilliant analysis for *The Guardian,* "How Feminism Became Capitalism's Handmaiden—and How to Reclaim It," published Oct. 14, 2013. http://www.theguardian.com/commentisfree/2013/oct/14/feminism-capitalist-handmaiden-neoliberal; last accessed Dec. 27, 2014.

82. Longhurst 2002, 468.

Notes to Chapter 5

1. http://www.sfgate.com/bayarea/article/Alameda-County-jail-s-pregnancy-test-policy-focus-5523839.php; last accessed June 3, 2014.

2. Alameda County jails had previously denied pregnancy tests to women who requested them and were under court order to provide them upon request. In light of that court order, country jail administrators mandated the test for all female inmates between the ages of fourteen and seventy. It is unclear why they thought that a sweeping mandate was better than provision upon request.

3. Hunt 1996, 277.

4. Hunt, 132–134.

5. Hunt, 389.

6. Ouellette and Hay 2008, 474.

7. Cruikshank 1999.

8. Young 2003; Beck 1992.

9. Scott 2012; Brown 1995.

10. Passavant and Dean 2002, 12; see also Cruikshank 1999.

11. Passavant 2006.

12. Passavant 2006, 395.

13. Solinger 2007, 169.

14. Lancaster puts it this way: "Virtually everyone who has written about the subject has marked connections among changing gender roles and anxieties about the status of the family, gay acceptance and antigay backlash, sexual revolution and sex panic" (Lancaster 2011, 233).

15. Brown 1995, 99–100.

16. Kliff 2014.

17. In *Stenberg v. Carhart* (530 U.S. 914 [2000]), the Supreme Court invalidated Nebraska's ban on the procedure; but in 2007's *Gonzales v. Carhart* (550 U.S. 124), the Court upheld a federal ban nearly identical to the state ban it had previously invalidated. See Wilson, 2013, for an excellent treatment of the jurisprudence relating to free speech and clinic protests.

18. The PPACA does not mandate insurance funding for abortion that is not intended to save the life of the mother; it also does not offer federal funding for non-life-saving abortion procedures. It does mandate that insurers offer plans that include well women and gynecological checkups, sexual health testing, family planning services

related to birth control and fertility treatments, breastfeeding support, postpartum depression screening, and intimate partner violence screening and education.

19. Guttmacher Institute, www.guttmacher.org; last accessed Apr. 20, 2015.

20. National Women's Law Center, www.nwlc.org; last accessed Apr. 20, 2015.

21. Kliff, 8.

22. http://thecontributor.com/civil-rights/tx-house-committee-approves-strict-abortion-restrictions; last accessed June 11, 2014.

23. http://www.huffingtonpost.com/2014/02/24/steve-martin-virginia_n_4847959.html; last accessed June 12, 2014. Emphasis added.

24. Legal and regulated abortion is "one of the safest common surgical procedures for women in the United States." And the earlier in the pregnancy the abortion is performed, the safer it is; therefore, laws that limit access and delay the procedure are laws that end up promoting abortion that is unsafe for the mother. The Guttmacher Institute reports that "complications from unsafe abortion procedures account for 13% of all maternal deaths," or 47,000 women worldwide ("Worldwide Abortion: Legality, Incidence, and Safety," https://www.guttmacher.org/media/presskits/abortion-WW/statsandfacts.html; last accessed Apr. 29, 2015).

25. http://boisestatepublicradio.org/post/idaho-woman-arrested-abortion-uneasy-case-both-sides; last accessed June 5, 2014.

26. http://www.huffingtonpost.com/2014/09/07/ann-whalen-abortion-daughter_n_5777120.html and http://www.reuters.com/article/2014/09/06/us-usa-crime-pennsylvania-abortion-idUSKBN0H10IR20140906; last accessed June 3, 2014.

27. http://www.thenation.com/article/160092/policing-pregnancy#; last accessed June 11, 2014.

28. Gross 2013.

29. The report and its executive summary are available at http://advocatesforpregnantwomen.org/main/publications/articles_and_reports/executive_summary_paltrow_flavin_jhppl_article.php; last accessed June 10, 2014.

30. As we can expect when we recall the jurisprudence of *Johnson Controls,* this is a responsibilization that lands squarely on the shoulders of women, even as men have direct roles to play in fetal health and viability. In the extreme cases where women are prosecuted for criminal harm to their unborn children, men are almost always absent. The executive summary of the NAPW report on women who have been prosecuted for fetal harm states that "although every pregnancy in [our] study involved a man, in 77% of the cases, the father or the woman's male partner was not even mentioned in any case document" (ibid.).

31. Gross 2013.

32. http://rhrealitycheck.org/article/2014/04/10/tennessee-legislature-passes-far-reaching-bill-make-pregnant-women-criminals; last accessed June 12, 2014.

33. http://www.newappsblog.com/2014/04/sb-1391-and-the-criminalization-of-pregnancy-in-tennessee.html; last accessed June 10, 2014.

34. Eckholm 2013.

35. Gross.

36. Ibid.

37. Ibid.

38. http://www.alternet.org/news-amp-politics/10-most-dangerous-places-be-wo man-america; last accessed June 12, 2014.

39. The Mayo Clinic offers a slightly more conservative estimate—stating that around 10–20 percent of pregnancies in the United States will end in miscarriage. The clinic website adds, however, that "the actual number is probably much higher because many miscarriages occur so early in pregnancy that a woman doesn't even know she's pregnant." http://www.mayoclinic.org/diseases-conditions/pregnancy-loss-miscarriage/ basics/definition/con-20033827; last accessed Dec. 22, 2014. The National Institutes of Health and Centers for Disease Control cite similar rates of miscarriage.

40. Gross.

41. Cassidy 2006, 122.

42. Ibid.

43. Ibid.

44. Pieklo 2014.

45. The Guttmacher Institute reports that in 2008, the most recent year for which good data is available, 51 percent of the 6.6 million pregnancies in the United States were unintended ("Unintended Pregnancy in the United States," http://www.guttmacher.org/ pubs/FB-Unintended-Pregnancy-US.html; last accessed Apr. 29, 2015).

46. Guttmacher Institute State Policy Brief: Contraceptives; current as of June 1, 2014. http://www.guttmacher.org/statecenter/spibs/spib_ICC.pdf; last accessed June 9, 2014.

47. *Burwell v. Hobby Lobby* 573 U.S. ___ (2014).

48. Arizona Senate Bill 2625. See http://www.huffingtonpost.com/2012/03/14/ari zona-birth-control-bill-contraception-medical-reasons_n_1344557.html; last accessed June 9, 2014.

49. http://legiscan.com/AZ/text/HB2625/2012; last accessed June 9, 2014.

50. http://www.dispatch.com/content/stories/local/2014/06/04/bill-would-restrict -abortion-coverage.html; last accessed June 10, 2014.

51. http://www.nytimes.com/2012/08/20/us/politics/todd-akin-provokes-ire-with -legitimate-rape-comment.html?_r=0; last accessed June 11, 2014.

52. http://www.motherjones.com/politics/2014/12/republican-wants-women-get -permission-father-having-abortion; last accessed Dec. 22, 2014.

53. Rubin 1984, 198.

54. These YouTube videos, produced for at least every week of pregnancy, have millions of views recorded.

55. http://thinkprogress.org/health/2014/03/27/3419669/arkansas-mother-arrested -breastfeeding; last accessed June 12, 2014.

56. http://www.theguardian.com/science/brain-flapping/2014/jan/28/pregnant -women-are-doing-it-wrong; last accessed June 12, 2014.

57. Readers may be interested to know that the prohibition on smoking is a relatively recent phenomenon in U.S. culture. In an interview on *Face the Nation* in 1971,

"the chairman of the board of Philip Morris, confronted with evidence that smoking in pregnancy leads to low birth weight, famously said: 'Some women would prefer having smaller babies'" (Cassidy, 24). Cassidy reports that the book *Safe Convoy,* published in 1994, argued "there is no scientific reason for a moderate smoker to stop when she is expecting, because 'to quit at that time might do more harm than good by upsetting the nerves.' A good rule for smokers is 'less than a pack a day.'"

58. http://www.bellinghamherald.com/2013/08/09/3139031/armed-man-gets-20-days -for-threatening.html; last accessed June 17, 2013.

59. Eggers 2014, 134.

60. Dean 2009.

61. Tom Whyman. 2014. "Beware of Cupcake Fascism." *The Guardian,* Apr. 8. http:www .theguardian.com/commentisfree/2014/apr/08/beware-of-cupcake-fascism; last accessed June 12, 2014.

62. Whyman.

Notes to Chapter 6

1. M.I.A. is the stage name of Mathangi "Maya" Arulpragasam, a British Sri Lankan born in 1975. I refer to her by her performer's moniker in this text, as it is the performance of her pregnancy and the press coverage of it that interest me most.

2. http://www.dailymail.co.uk/tvshowbiz/article-1139386/You-wont-Mothercare -British-rapper-MIA-performs-Grammys-sheer-dress-babys-date.html; last accessed May 9, 2014.

3. Bobel and Kwan 2011.

4. Fox 2012, 154.

5. Gullette 2004, 109. See also Fraser 1997; Foucault 1977.

6. There is a rich literature on "hedonic feminism," which emphatically places pleasure in the body as a path to women's emancipation. See in particular the work of Robin West (1987, 1988) and Katherine Franke (2001).

7. Fraser 1989, 14.

8. Lazarus-Black and Hirsch 1994.

9. Scott 1987; Piven and Cloward 1977.

10. Scott 2010.

11. Scott 2012, xviii.

12. For excellent histories of rock 'n' roll as antagonistic to dominant cultural norms and politics, see Frith, Straw, and Street (eds.) 2004, especially Keightly 2004, 109–142.

13. Whiteley 2013; Leonard 2007; Cohen 2004; Gaar 1992; Coates 1997; Cohen 1997; Reynolds and Press 1995; Frith and McRobbie 1990 [1978]).

14. Whiteley 2013.

15. Kuwahara 1992; hooks 1990.

16. Pough 2004, 28.

17. Berlant 1997.

18. Dean 2009.

19. Berlant, 223.

20. http://content.time.com/time/specials/packages/article/0,28804,1878293_1878 320_1878336,00.html; last accessed May 9, 2014. This list included only one other woman of color, Phylicia Rashad, who was pregnant during a season of the popular television series *The Cosby Show*.

21. As this book goes to press, Nicki Minaj has gone public with her story of a having an abortion as a teenager. The *Rolling Stone* article in which she is quoted places the abortion in a broader context of Minaj's life; she tells the magazine that the decision and the process were extremely difficult for her. The media picked up on the article's abortion reference, and headlines in late December 2014 highlighted what some in the press called her "regret" at having the procedure. http://www.rollingstone.com/music/news/ nicki-minaj-is-hip-hops-killer-diva-inside-rolling-stones-new-issue-20141230; last accessed Apr. 22, 2015.

22. http://www.huffingtonpost.com/2013/09/23/mia-nfl-video_n_3977513.html ?utm_hp_ref=entertainment; last accessed May 9, 2014.

23. Durham 2009.

24. Rasmussen and Brown 2005, 480.

25. Rasmussen and Brown, 469.

26. For instance, Aguilera performed at the KIIS FM Wango Tango festival on Mother's Day 2014 after previously headlining the New Orleans Jazz Festival—both while visibly pregnant. For Wango Tango, she wore a tight black minidress with cutouts near the "bump." http://www.usmagazine.com/celebrity-moms/news/christina-aguilera-wango -tango-pregnant-picture-2014115; last accessed May 9, 2014. *Us Weekly* reports that for the jazz festival, Aguilera "stunned in a short black bustier dress and matching jacket. She accessorized the look with a hat and sequined fishnet tights." http://www.usmaga zine.com/celebrity-moms/news/christina-aguilera-rocks-baby-bump-in-mini-black -dress-on-stage-photo-201435; last accessed May 14, 2014.

27. It is interesting to see Lana Del Rey evoke references to JFK and a bygone political era, in concert with African American rapper ASAP Rocky, in her video for "National Anthem" (2012). Thanks to Mikhala Stutzman for pointing this out in an unpublished paper on the video.

28. Madonna was pregnant before the "bump" became a cultural obsession; the press covered each of her two pregnancies (in 1996 and 2000), as well as the adoption of her two children, David and Mercy. However, the mania for celebrity pregnancies hadn't become entrenched enough to warrant the kind of extensive coverage that women post-2000 have been subjected to and profited from. It is fun to imagine how a post-2000 press would treat a pregnant Madonna or how a pregnant Madonna would treat the contemporary press.

29. P!nk, or Pink, was born Alecia Beth Moore. http://hollywoodlife.com/2010/11/16/ pink-confirms-shes-pregnant-with-her-first-baby-and-she-thinks-its-a-girl; last accessed Oct. 5, 2013.

30. Leigh Blickley. 2010. "Pink Plans to Take Her Baby Roadtrippin' on Her Tour Bus!" http://hollywoodlife.com/2010/11/24/pink-taking-her-baby-on-tour-carey-hart; last accessed Nov. 4, 2013.

31. http://www.mybabyradio.com/celebgossip/pink-reveals-her-pregnancy-side-effect; last accessed Apr. 22, 2015.

32. http://perezhilton.com/perezitos/2012-12-10-pink-feels-sympathy-for-kate-middletons-pregnancy#ixzz318lFmouT; last accessed Oct. 5, 2013.

33. http://www.mybabyradio.com/celebrity-gossip/pink-reveals-her-pregnancy-side-effect; last accessed Nov. 7, 2013. Rapper Lil' Kim conceived her first child in early 2014 and received treatment in the press similar to Pink, such as: "Rapper Lil' Kim announced her pregnancy at The Blonds Fashion Week after-party by turning up on the red carpet with a HUGE baby bump. The 39-year-old, who is keeping the father's identity private for now, insists she won't stop performing whilst she's expecting. 'I'm still going to work,' she said. 'I'm still going to be hardcore. The baby has made me even more of a beast!'" (http://www.usmagazine.com/celebrity-moms/news/lil-kim-pregnant-im-still-going-to-be-hardcore-after-baby-2014132; last accessed Apr. 22, 2015).

34. http://www.nydailynews.com/entertainment/gossip/american-music-awards-2010-pregnant-pink-shows-baby-bump-red-carpet-article-1.452700#ixzz318qz7PBY; last accessed Nov. 21, 2013.

35. Prior to the advent of formula feeding, breastfeeding was the only source of nutrition for babies before they were old enough to handle nonhuman milk and solid food. Therefore, until the 1930s, the vast majority of mothers in the United States nursed their babies, at least until six or nine months of age (Baumslag and Michels, xxi). The vast majority of those same women did not work outside the home for the period of time during which they were nursing their children. As women entered the workforce in larger numbers and took jobs that did not permit maternity leaves, the ability of women to nurse for an extended period of time was put into jeopardy. Simultaneously (and not coincidentally), convenience became the watchword of the day for all forms of food preparation; as such, formula feeding became both necessary and attractive. Bottle feeding became the norm.

By 1995, only 53 percent of women in the United States even attempted breastfeeding, and only one in five of all infants in the United States would receive any breast milk at all in the first twenty weeks of age (Baumslag and Michels, xxi).

36. I absolutely do not mean to imply a lack or denote that these parents are somehow "less than" when noting these absences. Lesbian-headed households do not "lack" fathers or men, but men and fathers are usually absent from the media coverage, unless it is a narrative that highlights the question of who the father "is." Moms who parent via adoption or surrogacy do not "lack" a bump, but their bumps or the bumps of their surrogates or birth moms are absent, usually, from the media coverage.

37. http://www.parenting.com/gallery/celebrity-single-moms; last accessed May 11, 2014.

38. The father of Minnie Driver's child is reported to be television writer and producer Timothy Lea.

39. http://www.dailymail.co.uk/tvshowbiz/article-2103668/Minnie-Driver-FINALLY-reveals-identity-son-Henrys-father.html#ixzz31iosfnEm; last accessed May 11, 2014.

40. Phelan 1994; Phelan 1993.

41. There is a tremendously rich literature on lesbians and popular culture that I cannot do justice to in this section. Beyond Phelan's extensive body of work, readers are advised to see Reed 2009; Beirne 2008; and Gever 2003—to start.

42. Foster and Bernard were reportedly together from 1988 to 2008. Foster is now married to Alexandrea Hedison, a photographer and actress. http://www.eonline.com/news/534871/jodie-foster-marries-girlfriend-alexandra-hedison; last accessed May 10, 2014.

43. http://abcnews.go.com/Entertainment/story?id=107291; last accessed Oct. 6, 2013.

44. *Qparent* also includes bisexual moms. With a photo of Ani DiFranco, her daughter, and her husband, the author writes that DiFranco is "unabashedly bisexual and fiercely independent." A few slides later, *Qparent* stresses that "biphobia" is alive and well and is typified by negative responses to pro basketball player Sheryl Swoopes's engagement to a man, after living and parenting with a female partner for seven years.

45. http://qparent.com/2012/12/28/12-lesbian-bisexual-celebrity-moms; last accessed Mar. 20, 2014.

46. Goodwin 2010, i.

47. http://www.msnbc.com/melissa-harris-perry/how-we-made-our-miracle; last accessed May 12, 2014.

48. http://www.nbcnews.com/health/kids-health/ivf-used-record-setting-1-100-babies-u-s-n32026; last accessed May 12, 2014.

49. Surrogacy is not without controversy. Just like parents (celebrity and not) who engage in international adoption, those who utilize surrogates are sometimes accused of being part of a "market in babies" that further entrenches racialized understandings of the worth of particular humans. Perry herself highlighted the potential ethical dilemmas of surrogacy in her statement to the press, writing that she first seriously considered surrogacy when she learned that "a dear friend and his husband were expecting their second child via surrogacy. He is a feminist scholar and a politically progressive intellectual. When I discussed my concerns with the ethics of surrogacy, he understood. He repeatedly talked with [husband] James and me, introduced us to a thoughtful attorney, and shared the good and bad of his own surrogacy story. I read everything I could find, consulted everyone I could, and prayed a lot." For some of the critiques of surrogacy as they relate to the coordination of capitalism and medicine, see Rothman 1989, who wrote, "This is where this is all heading: the commodification of children and the proletarianization of motherhood" (66)—the use of women's labor to create children-commodities who provide income (material, psychic, solidarity) to the family. See also Becker 2000; Gabilondo 2010; Goodwin 2010. For a critique of adoption and surrogacy as they relate to race, see, as well: Dorow 2010; Roberts 1998; Williams 1997; Berkowitz and Snyder 1988. There is a nice conversation about the use of "choice" in describing arrangements of surrogacy (and, by extension, adoption) and whether surrogacy can be considered "feminist," on the Reproductive Health Reality Check website, with scholars like Lisa Ikemoto weighing in (http://rhrealitycheck.org/article/2014/04/23/invoking-choice-discussing-surrogacy-feminist-concern-mistake; last accessed Apr. 22, 2015).

50. Appadurai wrote, "Commoditization lies at the complex intersection of temporal, cultural, and social factors. To the degree that some things in a society are frequently

to be found in the commodity phase, to fit the requirements of commodity candidacy, and to appear in a commodity context, they are quintessential commodities" (Appadurai 1986, 15). Music stars and actresses, no matter how "indie" they are, are quintessential commodities in communicative capital.

51. http://web.archive.org/web/20121025201853/http://www.hollywoodreporter.com/review/black-swan-film-review-29918; last accessed Jan. 8, 2014.

52. http://web.archive.org/web/20140324063741/http://www.incontention.com/2010/09/01/review-black-swan; last accessed June 9, 2014.

53. http://web.archive.org/web/20131027131555/http://articles.latimes.com:80/2008/oct/16/entertainment/et-mila16; last accessed June 11, 2014.

54. There are several versions of this video on YouTube. The version of PopSugar's YouTube channel devoted to Kunis has more than 700,000 views; the one posted by Holly Whoops has more than a million. I last accessed a version of the video on the TMZ channel, which said Kunis had gone "nuts" and "flipped out" in the interview and had more than 720,000 views. http://www.youtube.com/watch?v=2h_hbk_Ax5k; last accessed June 7, 2014.

55. http://www.eonline.com/news/547236/mila-kunis-flaunts-growing-baby-bump-in-tight-top-visits-her-parents-with-ashton-kutcher-see-the-pic; last accessed June 10, 2014.

56. http://www.usmagazine.com/celebrity-moms/news/mila-kunis-goes-casual-with-ashton-kutcher-see-the-pregnant-star-201426; last accessed May 1, 2015.

57. https://www.youtube.com/watch?v=onDCvHtHSkY; last accessed May 17, 2015.

58. http://www.usmagazine.com/celebrity-moms/news/mila-kunis-talks-pregnancy-ashton-kutcher-proposal-in-marie-claire-2014126; last accessed June 12, 2014.

59. Yes, of course, Kunis is a celebrity, and her image is being used to sell and commodify, to brand and associate her with particular practices that connect her to consumers. While her inscrutability may be enabling a feminist act of resistance against patriarchal norms associated with how we "should" be pregnant and parent, she is also engaging in activities that serve to commodify the experience. Indeed, Kunis's inscrutability might simply prompt us to watch her more, in order to understand her better.

60. Santos et al. 2008; Santos 2007.

61. Santos articulates this as a "sociology of silences" in an interview with Roger Dale published by the journal *Globalisation, Societies, and Education (Dale 2006)*.

62. Santos 1995.

63. Santos, Nunes, and Meneses 2008.

64. Scott 2012, 141.

65. Scott 2012, 121.

66. Gullette 2002, 134.

67. There is so much to be said about the expectations that women *will* reproduce and the nonnormative stance of women who do not parent. As this is a book on celebrity pregnancy and the baby bump, I do not pursue the topic here—but urge that we think about refusals to conceive and gestate as important refusals in and of themselves.

BIBLIOGRAPHY

Adorno, Theodor W., and Max Horkheimer. 1944. *Dialectic of Enlightenment.* New York: Verso Books.

Alford, Justine. 2014. "Diet of Mother Can Lead to Alterations in Her Child's DNA." IFL Science, Apr. 30. http://www.iflscience.com/health-and-medicine/diet-mother-can -lead-alterations-her-child's-dna; last accessed May 1, 2014.

Alexander-Floyd, Nikol G. 2012. "Disappearing Acts: Reclaiming Intersectionality in the Social Sciences in a Post-Black Feminist Era." 24 *Feminist Formations* 1: 1–25.

Althusser, Louis. 1997. *On the Reproduction of Capitalism: Ideology and Ideological State Apparatuses.* New York: Verso. (Originally published in 1971.)

Anzaldua, Gloria, and Cherrie Moraga. 1995. *This Bridge Called My Back: Writings by Radical Women of Color.* Watertown, MA: Persephone Press. (Originally published in 1981.)

Appadurai, Arjun (ed.). 1986. *The Social Life of Things: Commodities in Cultural Perspectives.* New York: Cambridge University Press.

Asimow, Michael, and Shannon Mader. 2004. *Law and Popular Culture: A Course Book.* New York: Peter Lang.

Baer, Judith A. 1999. *Our Lives Before the Law: Constructing a Feminist Jurisprudence.* Princeton, NJ: Princeton University Press.

Bailey, Lucy. 2001. "Gender Shows: First-Time Mothers and Embodied Selves." 15 *Gender and Society* 1: 110–129.

Banks, Taunya Lovell. 1999. "Toward a Global Critical Feminist Vision: Domestic Work and the Nanny Tax Debate." 3 *Journal of Gender Race and Justice* 1.

Bartky, Sandra Lee. 1999. "Foucault, Femininity, and the Modernization of Patriarchal Power," pages 129–154 in Janet Price and Margrit Shildrick (eds.), *Feminist Theory and the Body: A Reader.* New York: Routledge.

Bartlett, Katharine T., and Rosanne Kennedy. 1991. *Feminist Legal Theory: Readings in Law and Gender*. Boulder, CO: Westview Press.

———. 1991. "Introduction," pages 1–14 in Katharine T. Bartlett and Rosanne Kennedy, *Feminist Legal Theory: Readings in Law and Gender*. Boulder, CO: Westview Press.

Bassin, Donna, Margaret Honey, and Meryle Mahrer Kaplan (eds.). (1994). *Representations of Motherhood*. New Haven, CT: Yale University Press.

Baumslag, Naomi, and Dia L. Michels. 1995. *Milk, Money, and Madness: The Culture and Politics of Breastfeeding*. Westport, CT: Greenwood.

Beck, Ulrich. 1992. *Risk Society: Towards a New Modernity*. Vol. 17. Thousand Oaks, CA: Sage.

———. 1994. *Reflexive Modernization: Politics, Tradition, and Aesthetics in the Modern Social Order*. Palo Alto, CA: Stanford University Press.

Becker, Gay. 2000. *The Elusive Embryo: How Women and Men Approach New Reproductive Technologies*. Los Angeles: University of California Press.

Bedolla, Lisa Garcia. 2007. "Intersections of Inequality: Understanding Marginalization and Privilege in the Post-Civil Rights Era." *Politics & Gender* 2: 232–248.

Beirne, Rebecca. 2008. *Lesbians in Television and Text after the Millennium*. New York: Palgrave McMillan.

Bell, David, and Gill Valentine (eds.). 1995. *Mapping Desire: Geographies of Sexualities*. New York: Routledge.

Beltran, Mary C. 2007. "The Hollywood Latina Body as a Site of Social Struggle: Media Constructions of Stardom and Jennifer Lopez's 'Cross-over Butt,'" excerpted on pages 275–286 in Sean Redmond and Su Holmes (eds.), *Stardom and Celebrity: A Reader*. London: Sage Publications.

Bergman, Paul, and Michael Asimow. 2006. *Reel Justice: The Courtroom Goes to the Movies*. New York: Andrew McMeel.

Berkowitz, Jonathan M., and Jack W. Snyder. 1988. "Racism and Sexism in Medically Assisted Conception." 12 *Bioethics* 1: 25–44.

Berlant, Lauren. 1997. *The Queen of America Goes to Washington City: Essays on Sex and Citizenship*. Durham, NC: Duke University Press.

Besnier, Niko. 2009. *Gossip and the Everyday Production of Politics*. Manoa: University of Hawaii Press.

Block, Jennifer. 2007. *Pushed: The Painful Truth about Childbirth and Modern Maternity Care*. Cambridge, MA: Perseus Books.

Bobel, Chris, and Samantha Kwan (eds.). 2011. *Embodied Resistance: Challenging the Norms, Breaking the Rules*. Nashville, TN: Vanderbilt University Press.

Bordo, Susan. 1992. "Postmodern Subjects, Postmodern Bodies." 18 *Feminist Studies* 1: 159–176.

———. 1997. "The Body and the Reproduction of Femininity," pages 90–110 in Katie Conby, Nadia Medina, and Sarah Stanbury (eds.), *Writing on the Body: Female Embodiment and Feminist Theory*. New York: Columbia University Press.

———. 2004. *Unbearable Weight: Feminism, Western Culture, and the Body*. Tenth Anniversary Edition. Los Angeles: University of California Press.

Bottomley, Anne, Susie Gibson, and Belinda Meteyard. 1987. "Dworkin; Which Dworkin? Taking Feminism Seriously," pages 47–60 in Peter Fitzpatrick and Alan Hunt (eds.), *Critical Legal Studies*. New York: Basil Blackwell.

Bourdieu, Pierre. 1980. "The Production of Belief: Contribution to an Economy of Symbolic Goods." *Media, Culture, and Society* 2: 261–293.

———. 1990. *The Logic of Practice*. Palo Alto, CA: Stanford University Press.

Breese, Elizabeth Butler. 2010. "Meaning, Celebrity, and the Underage Pregnancy of Jamie Lynn Spears." 3 *Cultural Sociology* 3: 337–355.

Brewis, Joanna, and John Sinclair. 2000. "Exploring Embodiment: Women, Biology and Work," pages 192–214 in John Hassard, Ruth Holliday, and Hugh Willmott (eds.), *Body and Organization*. London: Sage.

Brown, Wendy. 1995. *States of Injury: Power and Freedom in Late Modernity*. Princeton, NJ: Princeton University Press.

———. 2001. *Politics out of History*. Princeton, NJ: Princeton University Press.

———. 2010. *Walled States, Waning Sovereignty*. New York: Zone Books.

Browner, Carole H., and Carolyn F. Sargent (eds.). 2011. *Reproduction, Globalization, and the State: New Theoretical and Ethnographic Perspectives*. Durham, NC: Duke University Press.

Bumiller, Kristin. 1997. "Spectacles of the Strange: Envisioning Violence in the Central Park Jogger Trial," pages 217–224 in Martha Fineman and Martha McCluskey (eds.), *Feminism, Media, and the Law*. New York: Oxford University Press.

———. 1998. "Body Images: How Does the Body Matter in the Legal Imagination?" pages 145–161 in Bryant Garth and Austin Sarat (eds.), *How Does Law Matter?* Chicago: Northwestern University Press.

Burchell, Graham. 1991. "Peculiar Interests: Civil Society and Governing 'The System of Natural Liberty,'" pages 119–150 in Graham Burchell, Colin Gordon, and Peter Miller (eds.), *The Foucault Effect: Studies in Governmentality, with Two Lectures by and an Interview with Michel Foucault*. Chicago: The University of Chicago Press.

———. 2009. *The Founding Fathers, Pop Culture, and Constitutional Law*. Burlington, VT: Ashgate.

———, Colin Gordon, and Peter Miller (eds.). 1991. *The Foucault Effect: Studies in Governmentality, with Two Lectures by and an Interview with Michel Foucault*. Chicago: University of Chicago Press.

Burgess, Susan. 2009. "YouTube on Masculinity and the founding Fathers: Constitutionalism 2.0." 64 *Political Research Quarterly* 1: 120–131.

Burgess, Susan. 2013. *Popularizing American Politics: Understanding American Government through Pop Culture*. New York: Routledge.

Butler, Judith. 1993. *Bodies That Matter*. New York: Routledge.

———. 1999. "Bodies That Matter," pages 235–246 in Janet Price and Margrit Shildrick (eds.), *Feminist Theory and the Body: A Reader*. New York: Routledge.

———, and Athena Athanasiou. 2013. *Dispossession: The Performative in the Political*. Oxford, UK: Wiley.

Buttenwieser, Sarah Werthan. 2007. "Hooray for Hollywomb!" 36 *Bitch* Summer: 23–26.

Calavita, Kitty. 2010. *Invitation to Law and Society: An Introduction to the Study of Real Law.* Chicago: University of Chicago Press.

Caldwell, Paulette. 1991. "A Hair Piece: Perspectives on the Intersection of Race and Gender." *Duke Law Journal* 365.

Carpio, Myla Vicenti. 2004. "The Lost Generation: American Indian Women and Sterilization Abuse." 31 *Social Justice* 4: 40–53.

Carter, Bill. 2004. "'Friends' Finale's Audience Is Fourth Biggest Ever." *New York Times,* May 8. http://www.nytimes.com/2004/05/08/arts/friends-finale-s-audience-is-the-fourth-biggest-ever.html; last accessed April 29, 2015.

Cassidy, Tina. 2006. *Birth: The Surprising History of How We Are Born.* New York: Atlantic Monthly Press.

Charles, Nickie, and Marrion Kerr. 1986. "Food for Feminist Thought." 34 *The Sociological Review* 3: 537–572.

Chase, Anthony. 1996. "Popular Culture/Popular Justice," pages 133–153 in John Denvir (ed.), *Legal Reelism: Movies as Legal Texts.* Urbana: University of Illinois Press.

Chodorow, Nancy J. 1999. *The Reproduction of Mothering: Psychoanalysis and the Sociology of Gender.* 2nd ed. Berkeley: University of California Press.

Clover, Carol J. 1998. "Law and the Order of Popular Culture," pages 97–120 in Austin Sarat and Thomas Kearns (eds.), *Law in the Domains of Culture.* Ann Arbor: University of Michigan Press.

Coates, Norma. 1997. "(R)evolution Now? Rock and the Political Potential of Gender," pages 50–64 in Sheila Whiteley (ed.), *Sexing the Groove: Popular Music and Gender.* New York: Routledge.

Cohen, Sara. 1997. "Men Making a Scene: Rock and the Production of Gender," pages 17–36 in Sheila Whiteley (ed.), *Sexing the Groove: Popular Music and Gender.* New York: Routledge.

———. 2004. "Popular Music, Gender, and Sexuality," pages 226–242 in Simon Frith, Will Straw, and John Street (eds.), *The Cambridge Companion to Pop and Rock.* New York: Cambridge University Press.

———, and Margaret L. Andersen (eds.). 1992. *Race, Class, and Gender: An Anthology.* New York: Cengage Learning.

Collins, Patricia Hill. 1994. "Shifting the Center: Race, Class, and Feminist Theorizing about Motherhood," pages 56–74 in Donna Bassin, Margaret Honey, and Meryle Mahrer Kaplan (eds.), *Representations of Motherhood.* New Haven, CT: Yale University Press.

———. 1998. "It's All in the Family: Intersections of Gender, Race, and Nation." 13 *Hypatia* 3: 62–82.

———. 2000. *Black Feminist Thought: Knowledge, Consciousness, and the Politics of Empowerment.* New York: Routledge.

Conby, Katie, Nadia Medina, and Sarah Stanbury (eds.). 1997. *Writing on the Body: Female Embodiment and Feminist Theory.* New York: Columbia University Press.

Coombe, Rosemary J. 1998. "Contingent Articulations: A Critical Cultural Studies of Law," pages 21–64 in Austin Sarat and Thomas Kearns (eds.), *Law in the Domains of Culture.* Ann Arbor: University of Michigan Press.

Cooper, Andrew. 2008. *Celebrity Diplomacy*. Boulder, CO: Paradigm.

Cortese, Anthony J. 2008. *Provocateur: Images of Women and Minorities in Advertising.* New York: Rowman & Littlefield.

Cramer, Renée Ann. 2009. "Sharing in Community while Interviewing 'Outlaws': Methodological Challenges and Opportunities." 1 *International Review of Qualitative Research* 4: 453–479.

———. 2012. "The Des Moines BirthPlace: Iowa's First Birth Center." 71 *Annals of Iowa*: 39–73.

Crenshaw, Kimberlé Williams. 1988. "Race, Reform, and Retrenchment: Transformation and Legitimation in Antidiscrimination Law." 101 *Harvard Law Review* 1331.

———. 1989. "Demarginalizing the Intersection of Race and Sex: A Black Feminist Critique of Antidiscrimination Doctrine, Feminist Theory, and Antiracist Politics." *University of Chicago Legal Forum*: 139–167.

———. 2001. "First Decade: Critical Reflections, or a Foot in the Closing Door." 49 *UCLA Law Review* 1343.

Cruikshank, Barbara. 1999. *The Will to Empower: Democratic Citizens and Other Subjects.* Ithaca, NY: Cornell University Press.

Currid-Halkett, Elizabeth. 2011. *Starstruck: The Business of Celebrity.* New York: Faber & Faber.

Cushman, Clare (ed.). 2001. *Supreme Court Decisions and Women's Rights: Milestones to Equality.* Washington, DC: CQ Press.

Dale, Roger. 2006. "From Comparison to Translation: Extending the Research Imagination—an Interview with Boaventura de Sousa Santos." 4 *Globalisation, Societies, and Education* 2: 179–182.

Dallek, Matthew. 1984. *Ronald Reagan: The Politics of Symbolism.* Cambridge, MA: Harvard University Press.

———. 2000. *The Right Moment: Ronald Reagan's First Victory and the Decisive Turning Point in American Politics.* New York: Free Press.

Darian-Smith, Eve, and Peter Fitzpatrick (eds.). 1999. *Laws of the Postcolonial.* Ann Arbor: University of Michigan Press.

Davies, Bronwyn. 2008. *Judith Butler in Conversation: Analyzing the Texts and Talk of Everyday Life.* New York: Routledge.

Davis, Joyce. 1997. "Introduction to Part III: Essentializing Gender," pages 171–176 in Martha Fineman and Martha McCluskey (eds.), *Feminism, Media, and the Law.* New York: Oxford University Press.

Davis-Floyd, Robbie E. 1992. *Birth as an American Rite of Passage.* Berkeley: University of California Press.

Dean, Jodi. 2009. *Democracy and Other Neoliberal Fantasies: Communicative Capitalism and Left Politics.* Durham, NC: Duke University Press.

Denvir, John. 1996. *Legal Reelism: Movies as Legal Texts.* Urbana: University of Illinois Press.

Denzin, Norman K. 2000. "Aesthetics and the Practices of Qualitative Inquiry." 6 *Qualitative Inquiry* 256.

DeVault, Marjorie L. February 1990. "Talking and Listening from Women's Standpoint: Feminist Strategies for Interviewing and Analysis." 37 *Social Problems* 1: 96–116.

Dillingham, Brint. 1977. "Indian Women and IHS Sterilization Practices." 3 *American Indian Journal for the Institute for the Development of Indian Law* 1: 27–28.

Dixon, Simon Winter. 2003. "Ambiguous Ecologies: Stardom's Domestic Mise-en-Scene." 42 *Cinema Journal* 2: 81.

Dorow, Sara. 2010. "Producing Kinship through the Marketplaces of Transnational Adoption," pages 69–83 in *Baby Markets: Money and the New Politics of Creating Families.* New York: Cambridge University Press.

Draper, Elaine. 2003. "Fetal Exclusion Policies and Gendered Constructions of Suitable Work." 40 *Social Problems* 1: 70–103.

Durham, Meenakshi G. 2009. "M.I.A.: A Production Analysis of Musical Subversion." Paper presented at the annual meeting of the International Communication Association, Chicago, IL; retrieved online at allacademic.com; last accessed May 9, 2014.

Dyer, Richard. 2003. *Heavenly Bodies: Film Stars and Society.* New York: Routledge.

———. 2007a. "Stars," excerpted on pages 78–84 of Sean Redmond and Su Holmes (eds.), *Stardom and Celebrity: A Reader.* London: Sage.

———. 2007b. "Heavenly Bodies," excerpted on pages 85–89 of Sean Redmond and Su Holmes (eds.), *Stardom and Celebrity: A Reader.* London: Sage.

———, and Paul McDonald. 2004. *Stars.* London: British Film Institute.

Dworkin, Andrea. 1974. *Women Hating: A Radical Look at Sexuality.* New York: Plume.

Earle, Sarah. 2003. "Bumps and Boobs: Fatness and Women's Experiences of Pregnancy." 26 *Women's Studies International Forum* 3: 245–252.

Eckholm, Erik. 2013. "Case Explores Rights of Fetus versus Mother." *New York Times,* Oct. 23.

Edwards, Mark Evan. 1996. "Pregnancy Discrimination Litigation: Legal Erosion of Capitalist Ideology under Equal Employment Opportunity Law." 75 *Social Forces* 1: 247–268.

Eggers, Dave. 2014. *The Circle.* New York: Knopf.

Eisenstein, Zillah. 1997. "Feminism of the North and West for Export: Transnational Gender and the Racializing of Gender," pages 29–49 in Jodi Dean (ed.), *Feminism and the New Democracy: Resisting the Political.* Thousand Oaks, CA: Sage.

Erlanger, Howard, Elizabeth Chambliss, and Marygold S. Melli. 1987. "Participation and Flexibility in Informal Processes: Cautions from the Divorce Context." 21 *Law and Society Review* 4: 585–604.

Ewing, Sally. 1987. "Formal Justice and the Spirit of Capitalism: Max Weber's Sociology of Law." 21 *Law and Society Review* 3: 487–512.

Faludi, Susan. 1991. *Backlash: The Undeclared War against American Women.* New York: Crown.

Featherstone, Mike. 1991. "The Body in Consumer Culture." 8 *Theory, Culture, and Society* 2.

Ferris, Kerry O., and Scott R. Harris. 2011. *Stargazing: Celebrity, Fame, and Social Interaction.* New York: Routledge.

Fineman, Martha. 1993. "Our Sacred Institution: The Ideal of the Family in American Law and Society." 387 *Utah Law Review*.

———. 1995. *The Neutered Mother, the Sexual Family, and Other Twentieth Century Tragedies*. New York: Routledge.

———, and Isabel Karpin. 1995. *Mothers in Law*. New York: Columbia University Press.

———, and Martha T. McCluskey. 1997. *Feminism, Media, and the Law*. New York: Oxford University Press.

Firestone, Shulamith, and Anne Koedt (eds.). 1970. *Notes from the Second Year: Women's Liberation: Major Writings of the Radical Feminists*. New York: Radical Feminism.

Fitzpatrick, Peter. 2008. *Collected Essays in Law: Law as Resistance—Modernism, Imperialism, Legalism*. Burlington, VT: Ashgate.

———, and Eve Darian-Smith. 1999. "Laws of the Postcolonial: An Insistent Introduction," pages 1–18 of Eve Darian-Smith and Peter Fitzpatrick (eds.), *Laws of the Postcolonial*. Ann Arbor: University of Michigan Press.

Fleury-Steiner, Benjamin, Kerry Dunn, and Ruth Fleury-Steiner. 2009. "Governing through Crime as Commonsense Racism: Race, Space, and Death Penalty 'Reform' in Delaware." 11 *Punishment & Society* 1: 5–24.

Fogel, Susan Berke, Francine Coeytaux, Marcy Darnovsky, Lisa Ikemoto, and Judy Norsigian. April 23, 2014. "Invoking 'Choice' When Discussing Surrogacy as a Feminist Concern Is a Mistake." *Reality Check*. http://rhrealitycheck.org/article/2014/04/23/invoking-choice-discussing-surrogacy-feminist-concern-mistake; last accessed Feb. 25, 2015.

Foucault, Michel. 1977. *Discipline and Punish: The Birth of the Prison*. New York: Vintage.

———. 1978. *The History of Sexuality. Vol. 1: An Introduction*. New York: Vintage.

———. 1977–1979. "Governmentality" and related lectures in Graham Burchell, Colin Gordon, and Peter Miller (eds.), *The Foucault Effect: Studies in Governmentality*. Chicago: University of Chicago Press.

———. 2010 (1978–1979). *The Birth of Biopolitics: Lectures at the College de France, 1978–1979*. New York: Picador Press.

Fox, Nick. 2012. *The Body*. New York: Polity Press.

Francus, Marilyn. 2012. *Monstrous Motherhood: Eighteenth-Century Culture and the Ideology of Domesticity*. Baltimore, MD: Johns Hopkins University Press.

Franke, Katherine M. 2001. "Theorizing Yes: An Essay on Feminism, Law, and Desire." 101 *Columbia Law Review* 1: 181–208.

Fraser, Nancy. 1989. *Unruly Practices: Power, Discourse, and Gender in Contemporary Social Theory*. London: Polity.

———. 1997. *Justice Interruptus: Critical Reflections on the "Postcolonial" Condition*. New York: Cambridge University Press.

Friedman, Lawrence. 2007. *Guarding Life's Dark Secrets: Legal and Social Controls over Reputation, Property, and Privacy*. Palo Alto, CA: Stanford University Press.

Frith, Simon, and Angela McRobbie. 1990 (1978). "Rock and Sexuality," pages 371–389 in Simon Frith and Andrew Goodwin (eds.), *On Record: Rock, Pop, and the Written Word*. New York: Routledge.

Frith, Simon, Will Straw, and John Street. 2004. *The Cambridge Companion to Pop and Rock*. New York: Cambridge University Press.

Gaar, Gillian G. 1992. *She's a Rebel: The History of Women in Rock and Roll*. Seattle, WA: Seal Press.

Gabilondo, Jose. 2010. "Heterosexuality as a Prenatal Social Problem: Why Parents and Courts Have a Taste for Heterosexuality," pages 118–131 in Michele Brachter Goodwin, *Baby Markets: Money and the New Politics of Creating Families*. New York: Cambridge University Press.

Gabler, Neal. 1995. *Winchell*. New York: Knopf.

Garber, Marjorie. 1998. "Cinema Scopes: Evolution, Media, and the Law," pages 121–160 in Austin Sarat and Thomas Kearns (eds.), *Law in the Domains of Culture*. Ann Arbor: University of Michigan Press.

Garth, Bryant, and Austin Sarat. 1998. "Studying How Law Matters: An Introduction," pages 1–14 in Bryant Garth and Austin Sarat (eds.), *How Does Law Matter?* Chicago: Northwestern University Press.

Geraghty, Christine. 2007. "Re-examining Stardom: Questions of Texts, Bodies, and Performance," excerpted on pages 99–110 in Sean Redmond and Su Holmes, *Stardom and Celebrity: A Reader*. London: Sage.

Gever, Martha. 2003. *Entertaining Lesbians: Celebrity, Sexuality, and Self-Invention*. New York: Routledge.

Gilliom, John. 2001. *Overseers of the Poor: Surveillance, Resistance, and the Limits of Privacy*. 1st ed. Chicago: University of Chicago Press.

Gimlin, Debra L. 2001. *Body Work: Beauty and Self-Image in American Culture*. Los Angeles: University of California Press.

Ginsburg, Faye, and Rayna Rapp. 1991. "The Politics of Reproduction." 20 *Annual Review of Anthropology*: 311–343.

Glenn, Evelyn Nakano. 1994. "Social Constructions of Mothering: A Thematic Overview," pages 1–32 in Evelyn Nakano Glenn, Grace Chang, and Linda Rennie Forcey (eds.), *Mothering: Ideology, Experience, and Agency*. New York: Routledge.

———, Grace Chang, and Linda Rennie Forcey (eds.). 1994. *Mothering: Ideology, Experience, and Agency*. New York: Routledge.

Goldstein, Jessica. 2014. "Meet the Woman Who Did Everything in Her Power to Hide Her Pregnancy from Big Data." *Think Progress*, Apr. 29. http://thinkprogress.org/culture/2014/04/29/3432050/can-you-hide-from-big-data; last accessed May 1, 2014.

Goodale, Mark, and Nancy Postero (eds.). 2013. *Neoliberalism, Interrupted: Social Change and Contested Governance in Contemporary Latin America*. Stanford, CA: Stanford University Press.

———. 2013. "Revolution and Retrenchment: Illuminating the Present in Latin America," pages 1–22 in Mark Goodale and Nancy Postero (eds.), *Neoliberalism, Interrupted: Social Change and Contested Governance in Contemporary Latin America*. Stanford, CA: Stanford University Press.

Goodman, Douglas J. 2006. "Approaches to Law and Popular Culture." 31 *Law & Social Inquiry* 3: 757–784.

Goodwin, Michele Bratcher (ed.). 2010. *Baby Markets: Money and the New Politics of Creating Families*. New York: Cambridge University Press.

Gordon, Colin. 1991. "Governmental Rationality: An Introduction," pages 1–52 in Graham Burchell, Colin Gordon, and Peter Miller (eds.), *The Foucault Effect: Studies in Governmentality, with Two Lectures by and an Interview with Michel Foucault*. Chicago: University of Chicago Press.

Gross, Terry. 2013. "Personhood in the Womb: A Constitutional Question." *Fresh Air* (National Public Radio), Nov. 21. http://www.npr.org/2013/11/21/246534132/personhood-in-the-womb-a-constitutional-question; last accessed Apr. 27, 2015.

Grossberg, Lawrence. 1988. "Putting the Pop back into Postmodernism," pages 167–190 in Andrew Ross (ed.), *Universal Abandon? The Politics of Postmodernism*. Minneapolis: University of Minnesota Press.

Gullette, Margaret Morganroth. 2002. "Valuing 'Postmaternity' as a Revolutionary Feminist Concept." 28 *Feminist Studies* 3 (Autumn): 553–572.

———. 2004. *Aged by Culture*. Chicago: University of Chicago Press.

Haltom, William, and Michael McCann. 1994. *Distorting the Law: Politics, Media, and the Litigation Crisis*. Chicago: University of Chicago Press.

Hancock, Ange-Marie. 2007. "When Multiplication Doesn't Equal Quick Addition: Examining Intersectionality as a Research Paradigm." 5 *PS: Perspectives on Politics* 1: 63–78.

Hanigsberg, Julia. 1997. "Glamour Law: Feminism through the Looking Glass of Popular Women's Magazines," pages 72–83 of Martha Fineman and Martha McCluskey (eds.), *Feminism, Media, and the Law*. New York: Oxford University Press.

Hardt, Michael, and Antonio Negri. 1994. *Labor of Dionysus: A Critique of the State-Form*. Minneapolis: University of Minnesota Press.

———. 2001. "Adventures of the Multitude: Response of the Authors." 13 *Rethinking Marxism* 3–4: 236–243.

Harrington, Christine B., and Barbara Yngvesson. 1990. "Interpretive Sociolegal Research." 15 *Law & Social Inquiry* 1: 135–148.

Harris, Mark. 2008. "The Mommy Track." *New York Times*, Oct. 19, AR 1.

Harstock, Nancy. 1983. *Money, Sex, and Power*. Boston: Northeastern University Press.

Harvey, David. 2005. *A Brief History of Neoliberalism*. New York: Oxford University Press.

hooks, bell. 1990. *Race, Gender, and Cultural Politics*. Boston: South End Press.

Huckle, Patricia. 1981. "The Womb Factor: Pregnancy Policies and Employment of Women." 34 *Western Political Quarterly* 1: 114–126.

Hunt, Alan. 1996. *Governance of the Consuming Passions: A History of Sumptuary Law*. New York: Macmillan.

Hunter, James Davison. 1992. *Culture Wars: The Struggle to Control the Family, Art, Education, Law, and Politics in America*. New York: Basic Books.

Ikemoto, Lisa C. 1991. "Furthering the Inquiry: Race, Class, and Culture in the Forced Medical Treatment of Women of Color." 59 *Tennessee Law Review* 487.

———. 1993. "Traces of the Master Narrative in the Story of African American/Korean

American Conflict: How We Constructed 'Los Angeles.'" 66 *Southern California Law Review* 1581.

Inglis, Fred. 1988. *Popular Culture and Political Power*. New York: St. Martin's Press.

Jolie, Angelina. 2013. "My Medical Choice." *New York Times*, May 14.

Jong-Fast, Molly. 2003. "View: Out of Step and Having a Baby." *New York Times*, Oct. 5. http://query.nytimes.com/gst/fullpage.html?res=9D00E3D6143CF936A35753C1A965 9C8B63&sec=&spon=&pagewanted=2; last accessed Oct. 28, 2014.

Jordan-Zachery, Julia. *Shadow Bodies: Black Women, Ideology, Representation, and Politics*. Unpublished manuscript, on file with author.

Joslin, Richard, Peter Leuck, Chad Martino, Melissa Rhoads, Brian Wachter, Robin Chapman, and Gail Christian. (n.d.). "Gap Inc.: Has the Retailer Lost Its Style?" Cengage.

Kaplan, E. Ann. 1994. "Look Who's Talking, Indeed: Fetal Images in Recent North American Visual Culture," pages 121–138 in Evelyn Nakano Glenn, Grace Chang, and Linda Rennie Forcey (eds.), *Mothering: Ideology, Experience, and Agency*. New York: Routledge.

———. 1994. "Sex, Work, and Motherhood: Maternal Subjectivity in Recent Visual Culture," pages 256–271 in Donna Bassin, Margaret Honey, and Meryle Mahrer Kaplan (eds.), *Representations of Motherhood*. New Haven: Yale University Press.

Karpin, Isabel. 1997. "Pop Justice: TV, Motherhood, and the Law," pages 120–135 in Martha Fineman and Martha McCluskey (eds.), *Feminism, Media, and the Law*. New York: Oxford University Press.

Keightley, Kier. 2004. "Reconsidering Rock," pages 109–142 in Simon Frith, Will Straw, and John Street (eds.), *The Cambridge Companion to Pop and Rock*. New York: Cambridge University Press.

Kellerman, Jonathan. 2013. *Guilt*. New York: Random House.

Kipnis, Laura. 1988. "Feminism: The Political Conscience of Postmodernism?" pages 146–166 in Andrew Ross (ed.), *Universal Abandon? The Politics of Postmodernism*. Minneapolis: University of Minnesota Press.

Kliff, Sarah. 2014. "Thirteen Charts That Explain How Roe v. Wade Changed Abortion Rights." *Washington Post*, Jan. 22. http://www.washingtonpost.com/blogs/wonkblog/ wp/2014/01/22/thirteen-charts-that-explain-how-roe-v-wade-changed-abortion -rights; last accessed June 9, 2014.

Kuwahara, Yasue. 1992. "Power to the People, Y'all: Rap Music, Resistance, and Black College Students." 16 *Humanity and Society* 1: 54–73.

Lancaster, Roger N. 2011. *Sex Panic and the Punitive State*. Berkeley: University of California Press.

Lavrence, Christine, and Kristin Lozanski. 2014. "This Is Not Your Practice Life: lululemon and the Neoliberal Governance of Self." 51 *Canadian Review of Sociology* 1: 76–94.

Lawrence, Jane. 2000. "The Indian Health Service and the Sterilization of American Indian Women." 24 *American Indian Quarterly* 3: 400–419.

Lazarus-Black, Mindie, and Susan F. Hirsch (eds.). 1994. *Contested States: Law, Hegemony, and Resistance*. New York: Routledge.

Lehman, Katherine J. 2011. *Those Girls: Single Women in Sixties and Seventies Popular Culture*. Lawrence: University of Kansas Press.

Lens, Vicki. 2003. "Supreme Court Narratives on Equality and Gender Discrimination in Employment, 1972–2002." 10 *Cardozo Women's Law Journal* 501.

Lenz, Timothy O. 1993. *Changing Images of Law in Film and Television Crime Stories*. New York: Peter Lang.

Leonard, Marion. 2007. *Gender in the Music Industry: Rock, Discourse, and Girl Power*. Burlington, VT: Ashgate.

Lichtenstein, Therese. 1994. "Images of the Maternal: An Interview with Barbara Kruger" (artist), pages 198–203 in Donna Bassin, Margaret Honey, and Meryle Mahrer Kaplan (eds.), *Representations of Motherhood*. New Haven, CT: Yale University Press.

Liesen, Laurette T., and Mary Barbara Walsh. 2012. "The Competing Meanings of 'Biopolitics' in Political Science: Biological and Postmodern Approaches to Politics." 31 *Politics and the Life Sciences* 1–2: 2–15.

Littler, Jo. September 2008. "Juliet Schor—an Interview by Jo Littler: Tackling Turbo Consumption," 22 *Cultural Studies* 5: 588–598.

Littleton, Christine A. 1991. "Reconstructing Sexual Equality," pages 35–57 in Katharine T. Bartlett and Rosanne Kennedy (eds.), *Feminist Legal Theory: Readings in Law and Gender*. Boulder, CO: Westview Press.

Longazel, Jamie G., and Benjamin Fleury-Steiner. 2013. "Beware of Notarios: Neoliberal Governance of Immigrants as Crime Victims." 17 *Theoretical Criminology* 3: 359–376.

Longhurst, Robyn. 1997. "Going Nuts: Re-presenting Pregnant Women." 53 *New Zealand Geographer* 2: 34–38.

———. 2001. "Taut, Trim, Terrific, and Pregnant," pages 1–28 in David Bell, Jon Binnie, Ruth Holliday, Robyn Longhurst, and Robin Peace (eds.), *Pleasure Zones: Bodies, Cities, Spaces*. Syracuse, NY: Syracuse University Press.

———. 2002. "Corporeographies of Pregnancy: 'Bikini Babes.'" 18 *Environment and Planning D: Society and Space* 4: 453–472.

Lorde, Audre. 1978. "Scratching the Surface: Some Notes on Barriers to Women and Loving." 9 *The Black Scholar* 7: 31–35.

———. 1984. *Sister Outsider: Essays and Speeches—Freedom*. Los Angeles: Crossing Press.

———. 1995. "Age, Race, Class, and Sex: Women Redefining Difference," pages 283–292 in Beverly Guy-Sheftall *(ed.)*, *Words of Fire: An Anthology of African-American Feminist Thought*. New York: New Press.

Lorenz, Aaron. 2007. *Lyrics and the Law: The Constitution of Law in Music*. Lake Mary, FL: Vandeplas.

Lujan, Carol Chiago. 1996. "Women Warriors: American Indian Women, Crime, and Alcohol." 7 *Women & Criminal Justice* 1: 9–33.

Luker, Kristin. 1985. *Abortion and the Politics of Motherhood*. Berkeley: University of California Press.

MacCannell, Dean. 2011. *The Ethics of Sightseeing*. Berkeley: University of California Press.

Manderson, Desmond. 2011. "Trust Us Justice: 24, Popular Culture, and Law," pages 22–52 in Austin Sarat (ed.), *Imagining Legality: Where Law Meets Popular Culture.* Birmingham: University of Alabama Press.

Mann, Susan Archer. 2012. *Doing Feminist Theory: From Modernity to Postmodernity.* New York: Oxford University Press.

Mantel, Hilary. 2013. "Royal Bodies." 35 *London Review of Books* 4: 3–7.

Marcuse, Herbert. 1964. *One-Dimensional Man: Studies in the Ideology of an Advanced Industrial Society.* Boston: Beacon Books.

Marshall, P. David. 1997. *Celebrity and Power: Fame in Contemporary Culture.* Minneapolis: University of Minnesota Press.

Marusek, Sarah. 2005. "Wheelchair as Semiotic: Space Governance of the American Handicapped Parking Space." 9 *Law/Text/Culture* 178.

Maschke, Karen. 1993. "From the Workplace to the Delivery Room: Protecting the Fetus in the Post-Roe Era." 12 *Politics and the Life Sciences*: 3–23.

Matson, Erin. 2014. "Is Preventing Surrogacy Feminist? No, It's Anti-Choice." *RH Reality Check,* Apr. 11. http://rhrealitycheck.org/article/2014/04/11/preventing-surrogacy-feminist-anti-choice; last accessed June 5, 2014.

McCall, Leslie. 2005. "The Complexity of Intersectionality." 30 *Signs* 3: 1771–1800.

McDonald, Paul. 2012. *Hollywood Stardom.* Hoboken, NJ: Wiley.

McMillan, Amanda. 2014. "Pre-Baby Body or Bust!" *Health.* http://www.health.com/health/gallery/0,,20603375,00.html; last accessed June 5, 2014.

McRobbie, Angela. 1993. "Shut Up and Dance: Youth Culture and Changing Modes of Femininity." 7 *Cultural Studies* 3: 406.

Mertz, Elizabeth. 1994. "New Social Constructionism for Sociolegal Studies." 28 *Law and Society Review* 1243.

Mezey, Naomi. 2011. "Law's Visual Afterlife: Violence, Popular Culture, and Translation Theory," pages 65–99 in Austin Sarat (ed.), *Imagining Legality: Where Law Meets Popular Culture.* Birmingham: University of Alabama Press.

Miller, Peter, and Nikolas Rose. 1995. "Production, Identity, and Democracy." 24 *Theory and Society* 3: 427–467.

Miller, William Ian. 1998. "Clint Eastwood and Equity: Popular Culture's Theory of Revenge," pages 161–202 in Austin Sarat and Thomas Kearns (eds.), *Law in the Domains of Culture.* Ann Arbor: University of Michigan Press.

Min, Janice. 2012. *How to Look Hot in a Minivan: A Real Woman's Guide to Losing Weight, Looking Great, and Dressing Chic in the Age of the Celebrity Mom.* New York: St. Martins Press.

Minh-ha, Trinh T. 1997. "Mother's Talk," pages 26–32 in Obioma Nnaemeka (ed.), *The Politics of (M)Othering: Womanhood, Identity, and Resistance in African Literature.* New York: Routledge.

———. 1989. *Woman, Native, Other: Writing Postcoloniality and Feminism.* Bloomington: University of Indiana Press.

Mitchell, Lisa Meryn. 2001. *Baby's First Picture: Ultrasound and the Politics of Fetal Subjects.* Toronto: University of Toronto Press.

Montoya, Margaret. 1994. "Mascaras, Trenzas, y Grenas: Un/masking the Self While Un/braiding Latina Stories and Legal Discourse." 17 *Harvard Women's Law Journal* 185.

Moore, Sally Falk. 1973. "Law and Social Change: The Semi-Autonomous Social Field as an Appropriate Subject of Study." 7 *Law & Society Review* 4: 719–746.

Morgan, Joan. 1999. *When Chickenheads Come Home to Roost: A Hip-Hop Feminist Breaks It Down*. New York: Simon & Schuster.

Munford, Rebecca, and Melanie Waters. 2014. *Feminism and Popular Culture*. Newark, NJ: Rutgers University Press.

Nadesan, Majia Holmer. 2002. "Engineering the Entrepreneurial Infant: Brain Science, Infant Development Toys, and Governmentality." 16 *Cultural Studies* 3: 401–432.

Nash, Meredith. 2005. "Oh Baby, Baby: (Un)Veiling Britney Spears' Pregnant Body." 19 *Michigan Feminist Studies*.

Natera, Miguel Angel Contreras. 2013. "Postscript: Insurgent Imaginaries and Postneoliberalism in Latin America," pages 249–281 in Mark Goodale and Nancy Postero (eds.), *Neoliberalism, Interrupted: Social Change and Contested Governance in Contemporary Latin America*. Stanford, CA: Stanford University Press.

Nelson, Jennifer. 2002. *Women of Color and the Reproductive Rights Movement*. New York: New York University Press.

Nelson, Margaret K. 1994. "Family Day Care Providers: Dilemmas of Daily Practice," pages 181–210 in Evelyn Nakano Glenn, Grace Chang, and Linda Rennie Forcey (eds.), *Mothering: Ideology, Experience, and Agency*. New York: Routledge.

Nonet, Philippe, and Phillip Selznick. 2001 (1978). *Law and Society in Transition: Toward Responsive Law*. New York: Harper and Row.

Norrie, Alan. 1999. "From Law to Popular Justice: Beyond Antinomialism," pages 249–276 in Eve Darian-Smith and Peter Fitzpatrick (eds.), *Laws of the Postcolonial*. Ann Arbor: University of Michigan Press.

Oakley, A. 1984. *The Captured Womb: A History of the Medical Care of Pregnant Women*. Oxford, UK: Basil Blackwell.

Olsen, Frances. 1991. "Statutory Rape: A Feminist Critique of Rights Analysis," pages 305–317 in Katharine T. Bartlett and Rosanne Kennedy (eds.), *Feminist Legal Theory: Readings in Law and Gender*. Boulder, CO: Westview Press.

———. 1993. "The Family and the Market: A Study of Ideology and Legal Reform," pages 65–93 in Patricia Smith (ed.), *Feminist Jurisprudence*. New York: Oxford University Press.

Ong, Aihwa. 1987. *Spirits of Resistance and Capitalist Discipline: Factory Women in Malaysia*. Albany: State University of New York Press.

Ouellette, Laurie. 2011. "Real Justice: Law and Order on Reality Television," pages 152–176 in Austin Sarat (ed.), *Imagining Legality: Where Law Meets Popular Culture*. Birmingham: University of Alabama Press.

———, and James Hay. 2008. "Makeover Television, Governmentality, and the Good Citizen." 22 *Journal of Media and Cultural Studies* 4: 471–484.

Passavant, Paul A. 2001. "Enchantment, Aesthetics, and the Superficial Powers of Modern Law." 35 *Law & Society Review* 3: 709–729.

———. 2005. "The Strong Neo-liberal State: Crime, Consumption, Governance." 8 *theory and event* 3.

———. 2006. "The Governmentality of Consumption." 6 *Interventions: International Journal of Postcolonial Studies* 3: 381–400.

———, and Jodi Dean. 2002. "Representation and the Event," 5 *theory and event* 41: 1–28.

Paul, Annie Murphy. 2010. "How the First Nine Months Shape the Rest of Your Life." *Time*, Oct. 4.

Paxman, Lauren. 2014. "Women Need a Whole Year to Recover from Childbirth Despite the 'Fantasy' Image of Celebrity Mothers, Study Claims.'" Daily Mail Online, Mar. 5. http://www.dailymail.co.uk/health/article-2102517/Women-need-year-recover-child-birth-study-finds.html; last accessed March 5, 2014.

Payne, Tom. 2010. *Fame: What the Classics Tell Us about Our Cult of Celebrity*. New York: Picador Press.

Pecora, Vincent. 2007. "Culture as Theater/Culture as Belief." 49 *Criticism* 4: 505–534.

Petchesky, Rosalind Pollack. 1987. "Fetal Images: The Power of Visual Culture in the Politics of Reproduction." 13 *Feminist Studies* 2: 263–292.

Petersen, Anne Helen. 2014. "Jennifer Lawrence and the History of Cool Girls." *BuzzFeed, Feb 28, 2014*. http://www.buzzfeed.com/annehelenpetersen/jennifer-lawrence-and-the-history-of-cool-girls?bffb; last accessed March 6, 2014.

Phelan, Shane. Summer 1993. "(Be)Coming Out: Lesbian Identity and Politics." 18 *Signs* 4: 765–790.

———. 1994. *Getting Specific: Postmodern Lesbian Bodies*. Minneapolis: University of Minnesota Press.

Pieklo, Jessica Mason. 2014. "Lawsuit: Staten Island Hospital Forced Patient into C-Section against Her Will." *RH Reality Check*, May 13. http://rhrealitycheck.org/article/2014/05/13/lawsuit-staten-island-hospital-forced-patient-c-section-will; last accessed Apr. 24, 2015.

Piven, Frances Fox, and Richard Cloward. 1977. *Poor People's Movements: Why They Succeed, How They Fail*. New York: Random House.

Pough, Gwendolyn D. 2004. *Check It While I Wreck It: Black Womanhood, Hip-Hop Culture, and the Public Sphere*. Boston: Northeastern University Press.

Quayle, Dan. 1992. "Address to the Commonwealth Club of California: May 19, 1992." Documented online at http://www.vicepresidentdanquayle.com/speeches_standing firm_ccc_1.html; last accessed Apr. 29, 2015.

Radin, Margaret Jane, and Madhavi Sunder. 2005. "Introduction: The Subject and Object of Commodification," pages 8–34 in Martha Ertman and Joan C. Williams (eds.), *Rethinking Commodification: Cases and Readings in Law and Culture*. New York: New York University Press.

Rapp, Rayna. 1994. "The Power of 'Positive' Diagnosis: Medical and Maternal Discourses on Amniocentesis," pages 204–219 in Donna Bassin, Margaret Honey, and Meryle Mahrer Kaplan (eds.), *Representations of Motherhood*. New Haven: Yale University Press.

Rapping, Elayne. 1997. "The Movie of the Week: Law, Narrativity, and Gender on Prime

Time," pages 91–103 in Martha Fineman and Martha McCluskey (eds.), *Feminism, Media, and the Law*. New York: Oxford University Press.

———. 2003. *Law and Justice as Seen on TV.* New York: New York University Press.

Rasmussen, Claire, and Michael Brown. 2005. "The Body Politic as Spatial Metaphor." 9 *Citizenship Studies* 5: 469–484.

Redmond, Sean. 2007. "The Whiteness of Stars: Looking at Kate Winslet's Unruly White Body," excerpted on pages 263–274 in Sean Redmond and Su Holmes (eds.), *Stardom and Celebrity: A Reader*. London: Sage.

———, and Su Holmes. 2007. *Stardom and Celebrity: A Reader.* London: Sage.

Reed, Jennifer. 2009. "Lesbian Television Personalities: A Queer New Subject." 32 *Journal of American Culture* 4: 307–317.

Reynolds, Simon, and Joy Press. 1995. *The Sex Revolts: Gender, Rebellion, and Rock 'n' Roll.* Cambridge: Harvard University Press.

Rhode, Deborah. 1993. "Reproductive Freedom," pages 305–321 in Patricia Smith (ed.), *Feminist Jurisprudence*. New York: Oxford University Press.

———. 1997. "Media Images/Feminist Issues," pages 8–21 in Martha Fineman and Martha McCluskey (eds.), *Feminism, Media, and the Law*. New York: Oxford University Press.

Roberts, Dorothy. 1992. "Punishing Drug Addicts Who Have Babies: Women of Color, Equality, and the Right of Privacy." 104 *Harvard Law Review* 1419.

———. 1998. *Killing the Black Body: Race, Reproduction, and the Meaning of Liberty.* New York: Random House.

Rodriguez-Trias, Helen. 1978. "Sterilization Abuse." 3 *Women & Health* 3: 10–15.

Rogin, Michael. 1987. *Ronald Reagan, the Movie: And Other Episodes in Political Demonology.* Los Angeles: University of California Press.

Rose, Lacey. 2002. "In Pictures: Most Expensive Celebrity Photos." *Forbes,* May 22. http://www.forbes.com/2009/07/01/michael-jackson-magazine-business-media-jackson_slide_2.html; last accessed June 3, 2014.

Rose, Nikolas. 1999. *Governing the Soul: The Shaping of the Private Self.* London: Free Associations Books.

———. 2008. "Commerce vs. the Common: Conflicts over the Commercialisation of Biomedical Knowledge," pages 79–110 in Saw Swee-Hock and Danny Quah (eds.), *The Politics of Knowledge*. London: London School of Economics and Political Science and Institute of Southeast Asian Studies.

Rose, Tricia. 1991. "'Fear of a Black Planet': Rap Music and Black Cultural Politics in the 1990s." 60 *Journal of Negro Education* 3: 276–290.

Ross, Andrew (ed.). 1988. *Universal Abandon? The Politics of Postmodernism.* Minneapolis: University of Minnesota Press.

———. 1998. "Components of Cultural Justice," pages 203–228 in Austin Sarat and Thomas Kearns (eds.), *Law in the Domains of Culture*. Ann Arbor: University of Michigan Press.

Rothman, Barbara Katz. 1982. *In Labor: Women and Power in the Birthplace.* New York: Norton.

———. 1989. *Recreating Motherhood: Ideology and Technology in a Patriarchal Society.* New York: Norton.

———. 1988–1989. "Motherhood: Beyond Patriarchy." 13 *Nova Law Review:* 481–486.

———. 1994. "Beyond Mothers and Fathers: Ideology in a Patriarchal Society," pages 139–160 in Evelyn Nakano Glenn, Grace Chang, and Linda Rennie Forcey (eds.), *Mothering: Ideology, Experience, and Agency.* New York: Routledge.

———. 2004. "Motherhood under Capitalism," pages 19–30 of Janelle S. Taylor, Linda L. Layne, and Danielle F. Wozniak (eds.), *Consuming Motherhood.* Newark, NJ: Rutgers University Press.

Rubin, Nancy. 1984. *The Mother Mirror: How a Generation of Women Is Changing Motherhood in America.* New York: Putnam.

Ruddick, Sara. 1983. "Thinking about Mothering." 11 *Women's Studies Quarterly* 4: 4–7.

———. 1995. *Maternal Thinking: Towards a Politics of Peace.* Boston: Beacon Press.

Ruskin, Gary, and Juliet Schor. Jan.–Feb. 2005. "Every Nook and Cranny: The Dangerous Spread of Commercialized Culture." *Multinational Monitor.* 20–23.

Russell, Margaret M. 1991. "Race and the Dominant Gaze: Narratives of Law and Inequality in Popular Film." 15 *Legal Studies Forum* 243–254.

———. 1997. "Law and Racial Reelism: Black Women as Celluloid 'Legal' Heroines," pages 136–145 in Martha Fineman and Martha A. McCluskey (eds.), *Feminism, Media, and the Law.* New York: Oxford University Press.

———. 1998. "Rewriting History with Lightning: Race, Myth, and Hollywood in the Legal Pantheon," pages 172–198 in John Denvir (ed.), *Legal Reelism: Movies as Legal Texts.* Urbana: University of Illinois Press.

Salter, Michael. 2010. "Resources for a Dialectical Legal Semiotics?" pages 107–144 in Anne Wagner and Jan Broekman (eds.), *Prospects of Legal Semiotics.* New York: Springer.

Sandberg, Sheryl. 2013. *Lean In: Women, Work, and the Will to Lead.* New York: Knopf.

Santos, Boaventura de Sousa. 1995. "Three Metaphors for a New Conception of Law: The Frontier, The Baroque, and the South." 29 *Law & Society Review* 4: 569–584.

———. 2007. "Beyond Abyssal Thinking: From Global Lines to Ecologies of Knowledge." *Review XXX* 1: 45–89.

———. (ed.). 2008. *Another Knowledge Is Possible: Beyond Northern Epistemologies.* New York: Verso Books.

———, and Maria Jose Arthur. 2007. *Democratizing Democracy: Beyond the Liberal Democratic Canon.* London: Verso.

———, Joao Arriscado Nunes, and Maria Paula Meneses. 2008. "Opening up the Canon of Knowledge and Recognition of Difference," pages xvix–lxii in Boaventura de Sousa Santos (ed.), *Another Knowledge Is Possible: Beyond Northern Epistemologies.* New York: Verso Books.

Sarat, Austin. 2011. "What Popular Culture Does for, and to, Law: An Introduction," pages 1–21 in Austin Sarat (ed.), *Imagining Legality: Where Law Meets Popular Culture.* Birmingham: University of Alabama Press.

———. 2000. "Imagining the Law of the Father: Loss, Dread and Mourning in 'The Sweet Hereafter.'" 34 *Law & Society Review* 1: 3–46.

————, and Thomas R. Kearns. 1998. "The Cultural Lives of Law," pages 1–20 in Austin Sarat and Thomas R. Kearns (eds.), *Law in the Domains of Culture*. Ann Arbor: University of Michigan Press.

Schickel, Richard. 2000. *Intimate Strangers: The Culture of Celebrity*. Lanham, MD: Ivan R. Dee.

Schneider, Elizabeth M., and Stephanie M. Wildman (eds.). 2011. *Women and the Law: Stories*. New York: Foundation Press.

Schor, Juliet. 1998. *The Overspent American: Upscaling, Downshifting, and the New Consumer*. New York: Basic Books.

Scott, James C. 1987. *Weapons of the Weak: Everyday Forms of Peasant Resistance*. New Haven, CT: Yale University Press.

————. 2010. *The Art of Not Being Governed: An Anarchist History of Upland Southeast Asia*. New Haven, CT: Yale University Press.

————. 2012. *Two Cheers for Anarchism*. Princeton, NJ: Princeton University Press.

Shapiro, Ian (ed.). 2007. *Abortion: The Supreme Court Decisions, 1965–2007*. Indianapolis, IN: Hart.

Sherwin, Richard. 2002. *When the Law Goes Pop: The Vanishing Line between Law and Popular Culture*. Chicago: University of Chicago Press.

————. 2011. "Law's Screen Life: Criminal Predators and What to Do about Them—Popular Imperatives from Screen-Based Realities," pages 107–132 in Austin Sarat (ed.), *Imagining Legality: Where Law Meets Popular Culture*. Birmingham: University of Alabama Press.

Shildrick, Margrit, with Janet Price. 1999. "Openings on the Body: A Critical Introduction," pages 1–15 in Janet Price and Margrit Shildrick (eds.), *Feminist Theory and the Body: A Reader*. New York: Routledge.

Showden, Carisa R. 2009. "What's Political about the New Feminism?" 30 *Frontiers* 2: 166–198.

Silliman, Jael, and Anannya Bhattacharjee (eds.). 2002. *Policing the National Body: Race, Gender, and Criminalization*. Cambridge, MA: South End Press.

Silliman, Jael, Marlene Gerber Fried, Loretta Ross, and Elena R. Guttieriez. 2004. *Undivided Rights: Women of Color Organize for Reproductive Justice*. Boston: South End Press.

Simon, Jonathan. 2001. "Governing through Crime Metaphors." 67 *Brooklyn Law Review*: 1035.

Sloane, David Charles, and Beverlie Conant Sloane. 2002. *Medicine Moves to the Mall*. Baltimore, MD: Johns Hopkins University Press.

Smith, Andrea. 2003. "Not an Indian Tradition: The Sexual Colonization of Native Peoples." 18 *Hypatia* 2: 70–85.

Smith, Dorothy. 1987. *The Everyday World as Problematic: A Feminist Sociology*. Toronto: University of Toronto Press.

Smith, Patricia (ed.). 1993. *Feminist Jurisprudence*. New York: Oxford University Press.

Solinger, Rickie. 2007. *Pregnancy and Power: A Short History of Reproductive Politics in America*. New York: New York University Press.

————. 2013. *Reproductive Politics: What Everyone Needs to Know*. New York: Oxford University Press.

————, and Elaine Tyler May. 2000. *Wake up Little Susie: Single Pregnancy and Race before Roe v. Wade*. New York: Routledge.

Stacey, Jackie. 2007. "With Stars in Their Eyes: Female Spectators and the Paradoxes of Consumption," excerpted on pages 313–324 of Sean Redmond and Su Holmes, *Stardom and Celebrity: A Reader*. London: Sage.

Sternheimer, Karen. 2011. *Celebrity Culture and the American Dream: Stardom and Social Mobility*. New York: Routledge.

Strebeigh, Fred. 2009. *Equal: Women Reshaping Law*. New York: Norton.

Strolovitch, Dara. 2007. *Affirmative Advocacy: Race, Class, and Gender in Interest Group Politics*. Chicago: University of Chicago Press.

Stone, Deborah. 2011. *Policy Paradox: The Art of Political Decision Making*. New York: Norton.

Stout, Hilary. 2014. "With New Rewards Card, Amex Focuses on Busy-Mom Market." *New York Times*, Mar. 3, *page* B3.

Sumner, Alexandra, Glenn Waller, Stephen Killick, and Max Elstein. 1993. "Body Image Distortion in Pregnancy: A Pilot Study of the Effects of Media Images." 11 *Journal of Reproductive and Infant Psychology* 4: 203–208.

Swigart, Jane. 1998. *The Myth of the Perfect Mother: Parenting without Guilt*. Chicago: Contemporary Books.

Torpy, Sally J. 2000. "Native American Women and Coerced Sterilization: On the Trail of Tears in the 1970s." 24 *American Indian Culture and Research Journal* 2: 1–22.

Tropp, Laura. 2006. "Faking a Sonogram: Representations of Motherhood on *Sex in the City*." 39 *Journal of Popular Culture* 5: 861–877.

Teubner, Gunther. 1983. "Substantive and Reflexive Elements in Modern Law." 17 *Law and Society Review*: 239–285.

Twitchell, James. 2004. *Branded Nation: The Marketing of MegaChurch, College, Inc., and MuseumWorld*. New York: Simon & Schuster.

Ussher, Jane M. 2006. *Managing the Monstrous Feminine: Regulating the Reproductive Body*. New York: Routledge.

Van Krieken, Robert. 2012. *Celebrity Society*. Hoboken, NJ: Taylor and Francis.

Vogel, Lise. 1990. "Debating Difference: Feminism, Pregnancy, and the Workplace." 16 *Feminist Studies* 1: 9–32.

Von Drehle, David, with Massimo Calabresi. 2013. "The Surveillance Society." 7 *Time* 182 (Aug. 12): 32–37.

Wagner, Anne, and Richard Sherwin (eds.). 2012. *Law, Culture, and Visual Studies*. London: Ashgate Press.

Walker, Alice. 2001. *The Way Forward Is with a Broken Heart*. New York: Ballantine Books.

————. 2004. *In Search of Our Mothers' Gardens: Womanist Prose*. iTunes eBook.

Weingarten, Kathy, Janet L. Surrey, Cynthia Garcia Coll, and Mary Watkins. 1998. "Introduction," pages 1–14 in Cynthia Garcia Coll, Janet L. Surrey, and Kathy Weingarten (eds.), *Mothering against the Odds: Diverse Voices of Contemporary Mothers*. New York: Guilford Press.

West, Robin. 1987. "The Difference in Women's Hedonic Lives: A Phenomenological Critique of Feminist Legal Theory." *Wisconsin Women's Law Journal* 3: 81–145.

———. 1988. "Jurisprudence and Gender." 55 *University of Chicago Law Review* 1.

Wetherbe, Jamie. 2013. "Nude Sculpture of Pregnant Kim Kardashian Unveiled in L.A." *Los Angeles Times*, June 6.

Whitehead, Fred. 1994. *Culture Wars: Opposing Viewpoints*. San Diego, CA: Greenhaven Press.

Whiteley, Sheila. 2013. *Women and Popular Music: Sexuality, Identity, and Subjectivity*. New York: Routledge.

Whyman, Tom. 2014. "Beware of Cupcake Fascism." *The Guardian*, Apr. 8. http:www.the guardian.com/commentisfree/2014/apr/08/beware-of-cupcake-fascism; last accessed June 12, 2014.

Wildman, Stephanie M. 1984. "The Legitimation of Sex Discrimination: A Critical Response to Supreme Court Jurisprudence." 63 *Oregon Law Review* 265.

———. 2011. "Pregnant and Working: The Story of *California Federal Savings & Loan Ass'n v. Guerra*," pages 253–276 in Elizabeth M. Schneider and Stephanie M. Wildman (eds.), *Women and the Law: Stories*. New York: Foundation Press.

Williams, Joan C. 1991. "Deconstructing Gender," pages 95–123 in Katharine T. Bartlett and Rosanne Kennedy (eds.), *Feminist Legal Theory: Readings in Law and Gender*. Boulder, CO: Westview Press.

Williams, Patricia J. 1997. "Spare Parts, Family Values, Old Children, Cheap," pages 168–180 in Jodi Dean (ed.), *Feminism and the New Democracy: Resiting the Political*. Thousand Oaks, CA: Sage.

Williams, Polly. 2006. *The Yummy Mummy*. New York: Hyperion Books.

Wojcik, Pamela Robertson. 2003. "Typecasting." 45 *Criticism* 2: 223–249.

Wolin, Sheldon. 2010. *Democracy Incorporated: Managed Democracy and the Specter of Inverted Totalitarianism*. Princeton, NJ: Princeton University Press.

Yanow, Dvora. 2003. "Interpretive Empirical Political Science: What Makes This Not a Subfield of Qualitative Methods." 1 *Qualitative and Multi-Method Research* 2: 9–13.

———, and Peregrine Schwartz-Shea. 2006. *Interpretation and Method: Empirical Research Methods and the Interpretive Turn*. Armonk, NY: M.E. Sharpe.

Young, Iris Marion. 1995. "Mothers, Citizenship, and Independence: A Critique of Pure Family Values." *Ethics* 105: 535–556.

———. 2003. "Feminist Reactions to the Contemporary Security Regime." 18 *Hypatia* 1: 223–231.

———. 2004. "Modest Reflections on Hegemony and Global Democracy." *Theoria* 103: 1–14.

———. 2005. *On Female Body Experience: "Throwing Like a Girl" and Other Essays*. New York: Oxford University Press.

———. 2006. "Taking the Basic Structure Seriously." 4 *Perspectives on Politics* 1: 91–97.

Zeisler, Andi. 2008. *Feminism and Popular Culture*. San Francisco: Seal Press.

Table of Cases Cited

Bellotti v. Baird 443 U.S. 622 (1979)

Bradwell v. Illinois 83 U.S. (16 Wall) 130 (1873)

Buck v. Bell 24 U.S. 200 (1927)

Burwell v. Hobby Lobby 573 U.S. _____ (2014)

California Federal Savings and Loan Association v. Guerra 479 U.S. 272 (1987)

City of Akron v. Akron Center for Reproductive Health 462 U.S. 416 (1983)

Cleveland Board of Education v. LaFleur 414 U.S. 632 (1974)

Doe v. Bolton 410 U.S. 179 (1973)

Eisenstadt v. Baird 405 U.S. 438 (1972)

Frontiero v. Richardson 411 U.S. 677 (1973)

Geduldig v. Aiello 417 U.S. 484 (1974)

General Electric Co. v. Gilbert 429 U.S. 125 (1976)

Gonzales v. Carhart 550 U.S. 124 (2007)

Griswold v. Connecticut 381 U.S. 479 (1965)

Harris v. McRae 448 U.S. 297 (1980)

Hodgson v. Minnesota 497 U.S. 417 (1990)

Maher v. Roe 432 U.S. 464 (1977)

Michael M. v. Superior Court of Sonoma County 450 U.S. 464 (1981)

Muller v. Oregon 208 U.S. 412 (1908)

Nashville Gas Co. v. Satty 434 U.S. 136 (1977)

Ohio v. Akron Center for Reproductive Health 497 U.S. 502 (1990)

Planned Parenthood Association of Central Missouri v. Danforth 428 U.S. 52 (1976)

Planned Parenthood Assoc. of Kansas City, Missouri v. Ashcroft 462 U.S. 476 (1983)

Planned Parenthood of Southeastern Pennsylvania v. Casey 505 U.S. 833 (1992)

Roe v. Wade 410 U.S. 113 (1973)

Rust v. Sullivan 500 U.S. 173 (1991)

Stenberg v. Carhart 530 U.S. 914 (2000)

Thornburgh v. American College of Obstetricians and Gynecologists 467 U.S. 747 (1986)

Turner v. Department of Employment Security of Utah 434 U.S. 44 (1975)

United Automobile Workers v. Johnson Controls, Inc. 499 U.S. 187 (1991)

Webster v. Reproductive Health Services 492 U.S. 490 (1989)

INDEX

Page references followed by "*f*" refer to photographs.

THE CULTURAL LIVES OF LAW
Edited by Austin Sarat

The Cultural Lives of Law series brings insights and approaches from cultural studies to law and tries to secure for law a place in cultural analysis. Books in the series focus on the production, interpretation, consumption, and circulation of legal meanings. They take up the challenges posed as boundaries collapse between as well as within cultures, and as the circulation of legal meanings becomes more fluid. They also attend to the ways law's power in cultural production is renewed and resisted.

Letters of the Law: Race and the Fantasy of Colorblindness
Sora Y. Han
2015

Our Word Is Our Bond: How Legal Speech Acts
Marianne Constable
2014

The Street Politics of Abortion: Speech, Violence, and America's Culture Wars
Joshua C. Wilson
2013

Zooland: The Institution of Captivity
Irus Braverman
2012

Better Left Unsaid: Victorian Novels, Hays Code Films, and the Benefits of Censorship
Nora Gilbert
2012

After Secular Law
Edited by Winnifred Fallers Sullivan, Robert A. Yelle, and Mateo Taussig-Rubbo
2011

All Judges Are Political   Except When They Are Not: Acceptable Hypocrisies and the Rule of Law
Keith J. Bybee
2010

Riding the Black Ram: Law, Literature, and Gender
Susan Sage Heinzelman
2010

Tort, Custom, and Karma: Globalization and Legal Consciousness in Thailand
David M. Engel and Jaruwan S. Engel
2010

Law in Crisis: The Ecstatic Subject of Natural Disaster
Ruth A. Miller
2009

The Affective Life of Law: Legal Modernism and the Literary Imagination
Ravit Reichman
2009

Fault Lines: Tort Law as Cultural Practice
Edited by David M. Engel and Michael McCann
2008

Lex Populi: The Jurisprudence of Popular Culture
William P. MacNeil
2007

The Cultural Lives of Capital Punishment: Comparative Perspectives
Edited by Austin Sarat and Christian Boulanger
2005